The Promise of Hope

How True Stories of Hope and Inspiration Saved My Life
and How They Can Transform Yours

9 Keys to Powerful Personal Change

EDWARD GRINNAN

Editor-in-Chief, *Guideposts* Magazine

Guideposts
New York, New York

The Promise of Hope

ISBN-10: 0-8249-4815-7
ISBN-13: 978-0-8249-4815-3

Published by Guideposts
16 East 34th Street
New York, New York 10016
Guideposts.org

Distributed by Ideals Publications, a Guideposts company
2630 Elm Hill Pike, Suite 100
Nashville, Tennessee 37214

Guideposts and *Ideals* are registered trademarks of Guideposts.

Acknowledgments

Every attempt has been made to credit the sources of copyrighted material used in this book. If any such acknowledgment has been inadvertently omitted or miscredited, receipt of such information would be appreciated.

Library of Congress Cataloging-in-Publication Data

Grinnan, Edward.
    The promise of hope : how true stories of hope and inspiration saved my life and how they can transform yours : nine keys to powerful personal change / Edward Grinnan.
        p. cm.
Includes bibliographical references and index.
ISBN 978-0-8249-4815-3 (alk. paper)
    1. Conduct of life. 2. Change (Psychology) 3. Hope. 4. Inspiration. I. Title.
II. Title: How true stories of hope and inspiration saved my life and how they can transform yours. III. Title: Nine keys to powerful personal change.
BJ1521.G84 2011
155.2′5—dc22
                                                    2011003241

Cover design by Georgia Morrissey and Audrey Razgaitis
Cover photograph by Gail Zucker
Interior design by Lorie Pagnozzi
Typeset by Aptara

Printed and bound in the United States of America
10 9 8 7 6 5 4 3

To my family;
to Julee and the dogs;
and for Van

Contents

Preface

I t was a raw, blustery late afternoon in early spring almost two years back now, and you couldn't tell if the howling was coming from the wind in the still-bare trees or the hungry pack of coyotes up the hill behind our getaway place in the Berkshires of western Massachusetts. The air still held an insinuation of winter, as if it might not be done with us yet. With the land still so barren, spring is tough on the coyotes and bears, and we had a golden retriever pup with us who was not even two yet. I'd have to keep an eye on her, but she wouldn't like it. She'd want to explore.

I brought in some more wood for the stove. My wife, Julee, glanced at a sheaf of legal-looking papers strewn across the dining room table. It was a book contract I was about to sign.

"Is Millie in?" she asked.

"Yeah."

"You can't leave her out with that bear around."

"I never do."

"A bear would make short work of her. You saw what it did to our trash can. Those coyotes too. They hunt in packs."

"She's in."

"So," Julee said, pointing to the papers, "what's this book about?"

"It's about the power of personal change and what I've learned from my years at Guideposts, helping people tell their stories of hope and transformation and redemption. It's a good subject. Change is one of the hardest things. Look at the stuff people go through. Just look at some of the stuff we've been through, Jules."

She paused for a moment, as if she was hoping I'd actually heard what I said.

"Are you going to tell your own story, Edward?" she finally asked.

It was the one question I hoped she wouldn't ask.

"I thought I'd touch on it," I said noncommittally.

Julee tended to the fire in the woodstove a little more vigorously than was strictly necessary. "Touch on it?" she said. "How do you just touch on a story like yours?"

I didn't have an answer—at least not yet.

"For twenty years, Edward, you've helped all kinds of people, from celebrities to ordinary people, tell their personal stories for millions of readers of the magazine every month. And it's good. It helps people. Millions of people. But nobody knows your story, not in all these years. Maybe it's time you come out of hiding and tried some of your own medicine. Did you ever think your story might help people?"

This would be a good time, I decided, to take Millie for a walk. I grabbed her leash and went back outside to mull the question over. I sat in a log chair and tilted back, looking up through the denuded branches at the graying sky, where streaks of sunset were already beginning to appear. Millie settled at my feet.

Julee was right. For all these years I'd been helping people tell their true, first-person stories of hope and inspiration in *Guideposts* magazine, urging them to find the spiritual and emotional truth of their experiences and bare their souls to millions of readers. Sometimes I felt more like a therapist than an editor. And yet these stories had changed me. They changed my life in ways I never could have dreamed. Perhaps it *was* time for a dose of my own medicine.

Our stories reveal and define us. They are the road maps of our lives. Our stories transform us and change the people around us. Human beings have been telling their stories since they could carve on cave walls, and probably earlier. We may be hardwired for storytelling. We are our stories, and all stories are about change. Our stories are as human as our flesh. So why was I afraid of mine?

In a way, I suppose, I thought my story was long behind me, almost as if it had happened to someone else. I would have to go back and find that person and get in touch with who he was and who, to a great extent, I still am at some level deep inside. That frightened me. I didn't want to go back there and look at parts of my life I thought I'd buried forever. But you never do bury anything completely. Who you are today is because of who you were yesterday. Life is a continuum, and our stories stretch across that continuum. We can only change ourselves so much within the context of who we are, though that change is often profound and transformative, even redemptive. And I was certainly a person redeemed.

Millie whined demurely, a pitiful sound coming from a ninety-pound dog. She was hungry for dinner. That was her story.

Back inside, Julee had stoked a fire that would have made Hephaestus proud, and the cabin was quite warm now.

"I see you are literally turning up the heat on me, Jules."

She was holding the pen and thrusting it toward me.

"If you are going to sign that contract, then sign it to write an honest book, because I don't think I want to spend a year never seeing you while you put together something about other people's stories and what you learned from them. They're great stories. Just put yours in there too. It's going to help people. It will give them hope. I promise you, Edward. Your story is why I married you."

The woodstove was throwing off so much light it hurt my eyes. I took the pen from Julee, sat at the table, pawed through the papers till I found the last page and signed my name where it said *author*.

Introduction

Find a Job, Any Job

I arrived for my job interview at *Guideposts* magazine one day in 1986 having barely heard of the publication. I only knew that there was an opening for an assistant editor. A friend thought that perhaps I was interviewing at a travel magazine. In a way, he was right—if you substitute the word *journey* for travel.

At the time, though, I was simply looking for a job, practically any job, to keep body and soul together: a body that, at age thirty-two, I'd subjected to almost unbearable abuse—and that had come all too close to an early end—and a soul that had long disappeared behind the clouds.

Just a few years out of graduate school, I was a freelance writer, which meant I was pretty much self-unemployed. Despite my very best efforts, I'd somehow managed to graduate (barely) from the Yale School of Drama with an MFA in playwriting; then I was shocked to discover upon my arrival in New York that there were no listings for "playwright" in the *New York Times* want ads. This left me to my own devices, which was not a good thing back then, and by the time I arrived at the *Guideposts* editorial offices on Third Avenue, my life was on the brink of disaster. No, it *was* a disaster. Had *Guideposts* checked more carefully into my recent background—and had I not been able to conjure up a few passable letters of reference and by some miracle avoid betraying my shaky emotional state—I would have never been hired. *I* wouldn't have hired me.

Yet it had been suggested in no uncertain terms by people who were trying to help me salvage my life and my self-respect that I find a job, any job, and stick to it for a year no matter what. That was asking a lot. Not because I was lazy or because I thought the world owed me anything—in some ways I was unbelievably driven—but because one of the more recent "jobs" I'd held was hustling spare change and bumming cigarettes on street corners in lower Manhattan. And I wasn't even very good at that.

I am getting ahead of myself though. This is not a book about me, except to the extent that you need to know who I am to understand what I learned. It is a book about change, that great immutable force in life that has the power to either destroy us or lead us on amazing journeys in growth, transformation and happiness. Change is good, but it is hard; it is necessary but often painful. Either we choose it or it chooses us, but no matter what, all of us are meant to deal with change. And if what I have learned as the editor-in-chief of *Guideposts* is any indication, most of us want to choose it.

We yearn for personal change, be it big or small, monumental or incremental, life-changing or life-saving. There is a place of transformation deep within us, a wellspring from which the power to change flows through our lives like a divine current and beckons us to triumph over our struggles and realize our human and spiritual potential. It is our discovery of that wellspring and the harnessing of that current that is both our greatest challenge and our surest path to joy and self-fulfillment. Without change, our souls are marooned in a kind of metaphysical inertia where growth and progress toward a better and happier self are impossible.

Nobody can tell you exactly how to change, or when, or even why. Those are the decisions only we can make for ourselves. They can be tough and lonely decisions, and they are usually the most important decisions of our lives. But in meeting hundreds of people with incredible stories of inspiring and lasting personal change, I have learned that certain essential qualities are universal to the change process. With these nine qualities, change of monumental proportions is possible:

Honesty

Willingness

Imagination

Commitment

Faith

Forgiveness

Acceptance

Resilience

Love

I haven't set out to write a self-help book. The term does not sit well with me. Actually, this is more of a not-by-yourself-help book. Arriving at *Guideposts*, I was certainly in no position to be of much help to myself. I mean, look where *that* had gotten me. But maybe Willingness was in play, just a little, in my "find a job, any job" approach, because at least it got me to a very special place where I was soon to discover not only a magazine of passionate influence in the lives of millions of Americans, but also an incredible variety of moving and personal stories from people of all walks of life, the famous and the rest of us, each and every story a true and inspiring saga of profound change. Founded in 1945 by Dr. Norman Vincent Peale and his wife, Ruth, the magazine was a model for what would one day be called user-generated content. My job was to help people bring their inspiring true stories to life on the page.

A year. That was all that was asked of me. All I had to do was show up, do my job, find a little time to work on my résumé, and figure out what to do with my life. Little did I know that through the people I was about to meet, through writing and editing their stories of personal change for *Guideposts*, life was going to figure out what to do with me.

1
Honesty

Biologically, we never stop changing. The molecules we wake up with are different from the molecules we went to sleep with. Hair grows and falls out, blood-sugar levels fluctuate. My fingernails lengthened slightly as I typed this. One of the first scientific factoids I remember hearing was that our bodies undergo a complete cellular makeover every seven years, roughly the time it takes for the billions and billions of cells that constitute our corporeal being to turn over. So how come, my innocent middle-school mind wondered at the time, we aren't completely different people at each septennial juncture?

Ah! said my science teacher, that's because our DNA stabilizes this process. Biological change is "process change"—change we have little or no control over. Nature just takes care of it, as it does the turning of the seasons and the rotation of the earth on its polar axis.

The kind of change I'm talking about, the kind that begins with honesty, is the kind *we* take care of (or not). Transformational change.

What part of us, exactly, are we changing when we engage in transformational change? Does it mean becoming less of what we are and more of something we want to be? A better version of ourselves, or a completely different person altogether?

Most of us tend to view our personal changes a little like nature's changes—as something that happens in our external world: we get a big promotion; we gain thirty pounds in the years after our kids are born; a loved one dies, and so on. But change at its most basic level is how we *react* to what happens to us in life, not the event itself. The big promotion or gaining thirty pounds or losing a loved one are what happens, but they're not change—not really. Positive change occurs when you do something about your exciting new responsibilities or those unhealthy pounds or your paralyzing grief.

We ran a contest at the magazine recently called "New Year, New You," in which we offered a total, yearlong mind/body/spirit makeover with four of our personal empowerment experts to the person who told the most compelling story about why she or he wanted to change. We had thousands of entrants and, as you might expect, many wanted to change the external things people usually seek to change—weight, health, fitness, career, finances, relationships. Yet more than all of those, there was *one* thing that people most wanted to change.

Negative thinking.

Now, these were not unhappy people. Most were solid members of their communities, worked hard, went to church, and took care of their families. Good people. Yet they were beset by negative thoughts—doubt, guilt, envy, resentment, worry and putting themselves down. A veritable epidemic of negative thinking. And negative thinking can only lead to negative results. Who could hope to change any of those other problems, from body-image issues to finances, if they didn't first address a change in their negative thought process? Then I thought about myself, the editor-in-chief of a magazine rooted in positive thinking. Was I so free of these attitudinal encumbrances?

No. I worry and complicate situations that should be simple. I fear that bad events will only get worse, and I wonder if good events might have a tarnished lining. I seem to have a capacity for giving myself a hard time and draining my life of the positive change that is there for me, the joy and satisfaction each of us is meant to experience and that are the keys to a happy life.

Which brings me back to the matter of honesty, and why it's the first indispensable prerequisite in transformational personal change. Unless we are willing to honestly recognize and admit a problem—unless we address our attitude before anything else—we have virtually no hope of changing beyond being struck by lightning on the road to Damascus, and few of us will ever hit that particular spiritual jackpot (though later in the book I will tell you about a couple who did).

Most of us are honest people. But being honest with ourselves is hard. It is not a perfect process. In fact, self-honesty can be a very messy business. There is no one easier to lie to than yourself. People who would never lie to their children or their friends have no compunction about deceiving themselves. We justify our faults and disappointments by blaming others or circumstances we believe we can't control. We think it is a shortcoming to admit unhappiness. We say we're not angry and resentful when we know we are, for fear that we'll be thought of negatively or even denied love. We say that we have strong faith, yet we mistrust the future. And maybe it's the bathroom scale that's five pounds over, not me.

We don't just hide from tough truths. We also hide from our true desires and dreams, afraid to admit what we yearn for from life. There's nothing wrong with wanting a better life and greater happiness; the journey of personal change is a journey toward joy. Yet unless we honestly believe that we deserve it, and then work to achieve it, happiness will always be beyond our grasp. It's not enough to simply believe in the dream; you have to believe you *deserve* it.

Fear of our problems and our dreams is the greatest obstacle to change. Change demands a hard and sometimes painful look in the mirror. I once wrote a cover piece with a remarkable man who literally couldn't do it: He couldn't look in the mirror. His story inspires me to this day and, as you will come to understand, it is also a story I identify with on a very personal level. In Bill Irwin's case, it took going blind for him to finally see and to ultimately embark on a journey of nearly unimaginable courage, determination and, yes, vision.

My wife, Julee, and I have a house nestled in the Berkshire Hills of Massachusetts that we use as a kind of retreat, a place to unwind and escape the endless stimulation of city life, though Julee likes to claim that we actually bought the property for our dogs and we're just the obedient caretakers. Winding along the upper border of our land is the storied Appalachian Trail, a gorgeous and rugged path that stretches through breathtaking woodlands, across rushing streams, and over rocky mountain-tops from Georgia to Maine. Few things are more glorious than hitting the trail with our golden retriever, Millie, for some serious hiking. And every so often I try something. With Millie ahead on the leash, I close my eyes and try to follow the trail. It is amazing how quickly the world feels as if it is falling away. If I make it twenty feet without stumbling, I'm lucky.

Bill Irwin made it 2,167.9 miles. Blind.

Bill began his colossal solo trek with his Seeing Eye dog, Orient, on March 8, 1990, at the southern trailhead at Springer Mountain, Georgia, elevation 4,161 feet, with the words, "Orient, forward." His improbable goal was to hike the entire trail, all the way to the summit of Mount Katahdin in Maine, in a single hiking season. It's a daunting effort for even the fittest, sighted hiker, with a failure rate similar to that of climbers attempting Mount Everest. On average, it takes a strong hiker more than five months of continuous hiking to complete the journey. And the fact was, Bill Irwin, at fifty-two, didn't even like to hike.

But Bill's change journey began long before he and Orient stood alone atop Springer Mountain that blustery March morning. Three years earlier Bill had been a bitter, depressed, middle-aged man with four failed marriages behind him, a five-pack-a-day cigarette habit, and an increasingly deadly dependence on alcohol. As Bill told me, "There wasn't enough room on a 747 for all my emotional baggage."

Far from being a skid-row bum, Bill was a hard-working professional, a toxicologist and owner of his own medical laboratory, until his blindness forced him to sell it. He was the son of a respected but inordinately strict Alabama surgeon who had been quick with the strap and not so much with his affection. From him Bill learned that the Irwins were better than other people in town, that they never quit or got beat. In short, Bill was given a simple mandate to live up to: perfection.

People who internalize their parents' expectation of perfection often become workaholic overachievers for whom no goal, once attained, is ever good enough. Nothing is ever good enough because *they* are not good enough; they are not perfect. There is no greater toxin to the soul than the self-expectation of perfection. It means we're trying to steal from God something only God can possess.

It's hard to attain perfection when one of your basic sensory powers starts to fail. Bill was in his late twenties and working three jobs—chemistry teacher, medical technologist, and owner of a fledgling toxicology lab—when his left eye was removed due to disease. Now he was a one-eyed man trying to be perfect. A one-eyed man with a drinking problem, among other issues.

Then the sight in his right eye began to deteriorate. As his eyesight inexorably diminished, Bill's anger and arrogance grew. He built a successful business only to sell it. He could still teach, so he taught. His mind was still brilliant, so he consulted. His marriages failed, one after another, and for the most part he was no different a father to his three kids than his father had been to him. The more his problems mounted, the more he used alcohol as an escape.

In 1976, the light in Bill's world went out completely. Swallowed up in that ineluctable darkness, he became isolated and self-pitying, swilling whiskey alone at home most nights and reeling from one broken relationship to the next.

If there was a bright spot, it was Bill's capitulation to a friend's prodding that he get a Seeing Eye guide dog. The relationship between service dog and human is something like a miracle: a profound partnership across the bounds of species based on trust, empathy and an ineffable understanding of each other's needs. Seeing Eye dogs are trained using techniques predicated on reward and praise. Bill Irwin was not a person accustomed to dispensing those things, even to himself. Perhaps only an animal could have awakened those impulses.

Yet even with the help of Jorie, his dog, Bill's thinking continued to be malignantly negative until one night in February of 1987, when he put down his drink to pick up the phone and hear his desperate son Jeff beg him for help—something Irwins didn't do. Jeff's addiction to cocaine was killing him, and he needed treatment *now*. The toxicologist in Bill understood the danger his son was in. He got Jeff admitted to a twenty-eight-day inpatient rehab program in Birmingham, Alabama. There was a catch though. It was called Family Week. Bill had to agree to spend a week in sessions with Jeff and his counselors, who were not particularly amused when Bill said, "Sure, no problem. Just let me know when happy hour is."

Before that week began, however, Bill had to face another shock—Jorie had to be euthanized because of hip dysplasia. Jorie's death devastated Bill. The Friday after Jorie's death, Bill bought enough liquor for a week. It barely lasted the weekend. And then it was time for Family Week.

"They went through my bag to make sure I wasn't smuggling in any booze," Bill told me. He would not be allowed any alcohol for the week and could only smoke at appointed times outside the building; this for a guy—a toxicologist, for crying out loud—who smoked upwards of a hundred cigarettes a day. "I immediately started planning my escape!"

In the no-holds-barred sessions between Jeff, his mother and Bill, Bill lied. He denied blacking out from alcohol. Denied drinking in the morning. Denied his anger, the distance he put between himself and others, and the distance he put between himself and his feelings. But inside Bill saw the truth behind every lie. That is the thing about a lie—you can't tell one without knowing what the truth is.

At night, Bill tossed and turned in bed, as if some force much greater than himself were awakening him to the miserable facts of his own existence. And there was something more—a single shaft of shimmering hope that cut through all his darkness, a hope that said to Bill, "If not now, when?"

By week's end, the staff had given up on Bill Irwin. He was arrogant, angry, abusive, and incapable of being honest with himself or anyone else. He was a total head case, a man who would never be deterred from his own defiant path of denial and self-destruction. At the commencement ceremony, when Jeff would get his medallion for his twenty-eight drug-free days, his father planned to stand up when it was his turn and say, "My name is Bill, I used to work for the company that makes Valium, and I love to drink."

His turn came. Bill stood. He held his head high and directed his sightless eyes forward. But the words that came from his mouth were not the arrogant declaration he had every intention of making. All he said was, "My name is Bill and I'm an alcoholic."

"Orient, forward."

Orient was Bill's third dog, after Jorie and Sailor. Jorie and Sailor had been special, but Orient was something else: a big, strong German shepherd with an extraordinary personality. The only worry Bill had when he got Orient was that a dog who received his early training in New Jersey would have trouble cutting through his new owner's muddy southern drawl. "Where I come from," Bill noted, "rest is a two-syllable word. But he got used to it."

Bill didn't get much farther along the trail than I did before he fell. He lay on the ground for a moment while Orient checked on him. When Bill fell, Orient felt it was his failure as a Seeing Eye dog. Bill knew this would not be the first time he would fall, not by a long shot. He still had more than two thousand miles to go. Was he up for it? Was Orient?

Bill rose to his feet, shifted his backpack, and he and Orient were on their way. Days and weeks passed as they trekked through northern Georgia, through North Carolina, and into Virginia. Out on the Trail thru-hikers adopt trail names; Bill and Orient were known as the Orient Express.

On July 1 the Orient Express hit the halfway point, Pine Grove Furnace, Pennsylvania. By then Bill had survived hypothermia, a spill down a mountainside, and a night spent out in a boulder field after missing a campsite. As for Orient, he was holding up well—though on several occasions he was mistaken for a bear by other hikers—and was learning that Bill's stumbles and falls weren't his fault.

And Bill fell. Over and over again. Through New York, Connecticut and Massachusetts, he slipped and stumbled, each time picking himself up and moving forward toward his goal. He'd left Springer Mountain with ninety pounds of supplies in his backpack. At the time it seemed so little, but Bill learned he needed much less, shedding unnecessary burdens along the way. The process liberated him physically and emotionally. The lighter his pack, the lighter he felt, the faster he and Orient traveled, and the less he fell—a life lesson not lost on him. By now, perhaps, his emotional baggage could fit into a Piper Cub.

The press got wind of Bill's quest. Bill was more than happy to talk. In the three years since he had gotten sober, Bill had followed a 12-step program of recovery that emphasized spiritual surrender to a loving "higher power," which in AA means a divine presence to whom he could turn over his will and his life. He had also become a committed Christian. Now he told the media that he was out on the Trail not to show what a man could do but what the Lord could do with a man whose life had seemed so hopelessly out of control. The media did not always know what to make of this. But for that matter, neither did Bill. How do you explain such a miracle of change?

For Bill Irwin, the explanation was to achieve the impossible: for a man with no sight to toil two thousand rugged miles through the eastern wilderness of America and emerge on a mountaintop in Maine alive. So on he and Orient went, into the most arduous terrain on the AT.

It was fall when they hit Vermont and the difficult White Mountains of New Hampshire. By now there were few hikers braving the cold and early snows. It was very late in the season for any northbound thru-hiker to still be this far from Katahdin, let alone a blind one. People started to worry about

Bill and Orient. The pair nearly froze in the remnants of a hurricane that pounded New England, and they found themselves struggling through punishing wind and knee-deep snow near notoriously storm-prone Mount Washington.

Finally, on October 24, in a chilly, misty wind, Bill and Orient stood atop Mount Katahdin. It had taken nearly nine months to do the impossible. Yet for Bill Irwin, the impossible had occurred on those sleepless nights in his son's rehab, when a voice seemed to whisper, "If not now, when?" A voice that promised that honesty could deliver him from misery and self-abasement and lead him to joys he had never known.

We scale mountains to gaze at the view from the top. What must that view have been to a man like Bill Irwin? For gaze he surely did—a gaze that went inward toward a soul he thought he'd lost, a view more beautiful than from any mountaintop on earth. Honesty brought change. Change, big or small, is a kind of personal miracle, and to experience the miraculous is to transcend all other human experience.

In helping prepare Bill's first-person account of his odyssey for *Guideposts*, I spent hours on the phone with him, faxed pages of the article to a friend of his who read it to him for his input, and studied the inspiring book Bill wrote with David McCasland, entitled *Blind Courage*. It was an intensive and rewarding process, and I was very proud of the story.

Not long after that, I was leaving Washington, DC, following a story interview, fighting the roiling Friday rush-hour throng at Union Station for my train back to New York when I spotted a tall man with steel-gray hair negotiating the crowd confidently—more so than I—with a magnificent

German shepherd in the lead. There was no doubt in my mind whom I was seeing, I just didn't know if I was more excited to meet Bill or Orient.

"Bill! Bill Irwin! It's me, Edward, from *Guideposts*."

I shook his hand, and then asked for permission to bury my fingers deep into the furrows of fur around Orient's powerful neck. Bill and I chatted quickly as I walked with him to his track. He was headed back to Burlington, South Carolina, after a conference. What struck me about meeting him in person was his serenity, the confidence with which he and Orient moved through the crowd. It was also impossible to reconcile this image with the person he once was, before that stark moment of honesty at his son's rehab graduation. Suddenly I had an idea. Would Bill be interested someday in my helping him prepare a series of devotionals for our annual book, *Daily Guideposts*? Bill was game, and we parted with the promise that we'd work together. Eventually, in the course of that project, Bill told me a story that both broke and lifted my heart, a poignant punctuation to his and Orient's Appalachian adventure and a reminder of the challenges of change.

The working life of a Seeing Eye dog is not very long— about seven years or so after they've been fostered, trained and paired with a human partner. There came a day when even Orient had to move on to the next, less demanding stage of his life. Orient was placed in a new home with a wonderful family so Bill and his new dog could fully bond. After six months had passed and Orient was settled in with his new family, Bill paid him a visit. He took the harness off the new dog and told him to rest; then he eased himself into a chair next to Orient, his hand falling to Orient's shoulders. They sat like that for a while, Bill thinking about how far he and this dog had come, the millions of steps they had taken together. All at once Orient stood and walked away. Bill was perplexed until a moment later when his old dog returned. In his mouth he held the harness.

Just one last walk, he was saying. *A little hike for old times' sake.* And perhaps, even for a dog, closure.

Orient slipped easily into the harness, and he and Bill stepped outside the comfortable suburban house that would be Orient's home for the rest of his days.

"Orient, forward."

And once again the Orient Express was on the move. Bill savored every step with his old companion. He replayed all their adventures on the trail, all the falls he had taken and the anxiety he knew Orient must have felt—Orient, who was trained never to let his master come to harm. An understanding had grown between them on the journey that Orient was not responsible for Bill's failings, and that together they were going to do something incredible if only they believed and persevered.

The last walk was over all too quickly and was probably against the rules anyway. Not that that mattered at this point, not between this man and this dog. Inside, Bill unharnessed Orient. Even if Bill could see, his tears would have blinded him. Orient circled a couple of times as if getting new bearings, and then settled with a contented sigh at Bill's feet.

Change is hard for dogs too.

Orient, forward.

At *Guideposts* we call a story like Bill Irwin's a "big" story. The magazine has published countless numbers of them in the past sixty-five years, starting with air ace Eddie Rickenbacker's heroic tale of survival in war. They are incredible true stories of personal courage and transformation. But what I love—and what readers love—are the small stories, the simple accounts from everyday people meeting life's challenges with hope and inspiration and bravery, changing themselves when they couldn't necessarily change their circumstances. I have always said that everyone has a *Guideposts* story.

Take the woman I'll call Stella, who lived in my building. Stella and I occasionally returned home from work at the same time and rode the elevator together. Stella was tall, or at least she seemed so to me, a guy who argues with his doctor over whether I'm five feet seven and three quarter inches tall or five foot eight. Stella had a great smile, one of those smiles you wait all day to see. She dressed conservatively for her age, I thought, including her shoes.

Especially her shoes.

Ugly black flats. Shoes that said, *Don't look at my feet*. And to accentuate the point, she always seemed to stand with her feet squished together and shoulders slightly stooped, as if to make herself smaller.

Arriving home one day, hearing the quick click of heels hurrying across the lobby as I entered the elevator, I held the door and in rushed Stella—wearing shoes with heels that were the footwear equivalent of the Empire State Building. She must have had some fancy event to attend, I figured.

A week or so later it happened again. This time I saw Stella striding off to work in a bright new pair of high-heeled shoes, very sharp, very fashionable. Very tall.

When it happened a third time, I couldn't help myself; I had to say something.

"It looks like you've been on a shoe-buying binge," I said.

Then came that smile and a laugh to match. "Thank you," she said. "You know, I just got sick of pretending I was something I'm not. I used to troll the Internet, looking at all the incredible, beautiful shoes out there I would never wear. I knew all the brands, all the designers. I was like one of those people visiting exotic travel sites staring at photos of places they would never actually visit, just dream about. Finally I thought, *Let's be honest about this. I am who I am: a tall woman with big feet.* I'm taller than most men, anyway; would it really matter if I did something I really wanted to do for myself and was just a little taller? Who cares? It's not my problem!"

Not any longer. Stella was tall and beautiful. You could literally see the physical manifestation of a whole new attitude in the way she carried herself, liberated from the futility of trying to be something she wasn't. She moved out not long after to get married. I never met her fiancé. Maybe she found someone as tall as she was. But I like to think it was someone who simply didn't mind how tall she was—someone, in fact, who found Stella as beautiful as Stella finally did.

Earlier I talked about biological and natural change and about process change—changes that are largely beyond our control. Then there is change we undergo as people—like the changes in Bill and Stella—human change, change that I think is metaphysical in the truest sense of the word: a transformation of mind and spirit that moves us in the direction of happiness. Just as biological change is largely governed by our DNA, so too, I believe, we possess spiritual DNA, an incorporeal genome whose genes are turned on—and sometimes off—by the events and the choices we make in life.

M. Scott Peck said famously at the start of his landmark book, *The Road Less Traveled*: "Life is difficult." Life is difficult most often because of change, change that demands we look honestly at ourselves. So often it is precisely these struggles that are the gateways to greater happiness. Falling in love, for example, is easy; it's like going over Niagara Falls in an inner tube. There's not much you can do but hang on. But recovering from the breakup of a relationship is more like swimming upstream from the falls, desperate not to be swept over the edge into despair. Usually we grow stronger at these times, even if we don't yet know it. So, yes, life is difficult, but those difficulties are the secret keys to growth and joy.

Just as biologists tell us that certain influences can switch certain genes on or off, honesty switches on a spiritual gene that readies us for change. Clarity is a moment of focused honesty, when a truth about ourselves become manifestly and irrevocably revealed, a truth from which we can never retreat.

When Bill told me about how he sat alone at night, drunk and isolated, I knew how he felt. I was once in exactly the same space Bill was.

I am not sure when the moment of clarity occurred in my own life, or if it was a series of moments that ultimately, even miraculously, led me to the revelation of truth that would free me from whom—or what—I'd become. But I remember one such moment that happened in 1983 or so.

I was sitting at a rickety table in a bar called the Victor on the ground floor of a flophouse in Hoboken, New Jersey, across the Hudson River from Manhattan. The Victor was located catty-corner from the slightly more upscale flophouse where

I tenuously resided, which meant that the Victor represented the grim symbol of at least one last rung of the ladder lower than the one I clung to. And my grip was slipping.

It was a few minutes after six in the morning but I'd been up since four, when I emerged in a dawning terror from the alcoholic stupor I'd fallen into a few hours earlier after a night of blackout drinking. Those two hours were pure mental and physical anguish as I waited in a kind of existential hell for the time when liquor could be legally sold in New Jersey, cursing this atavistic Puritanism that caused me such suffering, and pacing the streets of the square-mile town until the neon Victor light sputtered on, a merciful beacon of relief. Without a drink in me I couldn't think, I couldn't eat, I couldn't do anything. I was literally not me—not just not myself, but not anyone.

Now I was getting dizzy on the cigarette I bummed off the annoyed bartender and trying desperately to hold down the drink that would stop my hands from trembling so badly that I couldn't have written my own name on a piece of paper if my life depended on it. What my life depended on was this purely medicinal drink that I couldn't afford to lose from my foodless stomach, for there was very little money left in my pocket to buy another one, and this precious alcohol had to get into my bloodstream before the inner frenzy of fear would finally abate.

At age twenty-nine, I was thru-hiking the Jellinek chart, a diagnostic tool clinicians use to track the sad course and predictable outcome of alcoholism and drug abuse. At an age when most serious alcoholics were just getting started,

I'd pretty much crossed the addiction Rubicon. If I drank continuously for too long and stopped too abruptly, I suffered hallucinations and convulsions. I'd been to emergency rooms, detoxes, and even a rehab before there were many rehabs—and certainly before people talked about them and turned their experiences into cable TV shows. My final semester at Yale, I'd lived mostly in the psychiatric wing—just a couple of private rooms, actually—of the student health service, where I was dosed with Librium and Antabuse before heading out to class each morning.

I hadn't been to my job as a Manhattan-based telemarketer for four days now and had stopped calling in "sick" to my boss, Caroline, after two, all of which led me to the pretty firm conclusion that this must be Thursday. For some reason that fact comforted me as much as it terrified me that it was even in question. I was terrified of nearly everything at that moment. Terrified that I was still wearing the same clothes I'd been wearing Monday morning, when I set off for work and then stopped at the Victor for a quick nerve-steadier. Terrified by the fact that I'd destroyed a long-standing relationship with a woman I loved deeply but not as much as I loved—or at least was devoted to—alcohol. I did not drink because I lost that relationship; I lost that relationship because I drank and because, after four years, it had become unbearable for her. It terrified me to see the person I was. But nothing terrified me so much as not knowing where the next drink would come from.

The bar was loud and smoky and filling up with railroad workers who were just getting off the graveyard shift from the transit station across the way. For them it was happy hour.

It was anything but happy for me and the handful of other shameful, solitary morning drinkers with whom I never made eye contact.

Instead I stared out the grimy plate-glass window at the swarm of commuters making their industrious way into New York, swept underground to the PATH train that would speed them beneath the river and lift them, I imagined, onto the bustling streets of Manhattan like so many weightless figures in a Chagall painting. Why couldn't I join them? What stood between me and that life? Why was I sinking in the quicksand of my own psyche when I could be one of that tide of humanity passing before my eyes who lived completely manageable lives, had houses and cars and jobs and families and kitchen appliances, who weren't ashamed to look other people in the eye, who were moving on every day of their lives to something else, who were productive members of society? I didn't even feel like a member of the human race. It was alienation so profound and disturbing that only alcohol could quell it, even if it was alcohol that was, at least on the physiological level, causing it. At some point the night before—or was it the night before that?—I'd awakened on some steps somewhere with a little Hispanic girl standing over me screaming, "Muerto! Muerto!" Her father or uncle or someone quickly disproved this, jerking me up by the collar and sending me on my stumbling way. But that little girl had been more right than not. "Dead" described me pretty well.

Someone had put Jersey son Bruce Springsteen on the jukebox. "Badlands." I tried to tune out the song even though I liked Bruce. The tremors in my hands had pretty much subsided enough that I could lift my glass to my lips without fear of spilling anything. I took care to set it back down as quietly as I could, as if hoping no one would notice.

The glass was nearly empty. I found myself wondering very simply if there was a way, any way, I would not fill it up again. Could I imagine that? Could I envision the glass staying empty? Could I imagine altering something that had become such an elemental aspect of my quasi-existence that without it I couldn't imagine life? Not today maybe; not tomorrow necessarily. It wasn't about when; it was about if. Could I somehow pull out of this downward spiral? Did I want to? Could I look at myself with stark and unblinking honesty and see the potentiality of change and finally embrace it?

It wasn't a voice, not like what happened to Bill. It was something from within, welling up from a part of me that alcohol and shame had not killed: *Yes.* I could allow myself that. I could imagine the glass staying empty. I could change. I wanted to.

But how?

2
Willingness

I f honesty is a sail, willingness is the wind that fills it. It's not enough to say, "I know I should be a more attentive husband," or "I need to be a more patient boss," or "I'm closing myself off to certain people and experiences by being judgmental," or "I know my habit of gnawing on pens annoys people to no end (and is taking a toll on my incisors)."

I have to find the *willingness* to do something about it.

I wasn't joking about the pens. I devour them. In fact, I choose pens based on their chewability. I like nice, soft plastic ones. At the end of the day it looks like a cocker spaniel has been sitting at my desk. Pens have exploded in my mouth, on my clothes, in my eyes. I've written devotionals about it, blogged about it, been warned by dentists about it (and even been threatened with a mouth guard), been embarrassed by a colleague's ten-year-old daughter about it ("*Eeew!* Did you do this?"). Still, I can't break this mortifying habit.

I am not feeble-minded. I'm certainly honest about my problem. I just haven't committed myself to changing it. I have not applied the willingness that will lead to a new, non-pen-chewing, happier me.

Willingness is honesty in action. People who are happy are people who are willing to do the challenging work necessary to get that way.

We all know people who know that they need to change—yet who never do. They've memorized their weaknesses and shortcomings like the state capitals and are often eager to share them with you—how they always seem to choose the wrong partners . . . or they have a "problem with authority" . . . or they can't figure out what they "want to be when they grow up" . . . or whatever. Yet, maddeningly, they never seem to do anything about it!

We're all a bit maddening in this way at times, and it's not always a bad thing. Change rarely happens overnight; change is a process. I think there are two types of people in the world: those who dive straight into the pool and get used to the water right away, and those who ease themselves in inch by frigid inch. Neither can fathom the other's method. But both work.

Then there are those who just stand at the edge of the diving board and never move.

I once had an employee I dreaded giving performance evaluations to—not because he was combative or defensive, but because he was so eager to agree with me on his shortcomings. I'd say, "You're really good at X, but Y and especially Z need improvement." He'd say, "You're right, I totally stink at Y and Z." There would then follow a discussion in which I would ask him how he thought he could improve his performance in the coming year. We'd have a good, frank talk, draw up an action plan together—something doable and measurable—and shake hands on it. "I know you can do this," I'd say.

At the next evaluation we'd go over the plan. Inevitably he was still holding his own on X, Y and Z, but had shown scant improvement. Now, this was not a bad employee. He seemed to work hard and want to try. Yet there was something holding him back, something deeper than I was qualified to address. I asked in exasperation whether I was failing him as a manager. No, he said, he just wasn't very good at those tasks, but he was determined to improve. After several rounds of this, and even with some special coaching, Y and Z were still problems and we had to let him go. I remember wondering how I would write a recommendation for him if ever asked. The most I could say would be, "He's really good at what he's really good at." That would be X.

Looking back on it now, I can see his problem was a lack of willingness, not a lack of honesty. He knew what his problem was. Why are some people so fearful of change that they will not even attempt it, even when they know it's necessary? What keeps us trapped in unsuccessful behaviors?

Charles Darwin said change was inherently conservative. Whether or not you accept Darwinian evolution by means of natural selection as the ultimate explanation for life on this planet—and I'm not sure even he would have claimed that—Darwin had a lot to say about change. "It is not the strongest of the species that survive, nor the most intelligent, but the one most responsive to change" is a quote that is attributed to him.

Change *is* necessarily conservative. Too much or too rapid change results in instability. We're designed to stick with what works and resist change unless our hand is forced. Thus change is a paradox: We can both need and resist it simultaneously, and not necessarily be wrong either way.

Sometimes we keep doing things simply because they feel good even if they're damaging in the long run. Anyone who eats a typical American diet probably struggles with weight. Boy, do I love ice cream. I know what's good for me, but I also know what's *good*, and the two impulses do battle until I decide it's time to fit back into those jeans that used to be loose. I chew on my pens because it releases stress even if it's bad for my teeth, and going to the dentist just causes me more stress. Bad habits are rarely without a good reason.

This is evident in an adult who survived an abusive child-hood or dysfunctional family. Defense strategies that enabled the child to survive a pathological environment totally backfire in the adult world, where lying to your boss is not a good thing even if lying to your dad spared you a humiliating punishment. A friend of mine worked for a long time at a job he hated. It actually got to the point where he was verging on panic attacks before he walked into his office building. "Something has to change," he said one night over dinner.

"Why do you put up with it?" I wanted to know.

"I don't have a choice."

"You don't?"

"It's always been like this."

"Since when?"

"Since . . ."

He stopped. My friend had grown up in a family in which the tension at home was unendurable. "I remember coming home from school and being so nervous I'd sit outside for an hour before I went in. That's the way I feel now." He dropped his fork onto his plate. "That's *why* I feel this way now."

My friend has a new job and has learned that not every situation has to replicate his family dynamics, especially bad ones. It is almost axiomatic that we sometimes seek what we know rather than what we need. Yet patterns can be broken with recognition and a willingness to change.

I had a new manager once who, when upset or frustrated, would raise her voice. No, that's putting it mildly. She would yell at people, and we're not a yelling culture here at *Guideposts*. I finally talked to her about this and she said that growing up in her big family, you had to yell to be heard. "Nothing ever got done until somebody yelled," she said. Then she added, "LIKE THIS!" with a laugh that got me laughing with her. I reminded her that other people didn't necessarily grow up in homes where they were routinely yelled at and might not see it as such a normal, let alone effective, form of communication. They might just do their jobs better—or at least be happier about doing them—"if you didn't yell quite so much." I whispered the last seven words, and we resolved the problem.

Some negative behaviors have roots so deep that to rid ourselves of them seems impossible—addiction, anger, low self-esteem, anxiety, depression and other self-destructive patterns. It's almost as if without them there will be a terrifying void or unacceptable vulnerability. Changing these behaviors takes great courage and a powerful willingness. There is nothing braver or more inspiring than someone who seeks to deliver themselves from a profound state of discontent, to realize dreams they once thought were lost. Someone like Amy Pressley Palacio.

If there are two themes that seem unlikely companions, they would be September 11, 2001, and weight loss. Yet for Amy Pressley Palacio, they are forever linked.

We are a body-image-obsessed culture. We spend way too much time thinking about how we look. We have ourselves scraped and peeled and injected with otherwise toxic organisms in an endless quest for perfection. In a world full of starving people, we actually pay doctors to vacuum fat out of us. Most of the results are either temporary or illusory.

Collectively this country has an issue with weight. Some of us don't worry enough about it, and some of us worry too much. Amy Pressley had a lot to worry about—302 pounds, to be precise.

She'd never been skinny. Even as a toddler she was pudgy and loved to snack. Other kids teased her, but that didn't change things; it only made her self-conscious and unhappy. Kids outgrow their cruelty. But Amy did not outgrow her weight problem. She just grew.

Something else grew in Amy as well: a strange dream that she didn't understand. She saw herself as a member of the United States Navy. Amy didn't come from a military family. She didn't know any sailors or have any particular yen for seafaring. This dream just seemed to walk up and take a seat in her life, like a friendly stranger. Here I am, said the dream.

In high school in Waynesville, North Carolina, Amy felt the urge so strongly that she signed up for the school's Junior

ROTC program. There was no weight requirement at this level. There were no sharp Navy blues in her size either. They didn't make them that big. She had to go out and get a custom-made uniform and listen to her classmates' jokes about hiring a tentmaker. It hurt. But the dream said, "Navy."

At the end of high school Amy decided to cut the dream loose. Amy could barely walk outside to her car without stopping to catch her breath. And the prospect of being made to swim terrified her. So she went on with her life—and of course the weight problem went with her. She ate when she was hungry and when she wasn't. She ate when she was lonely or frustrated or just plain bored. She buried her feelings with food. And let's not forget: Amy loved food. Because food was the one thing that seemed to love her back.

She was under no illusions about her obesity. After high school Amy became a medical assistant, so she understood the damage overeating and lack of exercise were doing to her body. She moved to Florida, found a job, and bought a house. Not bad for a twenty-five-year-old. She was finally settled. Except she felt more unsettled than ever.

She volunteered to work with the youth group at her church, hoping that by giving guidance she might also find some. Yet the more she talked to teens about hearing the call of God in their lives and discovering their path, the more she felt she had lost hers. She decided to commit herself fully to nursing and went back to school to become a registered nurse anesthetist. Amy did well and her self-esteem inched up.

She also managed to lose a little weight by sticking to a diet-and-exercise program. But she'd done that before, always yo-yoing back up. Counting calories, taking the stairs instead of the elevator, rewarding herself in other ways than with food—she'd been there, done that, like so many of us. Nothing ever seemed to work for long, and with each failure she seemed to lose more willpower than weight. Was it just her destiny to be fat and alone?

On September 11, Amy was driving to class when she heard the news over the car radio that the World Trade Center and the Pentagon had been attacked. By the time she got to school, she began to grasp the terrible toll that had been taken in innocent lives. Like the rest of America she was in a state of shock and disbelief, unprepared for anything like this on such a flawless late summer's day in a time of peace and prosperity.

In the student lounge she could barely bring herself to watch the nightmarish images on TV. The more she watched, the more she knew that the world had changed forever. What she didn't know was that she too was about to change. She bowed her head to pray but instead she heard these words, as clear as if they were spoken out loud: *Join the Navy.*

That couldn't be right, she thought. That dream had died years ago. But the thought persisted: *Do something. Stand up for your country. Join the Navy.* The dream was back.

It made no sense to her, this urge, even as it continued through the days ahead and the country groped its way through the national pain and confusion. Amy had a good job, a house, her nursing classes. And the Navy, she knew, didn't make uniforms big enough for her. She'd found that out the hard way. Yet that unsettled feeling that had been haunting her seemed to merge with the imperative of the dream.

The moment of truth came one stifling afternoon a few days later. Driving along the freeway after work, Amy found herself suddenly taking an exit she knew led to a Navy recruitment center. Only a willingness to act would put her confusion to rest. She pulled into the parking lot, climbed out of her car, and walked up to the center's door. She paused to catch her breath in the hot and humid Florida air. Then she stepped inside, trying to ignore all the posters of fit young men and women in Navy uniforms, and approached a recruiter behind the desk.

"What are the requirements for joining up?" she heard herself ask him.

The recruiter looked her up and down for a moment, and then said, "First, lose fifty pounds. Second, lose another fifty pounds. Then maybe we'll talk to you."

With a laugh, he went back to whatever it was he was doing before Amy had walked up to his desk and dared to take the biggest risk she'd ever taken. Our dreams can humiliate us as often as they fulfill us. Up until this moment in her life Amy would have dropped her head and slunk away, intent on burying her feelings with food and self-pity. But something was different. She was meant to join the Navy and nothing would convince her otherwise. This dream wasn't going to give in, not this time. She turned on her heel and stalked out, more determined than ever. That night she made a vow to herself and to God: She would lose one hundred pounds by her twenty-sixth birthday on February 26. Moreover, she would be in shape to pass whatever physical the Navy threw at her. Inside her size twenty-four body, Amy already felt lighter and fitter.

One hundred pounds in five months. No one said it would be easy, and it wasn't. Amy knew exercise was even more important than diet, so she signed up at a Gold's Gym near her house. Anyone who has walked into a gym for the first time knows how daunting it can be. Your eye always picks out the lean runners pounding away on the treadmills or the guys bench-pressing massive weight and grunting like Bulgarian Olympians. Half the time you just want to turn around and get back in the car. Amy felt that way for about a nanosecond before she walked up to the gym's owner, a man named Tony, and told him what was on her mind. She didn't have the money to hire a personal trainer, but Tony was so impressed he offered to devise a training program himself for Amy.

"Can you be tough on me and whip me into shape?" Amy asked Tony. "Boot camp is going to be hard."

Tony grinned. "I like your attitude. You're going to be an inspiration to everyone in this gym. Boot camp will be nothing after I'm through with you!"

Every Tuesday, Thursday, and Saturday Tony pushed her past limits she never believed she could even reach. It was hard and it got harder, but with each session, with each milestone she passed, Amy began to see, for the first time in her life, her own potential—the potential that had been buried beneath fat and poor self-esteem but had never died. The realization and conviction that she could change her life was the biggest change of all. It was a revelation.

She didn't so much count calories as change the way she ate. Food was for nourishment, she told herself, not escape. She abandoned processed junk foods and switched to natural foods. "If God didn't make it, I wasn't going to put it in my body," she declared. She thought through her feelings before eating. Changing her thinking about food was a major challenge. For years she'd had a dangerously compulsive relationship with the thing that we all need to live but that was killing Amy. Now she rode her bike, ran on the beach, learned to swim and surf, and avoided weighing herself too often. She wanted to gauge her progress by how she felt on the inside, and she felt stronger by the day.

Amy would be the first to tell you that she had times of doubt and weakness. She used each one to forge her willingness to go on. In her mind she saw herself striding back into that same recruiting station and proudly signing her enlistment papers. She burned that scene into her mind.

One morning in late February Amy put one foot and then the other on her bathroom scale. She was almost afraid to look down. When she did, she had to look twice. It read 170. Incredibly, maybe even miraculously, she had lost *more* than a hundred pounds in five months. She was so elated she didn't even notice the tears streaming down her cheeks until she looked in the mirror.

Amy felt a lightness not just in her body, but in her soul. Now something glowed within her. Next stop was the Navy recruitment center. This time she strode in confidently and walked right past the recruiter who'd snubbed her in September. He looked at her with a puzzled expression, as if he were trying to place where he'd seen her before. Amy went straight to the office of another recruiter to whom she'd been talking on the phone and presented herself for service in the United States Navy. The paperwork was already in order. "Your entrance physical will be in"—he checked his calendar— "two days: the twenty-sixth," Amy's birthday.

On September 11, 2002, at almost precisely the same time that she had been listening to the shocking news on her car radio the year before, Amy stood in formation with her fellow recruits at a memorial service for the victims of the attack. She held herself erect despite powerful emotions within. She had answered the call of this tragedy, reaching for a distant dream she had nearly abandoned and finding the willingness to achieve it. She had made contact with something deep within herself that she had long believed lost. At five foot seven and a lean, strong 158 pounds, she was even more transformed than her size ten body showed. She was *happy*.

There was one other big crazy blessing to come for Amy. In the Navy she met and married her husband, Wilson Palacio, also a sailor, who said it felt as if he'd waited his whole life for Amy. She knew just how he felt.

People say you can't achieve lasting and meaningful personal change unless you do it solely for yourself. I'm not so sure that's right. Obviously you shouldn't change just to please or impress others. But I think we can and often do start a change journey for more than just ourselves. Sometimes we care about others more than we are able (at first) to care about ourselves, and it's our commitment to them that activates the powerful will to change. Amy found at least some of her motivation through her sense of duty to country and to her fallen fellow citizens. She also summoned loyalty to a dream that she felt came not from herself and was uniquely given to her. People change to become better for their children and their partners all the time, or to become better bosses and employees, better friends and neighbors, and better citizens. That leads to happiness with ourselves, and there's nothing wrong or shallow about that. It's right to care about what others think of us and to allow those perceptions to help shape us. That's the way we are made. We certainly change for God.

In finding the willingness to change, I think it's important to imagine the positive impact our change will have on others and to use that as a powerful motivation. As Tony the gym manager told Amy, we can all be an inspiration to someone. What an incredibly potent concept! A recent survey conducted on Guideposts.org revealed that most people want to be a positive influence on others. The power to influence others positively, especially those we love, is one of the greatest powers human beings possess.

Besides, who wants to be a disappointment to their family, friends or colleagues? Who wants to be an anti-inspiration? We fear letting others down—and negative motivation can be a compelling force for change. It certainly had a powerful, if painful, impact on me. In fact, it may have saved my life.

Let's return to that bleak morning from the previous chapter. I sat looking at my grimy, empty glass on the wobbly table at the Victor, imagining whether I could somehow find a way to not fill it again. Could I buck the tide I'd succumbed to for years? It was a searing moment of honesty, just as Bill Irwin's had been when he stood up in his son's rehab and called himself an alcoholic. I certainly knew what I was. The very circumstances of my life screamed it out at me, and never more empirically than on that nerve-wracking morning. I finally could accept the accusation. But could I *do* anything about it? Was I willing? Would I ever be?

The music had changed on the jukebox from Springsteen to Michael Jackson—"Human Nature." A knot of people at the bar were singing along, way off-key. I counted the change in my pocket. Not enough. I left the bar, crossed over to the Hoboken train station, found a pay phone, and called Michael, my best friend from Michigan, who'd moved East about the same time I had and who, after I'd fled New Haven, had talked me into moving to Hoboken, where he and his wife, Kate, lived. I didn't actually have any friends left at this point, but Michael was more like a brother to me. The phone kept ringing, and I feared he'd already left for work. Worse, I dreaded Kate might pick up. At last Michael answered.

"It's me," I said.

Long silence.

"Can you spare twenty bucks?" I asked, trying to control the tremor that had migrated from my hands to my voice.

"Not for you."

"Ten."

"No, Edward. No. Caroline called a few minutes ago just to see if you were alive. I told her I thought I saw you lurching down Washington Street last night."

"Caroline?"

"Don't bother. They don't want to see you again. The job is gone."

"Five."

This final entreaty was met with an exasperated sigh, more like a muted howl, and then a long pause. Finally: "If you need shoes, I will buy you shoes. If you are hungry, I'll give you food. If you need a haircut, I'll get you a haircut. But I will not give you money."

I hung up. I didn't need shoes or a haircut or even food, at that moment at least. I needed a drink. I wasn't angry. What right did I have? Michael was being perfectly reasonable, even forgiving. The other night at his house for dinner I'd surreptitiously drunk half his liquor supply on my frequent trips to the bathroom in retaliation for his rationing me only two glasses of wine with the meal, and even then doling it out warily. I was surprised his wife was even letting him speak to me. Right now Michael would be knotting his tie and slipping into his serious lawyer's suit, soon to join the gathering throng being swept into Manhattan to do an honest day's work. It made me sick with shame to know I disappointed him. And nothing made me want to drink more—or at least was a better excuse for drinking—than shame. Shame is pain inflicted by our conscience. Like physical pain, it's a signal that something is wrong. People talk about athletes "playing through pain." Most times I felt as if I were playing through shame. This was not supposed to be me. Yet it was.

The comparatively small amount of alcohol I'd choked down at the Victor was already beginning to burn off and the fear was coming back; my pulse was starting to race and I was sweating. The long, warm day stretched ahead of me like a desert I had to cross. My mind was gripped by a single imperative: figure out how to get more alcohol. Without it I'd grow increasingly frantic and panicky. Worst-case scenario: I risked going into convulsions and ending up, as I had before, coming to in an emergency room with a Valium drip plugged into a vein and trying to remember my name and

Social Security number for the gathered medical personnel. Then a doctor would strongly suggest that I submit to a CAT scan and perhaps—just to cover our bases—a friendly spinal tap. I'd been down that road and would try to explain that this was alcohol withdrawal and dehydration, not a brain tumor. I'd be okay. The Valium I.V. would do the trick, thank you. The doctor would just shake his head. I knew what he must be thinking. I was too young to be having alcoholic seizures and the DTs. There must be something wrong with my brain. That, at least, I couldn't dispute.

Rush hour was now at full boil. People bustled by me as if I were a minor obstacle. I tried to move to where I wouldn't be jostled, but it was fruitless: I was stuck like a hunk of flotsam in a tide of humanity. I looked into people's eyes as they rushed past, these purposeful strangers, trying to find someone who might say yes.

The first couple of prospects ignored me, and for a minute I thought I might start hyperventilating at the ignominy of what I'd reduced myself to. But then one man stopped and fished a dollar from his pocket. Every so often others did the same. Sometimes just a few coins, sometimes more. I don't remember what exactly my pitch was. I think I just mumbled something about needing money. I wasn't up to concocting a story. Why lie on top of it all? That would feel more like stealing than begging, and begging was bad enough. It felt like a nightmare, but I kept going and I kept getting money, small but accruing amounts of it.

Then a pair of eyes met mine and didn't turn away. There was a flicker of stunned recognition and the person slowed ever so slightly, keeping his eyes on me while he passed, looking me up and down. We were not strangers, not quite. I knew him vaguely from the grad-student dining hall at Yale. And without a doubt he was appraising me with barely disguised disbelief and disgust. Then he was gone, racing for his train into the city. Something told me we would be haunting each other's thoughts for the rest of the day.

The encounter shocked me out of my mendicant mode. I put my head down and rushed from the station, stopping at the first bodega I found to buy a tallboy of cheap warm beer and sucking it down through a straw within thirty paces of the door, willing myself not to vomit. It had been at least a day since I'd eaten anything, probably not since dinner at Michael's. I wanted to escape into Manhattan, where I would feel more anonymous, but first I stopped back at my room to put on cooler (though not necessarily cleaner) clothes. That necessitated passing Louie, the flophouse proprietor, who was perched on a stool in the rundown foyer that served as a lobby.

Because of Louie's bulk, the stool seemed to be growing out of him, like an appendage. A bout with throat cancer forced him to speak through one of those mechanical voice boxes, giving his voice a buzzing quality. For all his gruffness, Louie was a good soul, and there was a weary kindness in his perpetually puffy and dark-ringed eyes. Louie had made me promise to stop drinking as a condition of continued residency. In my more paranoid moments, I imagined that he somehow knew everything I did, that he was in contact with my family, that he had even talked to my mother. He activated his voice box by pressing his fingers to his throat.

"Heard you stopped in the Victor."

I stared down at the floor, inching my way toward the death trap of an elevator.

"Look, kid," he croaked. "I told you."

"I'm all right, Louie. Really. I'm fine."

"You need to do something about yourself. Are you willing to keep going like this?"

I wasn't sure what I was willing to do. I just wanted to get out of Hoboken in the next twenty minutes.

"What about your family? They know? Your mom?"

The elevator door clattered closed.

"Rent's due," I heard his voice box buzz as the lift jolted into action.

The PATH train squealed and jolted, worming its way down the tunnel and picking up speed under the Hudson. I love trains, even subways, and I felt momentarily protected, deep beneath the riverbed. If only I could stay down here, burrowed safely into the ancient sediment. What about my family? Louie had wanted to know. I wished he hadn't asked that question. Sooner or later they would have to find out what was becoming of me, and the thought filled me with guilt and dread. I hadn't lived at home since I left at seventeen for college at the University of Michigan in Ann Arbor. It was only about an hour away from home, but it felt like another continent altogether. I'd bummed around the hemisphere after that, island hopping across the Caribbean; then disappearing into the jungles and mountains of South America; then living at an artists colony in New Mexico; writing for a newspaper; crewing aboard an ore boat on the Great Lakes; and eventually, almost by default, ending up in grad school back east, studying playwriting and drama. Somewhere along the way, before I knew it was happening, my life began to disintegrate. I'd always been independent, a free spirit, an artist, the youngest child who got away with way more than the other kids ever did. As the baby, I was my mother's undisguised favorite. My father was getting old and just didn't have that much fight left in him, especially after my brother, Bobby, who had Down syndrome and was the apple of his eye, died. Consequently I got away with a lot. It was no secret that I drank, couldn't always stop when I should, and got into trouble sometimes because of it. Drugs too. But my primary mood-changing substance of choice, the first love to which I always returned and remained pledged, was ethanol. I'd been good in school and my academic achievements had acted as a kind of buffer, mitigating whatever trouble I found myself in: *Oh no; someone this bright doesn't turn into a derelict!* Thus I had been able to orchestrate everyone's collective sense of denial (including my own) to avoid any real scrutiny.

Until recently I'd been able to support myself, more or less. I recoiled at asking for help from my family and compromising what I still clung to as my dignity and self-reliance. Asking for help would also require disclosing too much, which would elicit the kind of help I didn't want and couldn't admit I needed. Then they would *know*. And I couldn't let them know. In fact, it occurred to me as the PATH train wound into the first station, I'd proven that morning that I'd rather ask strangers for help than my own family.

They had loved the woman I'd been seeing—almost as much as I did—and hoped I would marry her. When she called to tell them she was leaving me, they didn't really understand, and Daria didn't feel comfortable, I suppose, spelling out for them, in all its sordid and ultimately irreconcilable detail, the debris of a relationship that could never be reconstituted into anything positive. It was over. There was only so much emotional shrapnel she was willing to be ripped by. There was some vague talk of my having problems, a breakdown of some sort, and she had hinted to them that I needed help. But as usual I guarded my privacy with such vigilance that it had the intended effect of fending off any serious inquiries into my increasingly unstable and self-destructive behavior. Besides, I was nearly a thousand miles away and I made sure to call just often enough to keep everyone at bay while maintaining my emotional autonomy. They had their suspicions, to be sure, but they had no idea of my transmogrification and there was no way I would ever let them know. Never. They would be more likely to find out from the coroner than from me.

I got out at the World Trade Center and soon found myself ascending the huge escalators up to the massive ground-level lobby, all glass and steel and marble and filtered sunlight, feeling a bit more on my rails, thanks primarily to another beer on the train, along with one of those minibottles of vodka. I was well enough now to possibly keep down a doughnut. My anxiety was receding a bit. Maybe today was the day something would change. I wouldn't even call it hope. Just a sense of temporary relief, a moment-by-moment reprieve. There is nothing like the insanity of an addiction to compel you to live in the moment: Urgent priorities come into stark focus and leave little room for ambiguity. Yet in the back of my mind I couldn't quite extinguish the grim scene in Hoboken. The humiliation reverberated like an ominous minor chord through my being. Something was different now. I'd crossed some line and the soundtrack had changed.

I found the sheer scale of the Twin Towers comforting, these giant totems of commerce. Their solidity and symmetry gave the world a sense of order and stability. Never could I have dreamed what their fate would be and how it would change all of us. Anchored as they were deep in the bedrock of the island, the Towers felt to me that day like a lifeline, indestructible, a place to wander through and around and feel safe.

It was easy to get lost in the warren of the streets of lower Manhattan. I spent the afternoon ambling, deliberately losing my bearings to the extent that I had them. Yet I kept walking past St. Paul's Chapel near Trinity Church, just east of the World Trade Center, with its historic graveyard that seemed so incongruous amidst this teeming nexus of moneychanging. I bummed more change and drank a little, but my body was so weak and my legs so wobbly that I could only tolerate small amounts. I was in a state of profound exhaustion. At one point a tall black man with a loping stride and serious dreads looked at me, threw back his head and laughed. What was he thinking? How did I appear to him? I walked along Church Street and Broadway, past food carts and outdoor cafes, street vendors and newsstands. I wandered through Chinatown, up into Little Italy and back, and then over to the Fulton Street Market, where tourists were standing in line to buy stuff no New Yorker would wait five seconds for.

Time and again I found myself back at St. Paul's, almost as if repeatedly coming out of a trance in front of its old gates. The symbolism startled me. St. Paul was one of the great transformative figures in Christianity, miraculously converted, I'd been taught, on the road to Damascus. And then there was that old burial ground beside the chapel, a swath of earth marked by soot-darkened headstones, towered over by glass and steel and millions of living, breathing humans. Why did I keep coming back here?

I thought about going inside but stopped myself. What would I do in there? Enjoy the coolness? Pray? No, I didn't think I was quite ready for that. And what if somebody offered me help?

By now it was rush hour again and I made my way down to Battery Park at the tip of the island. There, from a weather-worn bench, I watched the sunlight fade over the harbor, throwing a blanket of shadows across Staten Island. The salty breeze blowing in off the bay felt good. A tanker was gliding toward the sea and I thought about my own sailing days, what it was like to watch the land behind you disappear and give way to the vastness of open water. In the gloaming, the Statue of Liberty seemed close enough to reach out and touch. She stood so stoically that she looked like a Hollywood prop or a giant actress who at sunset would lower her torch wearily and walk across the water to Jersey City to be relieved by her night double, vigilant in their guardianship of freedom and liberty.

A sprinkling of lights from the Verrazano-Narrows Bridge and beyond punctuated the dark. I drew myself up from my bench and turned back toward the World Trade Center. What now? Back across the river? To what? More of the same? A chill rattled through me and I half-wondered if I was having a heart attack. Or maybe hoped. Where would this end? Because it couldn't go on.

I walked through the doors of the South Tower and wandered among the closed stores, window-shopping and killing time before the inevitable descent on the escalators. I just didn't want to get back on the PATH train, not yet, going back to Hoboken, back to the squalid trap my life had become, to figure out a way to keep drinking because that was all that seemed to matter.

I stopped in front of Brooks Brothers and stuck out my tongue. I wasn't being insolent. I was looking at my reflection in the darkened window to see if I could detect a tremor in my tongue. I could. You can sometimes stop your hands from shaking but not your tongue. I learned that in the hospital. I pinched the skin on my forearm, and then released it. It returned to normal only slowly. Dehydrated. Learned that in the hospital too. I regarded my reflected visage for a moment. Was that really me or was it some doppelgänger, some awful impostor? Quickly I turned away.

Heading toward the massive escalator bank, now mostly empty, I felt as if I were about to be swallowed up in a terrible chasm, a pit I might never be able to climb out of. Suddenly I was veering away, my weary legs willing me toward a long row of pay phones. I picked up a receiver, dialed a number—collect— and let it ring until a familiar voice answered and accepted the charges.

"Mom?" I said.

3

Imagination

One of the most quoted of the many quotable things Albert Einstein said was: "Imagination is more important than knowledge."

The second, less frequently cited part of the statement is actually my favorite: "For while knowledge defines all we currently know and understand, imagination points to all we might yet discover and create."

Honesty and willingness are knowledge-based: We recognize a need and choose a course of action. The third change key, imagination, is directional: It points the way to the transformation we seek. Imagination is forward leaning. It brings to light what is possible. It weds insight and action to vision.

Imagination isn't just the province of artists and great minds. Every one of us is blessed with this amazing capacity, this gift of the mind. Through the power of our imaginations we can change our thoughts—and, as the philosopher and psychologist William James said, by changing our thinking we change our lives.

We use our imaginations constantly. Every time we think about something that hasn't happened yet, we're using our imaginations. In the morning, when we survey the prospects of our day, our minds roaming through our to-do lists, we're performing an imaginative, creative act. We're seeing ourselves as actors in the future through the medium of our imaginations. Thanks to imagination, we don't have to be who we were or do exactly what we did yesterday. We can change ourselves, and thus the future. So I'm with Einstein on this one. Imagination trumps knowledge.

Imagination differs from fantasy in that it identifies a potential outcome from a plausible reality. It brings to light what is possible. But similar to fantasy, it does turn us into time travelers. Daily life unfolds on a linear timeline: We're born, we live, we die. In between, we laugh, we love, we grieve, we forgive. We grow. Imagination lets us peer along the timeline to see who we might be down the road. Once we honestly decide to change and summon the willingness to commit to that change, it is absolutely necessary that we envision ourselves changed.

Close your eyes and clear your head of all thoughts. Concentrate your imagination on a single image: *You, changed.* What you look like. What you sound like. How you act. And of paramount importance, how you feel—strong, confident, grateful, happy. Through every step of your change journey, never let these images escape your thoughts. The more you imagine your change, the more you will become it.

Dr. Norman Vincent Peale called this process imaging, subtitling his book of that name, *The Powerful Way to Change Your Life*. To quote, "The concept of imaging is a mental activity that consists of picturing vividly in your conscious mind a desired goal or objective and holding that image until it sinks into your unconscious mind, where it releases great untapped energies. It works best when combined with the seemingly illogical technique of giving thanks for benefits before they are received. It solves problems, strengthens personalities, improves health and greatly enhances the chances for success in any kind of endeavor."

What made Dr. Peale such a convincing proponent of imaging and positive thinking? Because he was a practitioner too. Like a pioneering scientist testing a new cure first on himself, Dr. Peale applied his techniques to transform his own life. It is hard to believe that the man considered one of the great motivators and orators of the twentieth century was at one time in his life plagued by self-doubt, insecurity, shyness and a near-total lack of self-confidence.

I met Dr. Peale late in his life and early in my tenure at *Guideposts*. He had traveled to the city from his idyllic farmhouse in Pawling, New York, to give a talk for the Dutch Treat Club, a conclave of prominent writers and thinkers to which he belonged and who met periodically at Sardi's, a famous restaurant in the heart of the theater district. But first he stopped by the magazine's offices to visit Van Varner, the editor-in-chief who had recently hired me. Van wanted to introduce Dr. Peale to his newest employee.

It was a brisk day with a bright winter's sun streaming through the twenty-third floor offices. I was more curious than nervous to meet the great man, and I'd made certain to wear a respectable suit and tie. I also brought along my wife Julee's copy of *The Power of Positive Thinking* and was going to ask him to sign it for her.

My first startled impression upon laying eyes on him was that he was awfully old, well into his eighties, and seemed older, moving slowly and appearing distracted and even a bit irritated at times. Van introduced me and he was gracious, his eyes lighting up a bit with surprise, and happy to sign the book for Julee. For some reason he handed the book back to Van. He asked me where I was from and when I said Michigan, he said we were practically neighbors. He was born and raised in Ohio.

Our time together was not done, however. Van asked me to join them at the luncheon. He said he wanted me to see Dr. Peale speak. I suspected, though, that someone of much greater stature within *Guideposts* had bailed out and I was being used to fill the table—luncheon fodder, if you will. Still, the first rule of the young and impoverished editor is never turn down a free meal.

The time came to go down to the car to take us to Sardi's, and we were joined by several other *Guideposts* executives. By now I was growing increasingly alarmed by Dr. Peale's state. He seemed devoid of his legendary enthusiasm. I looked around at the others as we climbed into the town car. If they were concerned, they didn't show it.

We moved at a slug's pace through the clog of crosstown traffic, Dr. Peale staring glumly out the window. It was Wednesday, matinee day, and traffic was even more sludge-like than usual. Occasionally he muttered something to Van or one of the other men, and then checked his watch. I grew very uncomfortable. Who were these people I'd gotten myself mixed up with? How could they do this to a poor old man who should be resting on the back porch of his beloved farmhouse, gazing over the gentle hills of Dutchess County, quietly basking in the accomplishments of his impressive life and not slumped in the back of a hired car lurching and honking through a Manhattan traffic jam? What kind of organization was this?

Things did not improve at the luncheon, which was held in a private room on the second floor. Dr. Peale barely touched his food and said hardly anything, except to the many admirers who stopped by and to whom he was unfailingly warm, even the ones I didn't think he actually recognized. Then he would sink back into what I took to be a kind of silent despair.

The moment I dreaded arrived as dessert and coffee were being served with much clatter and chatter. It was time for Dr. Peale to speak. He was introduced by the celebrated futurist and writer Isaac Asimov as among the most influential men of the century, one of the innovative and dynamic thinkers of our time. *This cannot be happening to this poor soul*, I thought, sinking down in my chair.

Dr. Peale rose with the applause and made his way to the podium, haltingly at first. But on that short journey of thirty feet or so, I saw something absolutely astonishing. As he neared the speaker's platform, he appeared to undergo a physical transformation. He drew himself up and at once his whole being seemed imbued with a manifest enthusiasm, an energy that engulfed the room.

"How is everyone today?" he asked in a voice that boomed like a cannon shot. "Are you as glad to be alive as I am?"

Dr. Peale spoke for about twenty-five minutes. His mastery of his material and of the crowd was unmatched by anything I had ever seen in a speaker. He was funny—very funny—humble, comically self-effacing when he slipped up (which wasn't always by accident, I suspected), a vivid storyteller, utterly confident and relaxed, totally on top of his game and on completely equal footing with his esteemed audience. Even the busboys stopped and listened. No one dared to tell them not to.

"People can change!" Dr. Peale boomed, clenching his fist as he said it. If they faced their difficulties with a reliance on God and a positive attitude, any problem could be overcome, any obstacle would fall before them. They could find joy and happiness if only they believed they could, and believed that was God's desire for them.

It wasn't exactly a speech; it certainly wasn't a sermon—at least, not like any sermon I had heard. It was a call to personal action, a glorious exhortation, delivered with an utter certainty in the miraculous power of humans to change their lives, to grow and find the happiness and freedom to which they were divinely entitled. This was not fire and brimstone. It was bricks and mortar, steel and glass, sky and earth. It was inspiring and practical all at once. It said, *If I can do it, you can do it too.*

The crowd leaped to its feet when he was finished. Except for me. I was too flabbergasted to move. I just sat there knowing I had heard the greatest and most inspiring public speaker of the age, someone whom, moments before, I was ready to put in an old-folks' home.

Van and I opted to walk back to the office and I confessed the dread I'd had about Dr. Peale right up to the moment he took the podium. Van had a good laugh at my story and then said, "Well, Dr. Peale is getting old, but he can still make about a hundred of those talks a year, one just as good as the other and none completely the same. I suspect he was tired and saving his energy. He was also imaging, seeing himself on that podium connecting with those people, fixing that image in his mind."

I'd never heard the word *imaging* before. Van started to explain, but as we entered the *Guideposts* offices, he instead pulled Dr. Peale's book of that title off a shelf and told me to read it.

Dr. Norman Vincent Peale was a preacher's kid, the son of a very good preacher, in fact, who had high expectations for all his children, especially Norman. Norman didn't believe he possessed a natural aptitude for the pulpit. He was terrified of public speaking. He didn't even like to speak up in class, though he was a decent student. After college he pursued a career as a newspaper reporter in Detroit, reporting on events rather than being at the center of them.

One night, covering a story on a house fire, Dr. Peale witnessed several firemen imploring a woman to walk to safety across a shaky board that led to an adjacent rooftop. The woman was paralyzed with fear, her eyes frozen in a stare of terror. No threats that she would burn up if she didn't exercise her only avenue of escape seemed to sway her. Fear had completely taken over. It was a do-or-die moment if ever there was one, with the latter being the probable outcome.

Dr. Peale, standing nearby, suddenly started talking to her, telling her that he knew she had enough strength to put one foot in front of the other, and then the next, and when her courage faltered God would be there to help. "Don't look down," he said. "Look ahead and see yourself safe. Faith will give you courage and courage will give you faith!" In minutes the woman had crossed to safety. "You should be a preacher," one of the firemen said, yet Norman was as surprised as anyone by his actions.

Finally Norman's strong-willed mother persuaded him to enter the seminary. Again fears and insecurities took hold of him. Seminary was a struggle. One day in his sophomore year an eminent professor took him aside after class. He demanded to know how much longer Norman was going to allow bashfulness to hold him back. He lambasted him for being hesitant and tentative. "How long are you going to be like this, Peale?" he nearly shouted. "A scared rabbit afraid of the sound of your own voice?" The professor accused him of using shyness as an excuse. "You better change the way you think about yourself, Peale, before it's too late. That's all. You may go."

Norman was devastated. It was as if a bomb had gone off in his life. He ran from the classroom all the way to the steps of the chapel and collapsed, holding his head in his hands. All his insecurities were arrayed before him. He was angry, hurt and resentful, and he felt powerless: powerless to change the way people saw him and powerless to do anything about himself. Most of all he was frightened. He knew what the professor had said was as true as anything he'd ever known about himself. He *was* a scared rabbit, worse than the woman at the house fire, who at least had had something real to fear.

Now he prayed with the greatest intensity of his life, a do-or-die prayer: "God, please help me. I know you can do it because I've seen you make drunkards sober and turn thieves into honest men. Please take away these inferiority feelings that are holding me back, this awful shyness and fear. Let me see myself not as a scared rabbit but as someone strong and confident who can do great things."

After that moment on the chapel steps, Dr. Peale's life would never be the same. His insecurities and self-doubt did not evaporate overnight, and never vanished completely. But from then on he used the technique he called imaging to face down his problems, to see himself as a success rather than a failure, to envision overcoming challenges rather than succumbing to them. What was most remarkable about his plea was this: He didn't desperately ask for the divine intervention you would expect. He didn't beg God to change him, but rather to help him see himself as a person who could do great things in life. He prayed for the gift of imagination.

Imaging as Dr. Peale conceived it is not simply a mental snapshot or visualized wish list. It is a systematic reimagining of that aspect of ourselves that we want to change. When combined with faith and prayer, he believed it was one of the greatest powers human beings possessed to affect our future happiness.

Try this: At the beginning of any change effort, large or small, develop a change vision statement. Commit to your effort by stating explicitly

- what it is you want to change;
- why you want to change it;
- how you will be different;
- how you will feel different; and
- who will be positively affected by this change, in addition to yourself.

Then call on your imagination to fully envision how that change occurs in you. See the tangible, physical results, but also envision a change in the underlying dynamic. For example, I imagine, with great delight, my desk no longer littered with half-masticated pens, and I also see myself handling stress and frustration in a more healthy fashion, like chewing a stick of cinnamon gum or maybe just taking a deep breath. Be sure to imagine not just the change itself, but also how achieving that change will make you feel. Ultimately change is about feelings, not behavior.

At the time, Dr. Peale's concept of imaging was unique, even somewhat controversial. Today we see people using it all the time. A friend of mine was recently treated for cancer. Her oncologist urged her to continually visualize the cancer cells in her body being eliminated by the treatments. That's imaging.

The most powerful secret to Dr. Peale's imaging is what he himself admits is paradoxical: giving thanks for blessings not yet received. It is more than faith that is being expressed in such an unusual way. Gratitude in advance of success is the ultimate form of living confidently. Try it. You will be amazed by the sense of hope and optimism it engenders.

Any change is a journey, with all the unexpectedness and uncertainty that goes with it. We can't always see the end of the path, or even the way to find it. That's when we must trust our imaginations more than ever—even more than our knowledge—to guide us, to illuminate the yet-to-be-seen.

No one would come to understand this more than a businessman from Georgia named Millard Fuller. He could not possibly have foreseen the shocking and overpowering impulse that would both save his marriage and change the world.

Millionaire. Despite inflation, the word still conjures images of success, power and status. Millionaires are people who hit it big and have it made. They live in luxury and don't have to sweat the little stuff like the rest of us do. In the American lexicon, millionaires should be happy by definition.

Which is why Millard Fuller dreamed of being one from a very young age. Most kids would say "fireman" or "astronaut" or "doctor" if you ask them what they want to be when they grow up. Millard would have said, "Rich." His father, the son of a Georgia sharecropper, had been raised in backbreaking poverty and knew the value of a dollar, perhaps all too well. He worked hard and established a little country store in Lanett where Millard worked when he wasn't in school. Millard never forgot the day a couple pulled up to the store in a shiny black showroom-new Cadillac, all chrome and fins and grille, the paint polished to such a glistening sheen Millard could see himself reflected in it, standing there in his tattered jeans and grimy T-shirt, broom in hand. The engine purred so softly you could hardly tell when the man turned it off. The couple sauntered in as if they could buy the place with pocket change.

After they paid for their purchases and left, Millard's father nodded and said, "That man's a millionaire," as if there were nothing better you could be.

Young Millard took note. His family wasn't quite poor, but they struggled like most folks in rural Georgia. Millard vowed that he would someday rise above it all. He would become a millionaire and people would speak of him with reverence and awe. He was willing to work harder and try harder than anyone else. It was a good goal. A noble one, Millard believed.

And work hard he did. At the University of Alabama he met another student named Morris Dees, who shared his drive for wealth and success. "We were as alike as dollar bills," Millard said. Morris and Millard ran a number of businesses out of their dorm rooms. They sold a campus phone directory, Christmas decorations, and birthday cakes made to order. By the time they graduated, rather than owing money like most of their classmates, they had a substantial bankroll.

Millard had met the girl of his dreams, Linda, at Alabama and they married. Now he was ready to take on the world. He and Morris planned to start a mail-order business out of Montgomery, but first Millard had to fulfill a six-month military stint. Millard and Linda moved to Fort Sill, Oklahoma, where they vowed to subsist on a soldier's pay. The money they had saved was for the new business. But this would be the last time, Millard promised himself, that he'd ever be poor.

They had fun being poor. Fort Sill was their honeymoon. They bombed around base in an old jalopy that backfired and left a big puddle of oil everywhere it went. "This car uses more oil than gasoline!" claimed Millard. They lived in a tiny efficiency apartment with no hot water. Linda learned to stretch a dollar across a day of meals. They were happy.

With his six-month hitch over, Millard took Linda to Montgomery, where he and Morris opened up their business. On the first day of work Millard took out his diary and scrawled himself a promise: "A million dollars before I'm thirty."

They ran an honest business and the partners worked hard—real hard—often at their desks before dawn and until after midnight. They ate and slept the business and within three years they were the largest publishers of mail-order cookbooks in the United States. Millard was also a father by then and he moved Linda and their son, Chris, into a nicer house where he would occasionally return to sleep. It was the sixties, and a new generation was taking over. Everyone was going to be a millionaire. Heck, the president was a millionaire. It was the American Dream in overdrive.

One autumn day the treasurer of Millard's company walked into his office barely able to suppress a grin. Millard looked at her quizzically—finance people weren't usually the giddy kind. She spread out some papers and cleared her throat. "Congratulations, Mr. Fuller. As of today, you are a millionaire. Officially."

And a year early too. The treasurer excused herself, thinking Millard might want to be alone or call his family. Instead Millard pored over the figures, rows and rows of them across a spreadsheet, like tiny soldiers in some army of wealth. The numbers didn't lie. They were irrefutable proof that a dream that had begun in his daddy's little country store had been fulfilled, almost like a prophecy. He'd risen from a line of Georgia dirt farmers to be rich. A millionaire! Wasn't that what everyone wanted? Enough money never to have to worry about anything? To always have food on the table and a roof over your head? Millard practically glared at the numbers. Then why weren't they making him feel happier?

He took out his diary, flipped it open, and wrote, "Ten Million."

That night he got home a little early to tell Linda the news. "Oh, Daddy!" Chris cried, greeting him at the door and hugging his knees. "I'm so glad you're back."

It was the first time in weeks he'd gotten home before Chris's bedtime. It occurred to him that he could have been on the moon for all his son knew. He lifted Chris in the air, hugged him, spun him around, and then went to tell Linda about the million. He also told her about the ten million.

Two weeks later, another visitor surprised him in his office. This time it was Linda, and she wasn't smiling. She barged right into the middle of a strategy meeting her husband was having with senior management. "I'm here because it's the only place I can talk to you, Millard," she said. Heads turned away uncomfortably. "It's over, Millard," Linda continued. "This isn't a marriage."

Linda left the office and climbed into a car that took her to the airport for a plane that took her to New York, where she remained incommunicado.

Millard was as clueless as he was devastated. Hadn't she wanted to marry a millionaire? Didn't everyone? "I poured my heart and soul into this business," Millard wailed to his pastor. The pastor restrained himself, staring at the floor, and allowed Millard to hear, really hear, his own words. That was precisely the problem. Millard should have put his heart and soul into his marriage and his family. That's what a heart and soul are for.

But that's what I thought I was doing, he'd tell himself on sleepless nights, longing for Linda. *Taking care of the ones I love.* And love them he surely did. No one doubted it. Yet even with relatives helping out, Millard felt awkward around Chris and uncomfortable in their beautiful home without Linda. How amazing it was, he thought, that the absence of someone he saw so little of could leave such an aching emptiness. How he longed for those days at Fort Sill where they had nothing but each other.

Finally Linda called from New York. "Can you be up here tomorrow?"

Millard was on the first plane in the morning and soon found himself sitting uncomfortably in a Manhattan hotel room with Linda. It had just been a few weeks, but the sense of estrangement was smothering. They felt as self-conscious as two high-school kids on a blind date. *How's work? Fine. How's Chris? Fine.* Neither wanted to pull off the bandages that covered their wounds.

"Let's get out of here," Millard gasped, fearful he might hyperventilate, fearful that if they sat in this moribund silence one minute more, everything they'd ever had between them would be gone forever, swallowed up by the silence.

They walked briskly up Fifth Avenue, their coat collars pulled high against the bite of the November wind. *How could a man without a house ever survive conditions like this?* Millard found himself wondering, gazing on the occasional homeless person huddled over a subway grate. These Yankees were crazy to live up here. He was about to say something to Linda about the cold when he noticed her tears and eased her into a doorway.

"Tell me," he begged his wife. "Tell me."

Linda had been seeing a counselor in New York, trying to sort out her tangled and painful feelings. One thing she knew for sure: She was desperately unhappy. The more success Millard achieved, the more her misery increased. "Money seems to mean everything to you," she told him. "After Fort Sill, it felt like you deserted me for your business. Desertion, Millard. That's what it feels like."

It was a bitter pill for Millard to swallow. Being a material success was how he had loved his family. Now he saw how this quest to be a millionaire, this compulsive desire for wealth that had gripped him for almost his entire life had alienated him from them. A million wasn't enough. Would ten be? Twenty? Or would each million isolate him more? Linda and Millard stood in the doorway talking for an hour until the cold got to them and they hailed a cab. "Let's go back to the hotel," Linda said.

Millard stared out the cab window as they traveled down the rich canyon of Park Avenue. Block after block of luxury apartment buildings loomed above them, their entrances guarded by pretentiously uniformed doormen. What were they guarding that was so important?

He thought back to the couple in the shiny Caddy and his own bedraggled, distorted reflection in the paint. What had become of them?

Suddenly it all seemed so frivolous, so meaningless. Was this really what he had wanted? Was this really the dream he had imagined back in his daddy's store? There was only one answer, and it was overwhelmingly clear to him. What stood between him and Linda was money. It separated them emotionally, spiritually, even physically. The only thing that would bring them together again was to get rid of it, every dollar. Yes, he still wanted to be rich. But not like this. He would change. He would reimagine his dream, his life.

And that is what Millard did. After he and Linda returned to Montgomery, he sold his half of the business to Morris. He sold his boat, his cabin on the lake, his horses, even the beautiful plot of land he planned to build his mansion on. He donated the money to various charities that could do better things with it than he could. He was no longer a millionaire, not even close. The family moved into a little apartment and Millard found a job as director of development for a small Christian college. He wasn't about to let his fundraising talents go to waste.

In the ensuing years Millard and Linda became ever more deeply involved in charity and missionary work, especially in Africa, where Millard raised funds to provide clean water and housing for the poorest of the world's poor.

In 1983 Millard was again paying a visit to New York, just about the time I was undergoing my own agonies across the river in Hoboken. Millard was in the city to meet with some editors at *Guideposts*. He sat at a conference table telling them about the work he and an organization he helped found were doing for the poor in Africa and how he wanted to expand his efforts globally, including in America—for example, to the South Bronx, just a few miles away.

Van Varner patiently explained that *Guideposts* didn't normally publish laudatory articles about people doing good deeds. "We look for a personal story our readers can identify with," he said.

So Millard told them the story of how he saved his marriage to Linda by giving away a million dollars and how that impulse had transformed his dreams of wealth into something far richer by freeing him to imagine the good that could be done in the world. Then he talked more about his fledgling organization. "What I need, more than just money and material, is people who want to give of their time—people who can help build hope."

When he was through, the editors sat silently. Maybe there was something here for a piece in the magazine. "What do you call your project?" one of the editors asked.

"Habitat for Humanity," Millard answered.

Had I known Millard when he was a young man, I would have totally understood his obsession with money, and the deeper vulnerability it revealed. He thought money would make him whole; I thought alcohol and other substances and desires and reckless behaviors could make me whole.

We can spend our lives seeking wholeness, in our families, our work, our relationship with God. We seek wholeness in love. I believe it's our nature to seek wholeness. Yet not all of us seek it wisely or well. I didn't really stop and ask myself what my lack of wholeness meant or how it got there. I refused to allow myself to think about what was missing. Yet that "missingness" was profoundly painful in a way that took me years to understand and even longer to fill. And once I took my first drink at age twelve, a good hard pull on a bottle of Old Grand-Dad bourbon, it didn't seem to matter. Once I got past the choking burn of it, the alcohol lit me up as nothing ever had. It filled a void I couldn't even conceptualize at the time.

When I took a drink, I felt liberated from myself. It was like experiencing a dimensional shift, like Captain Kirk kicking the Starship Enterprise to warp speed, and I didn't want to go back. I remember saying to another underage drinker once, "I want to be like this all the time." I was serious. Way too serious, as it turned out. Even had I known where that first drink would take me—the degree of degradation and suffering it would cause, the despair and hopelessness and self-destruction it would unleash—I'm still not certain I could have resisted, or would have wanted to. Alcohol sings a siren song that only alcoholics hear, and by the time I picked up the pay phone in the World Trade Center, although I finally wanted to turn back, I wasn't sure I could. There were moments of increasing frequency when I was stalked by the thought, *This is your fate. It can't be changed. This is who you are.*

I hung up the phone with a strange feeling of relief and dread, two states of mind that have difficulty occupying the same conscious space without making its owner exceedingly uncomfortable. I managed to get myself down the escalators-to-hell and onto a Jersey-bound PATH train that deposited me back in Hoboken, where the spastic red neon light of the Victor greeted me immediately upon my emergence above ground. The bar was crowded and I was down to my last pocketful of panhandled change and a couple of half-smoked cigarette butts I'd collected off the street. I swung by my flop, knowing full well what to expect. Louie had left for the night, but not before throwing my few belongings into a corner of the vestibule with a note that said, "Sorry, kid." Louie was old-school like that.

I rapped my knuckles on the double-glass window behind which the night clerk dozed. I rapped harder and woke him.

"Louie says you're out . . . no rent."

I interrupted. There was no need to explain. "I'm going to grab a few things. Tell Louie I'll be back in the morning for the rest or he can mail them to me. I'll pay him back. Tell him not to worry. I'm sorry."

I stuffed a few items into the battered duffel that hearkened back to my sailor days on the Great Lakes, and then trudged up Washington Street. I walked past bars and clubs, each more alluring than the other, alive with possibilities, and if I'd had the money for a proper drink or two I would have stopped in every one of them, answering that call of the wild. But I was broke and technically homeless. I turned east and found an uphill path that brought me to a bluff above the Hudson where there was a Little League field and some weather-worn bleachers along the third-base line. I took a seat in the cool damp grass and lay back, staring up at a faint canopy of stars, thinking about those big lake boats I'd worked on and how elusive and phantasmagoric the northern lights looked from the middle of Lake Superior.

I could sleep here. I'd done it before. But really, what on earth was wrong with me? I knew what the word for it was. On one level I completely accepted what I was. I'd read everything I could on the subject. I would sometimes hole up in the Yale medical library and scour books on alcoholism, mesmerized by post-mortem pictures of cirrhotic livers and wet brains, thinking, I suppose, that I could control the condition if I understood everything there was to understand about it, if I could somehow know more about it than it knew about me. The problem was, it knew everything about me.

I knew about AA. I knew it wasn't for me. First, I wasn't a joiner or a "group hug" type of person. Not at all. Second, there was the God thing, which I didn't want to deal with. I once called AA and asked if there were any meetings where no one discussed God. I was put on hold and I finally hung up. I didn't mind other people having God in their lives. I grew up in a religious home and saw how my parents' faith saved them after my brother Bobby's death. I just wasn't born with the religion gene, I figured. When I closed my eyes and tried to imagine God, all I could envision was a big hole in the cosmos, a vacuum. God was a metaphysical placebo. The concept worked if you believed it worked, and didn't if you didn't. I didn't, or at least couldn't.

And if God did exist, of what possible use was I to him, her or it? Why would I be doing this to myself if there was a God? God wouldn't put up with this. The closest thing to God in my life was alcohol. It controlled everything. It must be God.

I heard feet softly pounding the ground. I lifted my head to see a figure running toward me across the ball field in jogging clothes. Michael. I knew he would find me here, only a few blocks from his apartment. He climbed up several rows in the bleachers, stretched his legs out, and checked his time. He was never a fast runner. I used to be able to beat him easy.

"I talked to your family," he said, catching his breath.

"So did I."

"I told them I'd buy the ticket and they could send me a check."

"That's fine."

"I'll drive you to the airport."

"Tomorrow?"

"Yes."

"Then what?"

"You get on the plane—I'll make damn sure of that—you go home, you figure this thing out."

"How?"

"You do what you have to do. Just *do* something."

He wiped his brow with the sleeve of his maize and blue University of Michigan T-shirt. It was a good night for a jog.

"You don't have a cigarette, do you?" I asked.

Michael looked at me like I was insane—he'd probably just done five miles around Hoboken—and laughed.

"You can probably crash at the apartment tonight," he said.

"That's okay. I doubt I'll sleep anyway and the sun will be up soon enough. I'm sure Kate's still mad at me from the other night. She'll probably stay up guarding the liquor cabinet."

"She's cooled off."

"I won't cause her any more trouble."

Michael climbed down the bleachers and sat beside me in the grass. He gazed out over the Hudson, rippling in the light of a half-moon, and beyond to a postcard skyline of New York. From here at night the city looked like an open treasure chest glittering with possibilities.

"Look at that," he said. "Look what you're missing, Edward. You came all the way from Michigan for this. What happened to you?"

Ridiculously, a bit perversely even, the Bible story of Satan tempting Christ in the desert with the vista of Jerusalem before them flashed through my distorted mind. I tried to put myself in that jeweled cityscape across the water, tried to think of a place for myself. It was hard to picture. It was hard to imagine anything beyond this moment of my life.

Michael stood, brushing the grass from his running shorts, and I stood with him, tottering a bit, more from weakness than drink. He grabbed my arm. Close up I could see the concern in his eyes, and that alarmed me. Michael was usually quite self-possessed, with the polished cynicism of the third-generation lawyer he was. It was troubling to see the mask slip, to realize just how close to the edge I really was.

"Come by about seven. I'll buy you breakfast," he said.

"I've stopped eating."

"You'll try."

Then he turned and jogged off into the night, casting me a glance over his shoulder as if to say, *This is your last chance.* I waved like a fool and sat back down, thinking that I certainly must have run out of last chances by now. My eyes were tired but my heart hammered in my chest. I watched the running lights of a barge sliding downriver and tried to see if there was a sailor lounging on deck staring up at the sky like me, but there was no one. The barge looked deserted. I followed it until it disappeared on the other side of the darkness and wondered: *What next?*

4
Commitment

I f willingness puts us on the path to change, commitment keeps us moving forward when the going gets tough and we risk losing sight of the dream. Commitment is willingness reaffirmed. It is you, keeping a promise to yourself.

I don't know anyone who has tried to change something who hasn't encountered failure and setbacks, who hasn't lost a battle or two in winning the larger war. During those times, commitment keeps us focused on our larger purpose. It drives the mission, permitting us to delineate a goal from a fantasy, a plan from a wish. Without it, we grope for meaning in the darkness, like someone fumbling for the light switch in a strange room.

For me, and for many of the people I've met, commitment is the hardest demand of change. Discovering our willingness and the poetry of imagining ourselves transformed are stirring moments in our change journeys; they are the dockside jubilance as our ship leaves port, streamers streaming and horns blaring. Commitment keeps us going on the open seas. It is the engine of personal change. It is a form of power.

Most of us define commitment as tenacity, stubbornness and determination. It's all those things, but much more. I like to think of commitment as a transformation in itself: the potential released when our will and our actions are totally aligned. To become fully committed is the true beginning of personal change, an engagement of not just the will but also the soul, for the state of being committed is itself transcendent and deeply gratifying.

Commitment is necessary to all personal change, but I think it's even more essential for change that we do not necessarily choose. Take my friend Al. I see Al at the gym most mornings: a trim, well-conditioned forty-something music lawyer who could pass for thirty-something. The other day in the locker room he was showing some pictures of an Alaskan cruise he and his wife took with a group from their synagogue a few years ago. I almost didn't recognize Al in the pictures. For one thing, he had a lot more hair. But most noticeably, he had a lot more flab. He must have noticed my puzzled expression.

"Yep, that's me, all right."

"Wow. What happened?"

Al laughed. "The best thing that could have. I went bald!"

Al began losing his hair very quickly at a fairly young age, and it troubled him a great deal, especially in a business where his clients usually have a lot of hair. At first he worried that his thinning hair would make him look old and unhip. Soon he started believing it: Worry itself produced a negative personal change. "My confidence and my aggressiveness faltered," Al says, "and those are two things lawyers need. I felt like Samson, losing his powers: the more bald, the less bold. It was as if I was mourning my hair, this stuff that had been a part of me for all my life."

He tried growing compensatory facial hair and even considered getting a tattoo, "though, thank God, I eventually realized that's just not me." Finally he resorted to the desperate measure of a comb-over while he still had some growth on the sides, plastering it over his scalp like a hair tarp. "I practically had to glue it down. But it didn't fool anyone, least of all me."

Soon there was not enough hair even for that desperate tactic. "Most of the men in my family go bald, but not in their thirties! I tried everything out there. Hair replacement and regrowth is a multibillion-dollar business and nothing worked. Nothing. I was miserably unhappy. I even had my rabbi say prayers. I guess God didn't want me to have hair anymore."

Al was in despair. He'd even begun to fear that his wife found him less desirable, though it didn't occur to him at the time that his negative fixation on his hair loss might be a more plausible explanation. (Nothing turns a partner off more than complaining about how unattractive you think you are. I mean, if you don't find yourself attractive, why should your partner?)

One day Al saw his doctor for a check-up and asked him if any new hair-loss treatment was coming onto the market, a drug, a procedure, a magic elixir—anything.

"No," he said. "But you could lose a few pounds. Your weight is up again and I'm concerned about your cholesterol.

My prescription for you is to forget about your hair and get in shape. Find something physical you love to do. No one ever died of hair loss, Al."

"Easy for him to say, I thought," recalls Al. "He still had his hair. But on the way out of his office, I caught a look at myself in the mirror. The doctor was right. I'd been thinking about this small part of me that existed pretty much above the ears. What about the rest of me? What about between the ears? A huge bell went off: 'Dummy! You've been worried about all the wrong stuff!'"

In a moment of what he calls "life-altering revelation," Al realized hair loss wasn't the issue. Self-acceptance was. "It was almost as if God was challenging me: 'Are you going to work with what I gave you, or are you going to try to be someone you're not? Well?'"

The latter strategy had brought nothing but frustration and unhappiness for Al. "I'd begun to feel completely alienated from myself," he told me. So Al took his doctor's advice and joined a gym. He was not especially overweight, but he hadn't done any regular exercise since high school and was way out of shape. "Too many business lunches and too much late-night takeout. I'd do these crash quick-fix diets that never lasted. So I got on a program. I found a trainer and signed up for classes. I got totally into it. I became a real gym rat."

It was easy. At first. "You get such a great endorphin high when you start exercising," Al says, "but then you hit a wall." Soon Al reverted to his old ways and his attitude went south again. Finally his trainer, an ex-Navy Seal, read him the riot act. The wall, he said, represented commitment. "You are either committed to what you started or you give up," the trainer told him. "There's no in between. What's it going to be?"

That was the second revelation, Al says. "This was something I had to be committed to for the long haul, for the rest of my life. But it started with a daily commitment to show up for myself, even when I didn't want to. That was the real personal change for me. Sticking to it no matter what, learning to be committed. I mean it's easy to be committed to my wife, my kids, my clients. But to myself? To change? To taking responsibility for my own happiness and not ascribing it to some external superficiality, like my hair? That was something new."

You practically need a magnifying glass to find any hair on Al's head these days but he is incredibly youthful, energetic, and self-confident. "I'm happy," he says. "Going bald may not seem like a life crisis for most people, but for me it was a turning point. It taught me an incredible life lesson and produced permanent changes in behavior. I had to face a change I couldn't control and undertake a change I could. Commitment to taking care of myself has been a gift because it's taught me to be committed to other things too: a richer spiritual life, deeper friendships, better nutrition, more involvement in my community. You name it. All of it requires commitment and dedication. Commitment is a discipline that spreads throughout your life. You learn to show up, especially for yourself. Who knew that going bald would be such a blessing?"

For many men—and women too—hair loss is a fact of life, a relatively minor concession to the aging process, change we can deal with. But what about the far more serious physical challenges so many of us will have to face eventually—a serious illness, or a disabling injury? Nothing turns our lives inside out like health problems, either our own or those of someone close to us. Yet they can also lead us to amazing transformations. A woman from Wisconsin named Lori Schneider is a testament to that.

There is probably no place on earth more inhospitable to life than the summit ridge of Mount Everest. Nothing lives there except for those rare human beings who are driven by a consuming desire to attain the highest point on earth, and even then life cannot be sustained for long at those extreme heights. At 29,035 feet above sea level, the summit of Mount Everest is approximately the cruising altitude of a 747, more than five miles above the earth, the air so rarefied it contains only one-third the concentration of oxygen we normally need to live.

The ridge itself is a harrowing knife-edge of dreadfully exposed rock and snow with sheer drop-offs of ten thousand feet down the Kanchung face into Tibet on one side, and an eight-thousand-foot plunge onto the Khumbu glacier in Nepal on the other. Veteran climbers have been known to joke that if you fall, fall into Tibet and enjoy the extra two thousand feet of life. Or not.

It was on this very crest of the earth that fifty-two-year-old Lori Schneider found herself on May 23, 2009, the culmination of an epic quest to become only the twenty-sixth woman to climb the illustrious "seven summits," the highest points on each continent. Now, clipped onto a fixed rope and just several hundred feet from the top of the world, every mental and physical effort she made through the merciless cold took the full commitment of her will and spirit. With gusts of up to sixty miles per hour, the wind chill was close to one hundred degrees below zero. She could only take several steps at a time before having to stop and rest, panting furiously. Even when breathing supplemental oxygen, the body and mind scream out for air at this altitude. The most experienced mountaineers frequently succumb to the hazards of hypoxia, or oxygen deprivation. Extreme lethargy and even hallucinations are not uncommon. Climbers sit down in the snow, never to rise again. There is no possibility of rescue this high on the mountain. The people who climb Everest call it "the death zone" for a reason.

Lori concentrated on each laborious step, putting one cramponed foot in front of the other, and thought about the banner she carried in her backpack, the one she would plant at the summit if she made it. And she definitely planned to make it, though many climbers have been defeated even closer to the top of Everest, forced to turn back because of cold, lack of bottled oxygen, or the stark realization that if they took just one more step they would not have the energy to descend the mountain. What drove her on was the thought of the thousands of people around the world for whom walking from the bedroom to the kitchen took a similar supreme effort of will and body—people with MS, like Lori.

Lori had not grown up an athlete—"Girls really weren't encouraged to take sports when I was in school"—but when she moved with her husband to Colorado to teach special education, the great outdoors beckoned. Before long Lori was hiking, then climbing, mountains. In 1993, she climbed Mount Kilimanjaro in Tanzania, the highest point in Africa.

At her side was her father, Neal, who celebrated his sixty-first birthday at the snow-capped, 19,330-foot summit. "We did it as a challenge to ourselves, in a try-anything kind of spirit." Climbing with her dad was a thrill, but Lori attributes that "try anything" spirit to her mother, Darlene, who taught her that nothing was beyond her reach as long as she had the desire and the faith—the commitment.

As she and her father gazed out over the Tanzanian plains, the ambition to climb all seven of the highest continental summits began to form inside her, a dream that like a fire started to give off heat and light as it grew. Between her teaching career and her busy life, though, Lori delayed the dream. There would be time, she thought. She was still strong and young.

Until she woke up on the morning of January 4, 1999—or half of her did. The other half of her body, the right half, was completely numb.

"It was an incredibly scary sensation," Lori says, "like someone had drawn a line down the center of me."

She had MRIs, brain scans, a spinal tap, even a brain biopsy. Months of tests later, she learned the devastating diagnosis: multiple sclerosis, a baffling autoimmune disorder that attacks the central nervous system and can lead to paralysis, vision loss, dementia, and death. Even its milder symptoms can be debilitating. It strikes women more often than men and usually strikes young. Lori was only forty-two, in her prime, yet doctors were telling her to get ready to live the rest of her life in a wheelchair.

Lori thought about her dad climbing Kilimanjaro with her at sixty-one and her mother's incredibly affirming spirit and commitment to living life as it was meant to be lived—with faith, hope and optimism. She thought about her own faith. *No*, she said, *MS or no MS, I'm going to get ready to climb Mount Everest.*

Yet those two little letters stood in the way. Her symptoms worsened. She began fainting in the classroom and had to leave her teaching position. Her marriage fell apart and sometimes it felt like her whole life had too. "There were days," says Lori, "when it was hard to imagine going on." She told only those closest to her about the diagnosis. "I just couldn't talk about it," she says, as if speaking the words out loud would give the disease more power.

The hardest thing, Lori told me, was facing the fear of being sick. "I'd always striven to be the perfect teacher, the perfect wife, the perfect friend. Now I had to face those two little letters that reminded me I wasn't invincible." The change that MS brought on was hard. She was no longer Lori, the woman who climbs mountains. She was Lori, MS victim.

With treatment, the more severe symptoms abated. Something drew Lori back to Wisconsin, back to her family, to where she had grown up. Maybe it was the need to be close to the mother and father who inspired her so much, to draw on that positive energy and unconditional love. Slowly she grew stronger, fed by this spiritual spring.

There was another fear that plagued her, however—the fear of not attaining her goal of the seven summits, the commitment she'd made to herself standing atop Mount Kilimanjaro to travel the world in pursuit of that goal.

Did MS make that dream unattainable?

No, decided Lori. In fact, the seven summits became even more of a life imperative, a way to silently fight back against

MS. By conquering mountains she could conquer her fear and push back against a disease whose course could be so unpredictable. "I stopped thinking of myself as a victim of MS. I was a person with MS, a person first. The disease was not me." Recommitting to the seven summits would prove that to herself. When people talk about conquering a disease, they usually think about finding a cure. In the absence of such a medical breakthrough, Lori would conquer MS on her own terms.

She'd already knocked off the first summit, Kilimanjaro. Standing upon the primordial mountain with her dad was still one of the most joyous moments of her life, a memory she often drew upon for strength. Why not have her dad climb the next summit with her?

Lori set her sights on Cerro Aconcagua in Argentina, the highest point in South America at 22,841 feet, three thousand feet higher than Kilimanjaro and requiring technical climbing skills. Neal was ecstatic. Of course he would tackle the Andean giant with her. They made plans to join a commercial expedition going to Aconcagua in December of 1999, in honor of the millennium.

The climbing went well and Lori was surprised at how strong she felt, even at an altitude she had never scaled before. Then, at about twenty thousand feet, Neal faltered. They rested on a small shelf of rock and drank some hot tea from a thermos. Lori tried to urge him on, but it was no use. The altitude was draining the strength from her father. He'd need all his energy just to get down the ropes safely. Lori prepared to descend. Neal stopped her. No, he protested. Lori must go on.

Lori's dream was to stand atop Aconcagua with her father. How could she go on without him? But Neal was insistent.

She was so close. She couldn't quit now, not because of him. Neal wouldn't hear of it. She had to top out, for herself, for the commitment she'd made before she got sick, and to others who live in the shadow of MS every day of their lives. Lori's climb could cast some light on those shadows.

Leaving her dad in the hands of a guide, Lori resumed her ascent. Several hours of hard climbing later, she stood at the summit of Aconcagua. Gazing out over the jagged spine of the Andes, she thought about her father's words. Yes, she had made the climb for herself, to prove she wouldn't be held hostage by a disease, even one as debilitating as MS. Yet she was afraid to speak out. Almost a year after her symptoms first struck, she'd still told virtually no one of her diagnosis. Even her fellow expedition members didn't know. She was afraid people wouldn't treat her as Lori, but Lori with MS. Yet didn't this climb prove she was more than the disease? What else could it prove?

Suddenly Lori realized what she must do: go public with her MS and her commitment to climb the seven summits. Her father was right. Her climbs would mean more if they helped others fighting the disease, and they would mean more to Lori too.

Before Lori started down, she took one last look at the sweeping view. She imagined being able to see all the summits from here, one after the other. Aconcagua was the second tallest of the seven, the highest mountain in the world outside of Asia. Only one summit loomed larger: Everest, towering a mile higher into the troposphere than where she now stood. Even some of the world's most elite climbers avoided it. It was simply too hard and too dangerous. Lori wasn't at all sure she could do it. But she was sure she would try. And time was running short. Who knew when her symptoms might return?

Lori continued her quest, renewed by a deeper commitment to the higher cause of helping MS patients everywhere. Her next stop was Europe's tallest peak, Mount Elbrus, in Russia. Then came Alaska's Denali, also known as Mount McKinley and often called the coldest mountain in the world. After returning from the summit, horrific and persistent back pain forced her to take time off. A cyst had formed on a nerve in her spine, the result of a botched spinal tap when doctors were trying to diagnose her MS. Surgery stopped the leakage of spinal fluid in 2006, but it required a long period of recuperation and it was months before Lori had her climbing strength back.

In July of 2008 she scaled Australia's Mount Kosciuszko, the "easiest" of the seven summits. A rare snow squall made it not so easy. Late that same year, Lori traveled to Antarctica to attempt the daunting Mount Vinson. Conditions were brutal. Lori was turned back on her first attempt in temperatures of thirty-five degrees below zero. She was only two hundred vertical feet from the summit, but the wind at the bottom of the earth is like a cyclone and it was just too dangerous to continue. The expedition leader turned the group around.

But there would be one last try. After only a few hours of sleep at their high camp they started back up, attacking the grueling route that had defeated them the day before. They struggled for hours over ice and rock and snow. This time the weather was perfect: a mere twenty-five degrees below zero and only a light wind stirring the crystalline sky.

As she stood at the top of the bottom of the earth she thought of her mom, Darlene, who had lost her battle to cancer a couple of years earlier. Lori's tears froze to her cheeks. She raised a hand to heaven and yelled, "Hi, Mom! I made it!"

And now she was within a few hundred feet of the final summit, Everest. A few hundred of the most impossible feet on earth, a distance that had defeated and killed so many. Scores of men had died before Everest was finally climbed in 1953 by Edmund Hillary and Tenzing Norgay, and many more men and women attempting the peak had died since. The mountain is littered with bodies frozen forever in its icy slopes, each a deathly testimony to ambition gone wrong. Had Lori been too ambitious? Had her commitment to the seven summits been stronger than her abilities? No one would have blamed Lori Schneider if she skipped this one.

Just before reaching this point on the ridge, Lori had hauled herself up the fixed ropes over the Hillary Step, the one technical challenge between high camp and the summit: a sheer rock outcropping about five stories high. Edmund Hillary, for whom the step is named, said it would have been an interesting problem for a group of weekend climbers at sea level. At 28,500 feet, it is a potentially lethal obstacle. The effort can exhaust a climber, and it had left Lori gasping in her mask for more oxygen. After a rest, she'd struggled on, but slower than before. Each step was a single concentrated effort, an act of will and determination in and of itself. Again Lori thought of all the people with MS for whom an effort like this is virtually an everyday occurrence.

She started climbing the final slope to the summit, driving her ice ax into the snowpack. Almost ten years earlier, the doctors had been talking to her about a wheelchair. A wheelchair! And here she was taking the final step to the top of Everest, the highest spot on earth, a point beyond which there is nothing but air and sky and clouds and heaven.

Lori has always said that climbing made her feel closer to God. She had never felt closer than she did at that moment atop Mount Everest at 8:39 AM on May 23, 2009. Ironically she could not enjoy the view because cloud cover had rolled in, presaging that the weather was about to turn bad, and that meant turning around quickly. Her view turned inward, toward the inner journey she had taken since her diagnosis. She had conquered much more than seven mountains. She had conquered her fear of a terrible illness by committing herself to a cause. And that commitment changed her.

Lori unfurled a banner in honor of World MS Awareness Day, scheduled for May 28, and then posed for a few obligatory summit shots, literally the tallest person in the world at that moment. Then she turned and headed home toward Wisconsin.

I have had an obsession with Mount Everest since I was ten years old, when I read a National Geographic article on the first American ascent of the peak. Since then I have read nearly every book on Everest and on high-altitude mountaineering that's ever been published. My obsession does not necessarily have to do with climbing the world's highest peak myself; I'll stick to the modest mountaintops of New England. No, it's more about wanting to know what it feels like to push human endurance and suffering to its farthest margins. And that I do know, as my own story proves to me. Time and again I kept pushing myself further, deeper, when I should have turned back. It wasn't a mountain I was climbing though; it was a pit into which I was descending.

Lori Schneider reached both the peak of her change journey and the highest summit on earth, traveling a seemingly impossible path through an extraordinary act of commitment. Sometimes, though, before we can change, we have to hit bottom, encountering ourselves in a state of being so painful and damaging that change is the only option—or we die. Whether it's actual death or metaphorical death makes little difference. The latter could be worse, for when our spirits die, our joy in living is snuffed out. We press on physically, but life has no passion or deeper meaning. We become trapped in ourselves, hostage to our own spiritual inertia. We die.

"Life as you know it is about to end."

The words came from a lecturer behind an imposing but somewhat decrepit podium at a drug-and-alcohol rehab facility in Lapeer, Michigan, where I was now a new and relatively compliant inmate. It had not been easy to get in here, and as uncomfortable as I found my dismal surroundings, I also felt a stubborn entitlement to my hard-fought twenty-eight-day treatment residency.

Much to my own surprise, I'd actually shown up for breakfast with Michael that muggy morning in Hoboken several weeks earlier, staring silently at my plate of eggs while he wolfed down his and occasionally glowering at my warm glass of beer, which he was paying for. But I was long gone into alcoholic anorexia and the sips of beer were the only thing steadying me. I could no more swallow a bite of food than I could swallow my own head.

"At least drink some water," Michael grumbled through his toast. "You look like crap." For some reason I noticed how he said water and crap with that flat, nasal, distended Michigan "a" and thought about how I'd be hearing a lot of that accent soon. Crap. Water. Lap. Tap. Sap. Map.

We didn't talk much in the car on the way to Newark Airport. It was one of those incredibly hot and slimy days, when the temperature on the Jersey side of the Hudson is about ten degrees higher than on the New York side, and the air is so thick with humidity you could choke on it. I was feeling the dry heaves coming on, so I rolled down my window and stuck my head out like a dog, riding most of the way to the airport like that.

Michael walked me to the gate for the Northwest Airlines flight to Detroit, more to make sure that I got there, I expect, than out of any tender reluctance to take his leave of me. I'm certain his appointed role was to make sure I was on that plane, and back then you could still accompany people to their flight gates. I'd wanted to stop for one more drink at the bar across from the waiting area, but Michael wasn't going to pay for it, so I couldn't. Now I walked toward the jetway like a man going to his doom. It wasn't so much that I wouldn't be drinking and wandering the streets anymore, at least nominally a free man. That was a relief of sorts. But that relief threatened to be outweighed by dread of the encounters that lay ahead. My family would be waiting for me. What could I possibly say to them? How could I look them in the eye? I didn't know if I could endure the shame and humiliation, the invasion of my life that would have to take place.

Then, right before I surrendered my boarding pass to the gate agent, Michael hugged me.

It was really uncomfortable and, I thought at the time, really uncalled for. The emotion from the night before was bad enough; it felt radioactive. Now we were hugging. This was unbearable. Did he think I wasn't coming back? That he would never see me again? Was I that bad off? So pathetic and broken that I had to be hugged?

"Thanks, Michael," I muttered and shuffled down the jetway, so weak that it felt as if I were being sucked through a vacuum-cleaner hose into the guts of the plane.

The next few days are a jumble of memories. I spent a lot of time in my childhood bedroom at my parents' house in suburban Detroit, a room I hadn't inhabited regularly since I went off to college in Ann Arbor. It felt both familiar and unfamiliar; a person I knew used to live here but it wasn't exactly me. More like a distant relative of me, someone I might run into on the street but would fumble to find something to say to.

The atmosphere was tense. What exactly was my problem and why had I come home to Michigan? We conversed around the issue a lot. My father, never much of a talker, did try to talk to me, and to this day I appreciate what must have been an excruciating effort for him. Was alcohol the problem? Couldn't I just control myself? Was it something else? But his sentences usually trailed off, as if this were a difficulty he had no idea how to address, though he did say I might consider contacting AAA. Whether he knew he misspoke or not, I'll never know, but it gave me something to laugh about. Yes, I could use a tow all right, and a decent map.

My mother, I noticed, was reading a book on depression, which it turned out my sister, a school psychologist, had given her. It was my sister who eventually cut through all the emotional red tape of denial and got the ball rolling on the rehab. But it was left to me to find someplace to go. That's where my medical insurance stepped in and made everything insanely complicated and nearly impossible.

Rehabs were relatively few and far between back then. The Betty Ford Center had only just opened, and the act of seeking treatment had yet to gain wide acceptance, much less become a celebrity badge of honor. According to my insurance company, I could only be treated in a medical facility, specifically a hospital. Most rehabs were independent of hospitals even if they did maintain an affiliation. That wasn't good enough. The rehab facility had to be physically connected to a hospital.

Forget this, I thought, after about a hundred frustrating phone calls I made from a list of Midwest treatment centers my sister provided. *This is nonsense.* By now I'd been about a week off alcohol and was feeling a bit more back on my rails. With sobriety came arrogance. I'd get a job out here, maybe go out on the boats again, sock away some money, and move back to New York as soon as it became financially feasible. I'd take another stab at it and do it right this time. I could control myself. I could control my drinking. All I needed was a little personal discipline. I was not going to allow myself to stay trapped in my childhood bedroom with the six-shooter lamp and an old Detroit Tigers pennant on the wall. That was *not* what was going to happen to *me*.

"Have you found a place that will take you?" my mother asked one day while we ate tuna sandwiches for lunch and looked out the back window at the birds feasting on the seeds she'd scattered around the yard.

"I don't think I'm going. I can do this on my own."

She stared silently at her sandwich, knowing better than to argue with me. She stood up to take her plate to the sink, and the birds took off with her.

That evening, though, John Cavanaugh appeared unannounced (to me, at least). John was an old friend of my parents' and an usher from our church. He used to playfully admonish me when I was an altar boy at St. Owen's about wearing white socks under my black cassock. John had run into his own problems with drinking and it had very nearly killed him. He'd finally had a heart attack on a transcontinental flight and when they eventually got him to a hospital, he went into the DTs. He'd been sober for years now and was one of the most decent and kindest people I knew, with a craggy but still handsome face and striking blue eyes. He'd grown up Boston Irish but had always wanted to be a cowboy and even now wore western boots and jeans with a belt buckle Gene Autry would have lusted after.

John and I went out back to talk by ourselves, hunched confessionally in our patio chairs. He asked me the usual questions and in a voice soft with shame I answered as truthfully as I could. It was clear John had my number.

"What are you going to do about it, Edward?" he finally asked. I looked him in the eyes. Or tried to, at least, because one of John's eyes was glass and looked like a marble, and I knew somehow the loss of that eye had something to do with his drinking. So instead of answering his question, I asked him what I'd wanted to ask since I was a little kid living in that bedroom right above where we were sitting in the dusk.

"What the hell happened to your eye?"

I'd actually heard rumors but I'd never heard the real story. Now John told it to me unflinchingly. It was difficult for me to listen to, not so much because of the physical details, though they were gruesome, but because I found myself identifying intensely with the feelings he shared, enduring an almost horrifying recognition of myself in another human being at his worst. I will not tell you how John lost that eye because it is too brutal and too personal and too explicit, but I will tell you that at the time, it was not enough to get him to stop drinking. By the grace of God, he said, a few years later his heart attack landed him in a hospital, where they finally convinced him to seek treatment at an addiction facility.

I took a deep breath when he was finished, as if trying to clear the toxins of the story out of my body and mind. And there was John, staring at me with a marble eye and the map of Ireland on his face.

"Nothing in my life means more to me than my sobriety, Eddie," said John, reverting to my boyhood moniker, aptly so, considering where we sat. "It's a commitment, a day at a time, for the rest of my life. And sometimes it's more like an hour at a time. But no matter what, I am committed to my sobriety. That comes first."

"John, I'm going to try and pull myself together," I said, evading the real question. "I think I can do it."

"Alone?" he asked. "By yourself?"

I looked off into the dark, searching for an answer. There was a long silence. Then John slapped me on the leg and stood.

"I always thought you'd amount to something, Eddie. I still think you might." At least he didn't hug me.

John went inside, said good night to my parents, and was out the door, the heels of his cowboy boots clicking on the front walk. I sat on the patio for a long time, watching the night turn different shades of gray and green, until my parents went up to bed and the glow of the TV through their bedroom window eventually went out. I could imagine the two of them lying in bed, worrying about what to do with me but not talking.

I retreated to my room, rummaging aimlessly through an old trunk of letters and notebooks and diaries. Everything I had ever written now made me cringe. Trite, self-important, derivative. Was it writing that was driving me crazy? The honesty and self-exposure it demands? Yale had been difficult. I'd had to put my work out to be savaged and torn apart, and I'd felt torn apart with it. Was it time to walk away and start a completely new life, in a job far away from writing and New York?

John had said, or at least implied, that I needed to make a commitment. I sat up till dawn thinking about that, what that word meant and if I even understood it. Had I ever really been committed to anything in my life, as John was to his sobriety? I thought about it so much that the word began to fall apart in my brain, as if it were dissolving typographically under scrutiny . . . syllables, letters, vowels, consonants.

At dawn I went for a walk. When I got home I dug out my sister's list and began making calls again, searching for someplace my insurance would find acceptable for me to be confined. But there was that maddening provision about it being part of a hospital facility. Late that afternoon I called a place in little Lapeer, Michigan, a down-at-the-heels town one hundred miles or so north of Detroit, up in what we Michiganders call "the thumb."

"Is your rehab inside or outside the actual hospital building?" I demanded, probably sounding a bit crazed by now.

"I'm not sure what you mean," the intake person replied warily.

"It has to be connected physically to the hospital, not a stand-alone."

"You'll only come if it's connected?"

"No, no, it's not me. It's the insurance company. They insist on it."

"Well, there is a walkway between the rehab facility and the main hospital. It's very close."

"It has to be actually physically connected."

"It's more like a breezeway. It has like a canopy over it."

"It does? Will you go outside and see if the canopy touches the two buildings?"

There was a pause, and then I heard the phone being put down. He was back on the line after a few interminable minutes.

"Yes, the canopy actually touches both the hospital building and the rehab center itself and it covers the entirety of the walkway in between."

"So they're connected?"

"I'd say they're connected, yes."

I paused. This could be it.

"I think we can work with that," I said.

The man at the podium was a guest speaker from the hospital who had traversed the celebrated breezeway to address us on the progressive nature of addiction. Behind him, propped on an easel, was the Jellinek Chart in all its pathological glory. I'd studied the chart in textbooks (in between looking at pictures of diseased livers and atrophied brains) but seeing the famous chart now in full-blown form made me shudder. It looked like some sort of malignant board game. I half expected to see a little magnetic figure representing me put somewhere on the alcoholic continuum. *Where exactly?* I wondered.

The presentation was actually quite thorough and humane, but the podium was a bit unstable and every so often it would clunk to one side or the other, and I kept wanting to scoot up and helpfully slip a matchbook under its broken foot.

I was the newbie, having arrived a few days earlier after a very quiet ride up to the thumb with my parents. The intake was much how Bill Irwin would describe it to me nearly a decade later when I would work with him on his article about the Appalachian Trail. They went through my belongings with a thoroughness that would be the envy of the Transportation Security Administration, sniffing my toothpaste in the event I might have emptied the tube and replaced its contents with contraband, took away my vitamins (I'd get them back when I was discharged), and confiscated my spray deodorant.

"That's a problem?" I asked. Boy, if I had only known.

Then came a shock: Tommy.

Tommy was to be my roommate, and not for the first time. Tommy was a gateman I'd bunked with on one of the lake boats. I remembered him pulling a bottle out of his sea bag most mornings and taking a shot of straight whiskey, giving me a congenial smirk as it went down. Now here he was.

He didn't recognize me at first, until I reminded him that he once had to help fish me out of the water in Escanaba when, following a night of carousing ashore with some crewmembers, I'd slipped off the dock as we were getting back onto the ship, landing between the dock and the hull, which is a perilous place to find yourself, especially when you are not in complete possession of your senses. Only a few feet of water separated the dock pilings from the hull of the nine thousand-ton vessel. I would be crushed to death in an instant if the boat moved, and floating boats tend to move, bumping up against the dock. One gentle bump and my entire skeleton would collapse.

I screamed drunkenly at my jeering shipmates to help me. Finally, up in the pilot house, the third mate yelled down to throw me a line lest he be burdened with a ton of paperwork connected to my absurd demise. My hands were raw with rope burns by the time I got back to my cabin and sat wet and bleary-eyed on the edge of my bunk. Above me Tommy laughed himself to sleep, but not before he said, "Edward, you're just like me. There ain't no difference between us."

Twenty years separated us in age and a much greater distance sociologically, but on a level I didn't want to accept I knew what he meant.

This was a different Tommy, though, than the one I'd crewed with. That one was loud, profane and boastful. This Tommy seemed meek and compliant but also very cagey and edgy. His energy made me nervous.

"Here we are again," I'd said when I threw my bag down, the same bag I carried over my shoulder the last time I'd seen him, making my way off the ship for good.

Sailing was a fine gig for drinkers. Ninety days on and thirty days off, a month of continual inebriation if that was your wont. Then you white-knuckled it for the next three months and began the cycle anew. I saw my first case of the DTs onboard a lake boat. A steward named Kenny came back from leave and passed out in his cabin for half a day. I encountered him about an hour after he woke up, naked and shrieking, running down a passageway clawing at his skin. We had to lash him to his bunk until we got to port. I heard he went into cardiac arrest at the hospital. That is known as dying of alcoholic panic.

"They treat you right here," Tommy said as I put my stuff away. "You listen to them and you'll be okay. Me, I'm done with it. The union made me come here. I've had my last drink. Been twenty-five days. Doc says my liver's fine."

"Congratulations." Only a half dozen years or so had passed since we'd sailed together, but Tommy, sallowed and bent, looked like he had a lot more than twenty years on me now.

"Never thought I'd see you again," he said.

Tommy had skipped the lecture. This was his last day and he was leaving, headed for the union hall in Algonac on the St. Clair River to find a boat. I slipped out to say good-bye to him. He was standing by the door, stooped under the weight of his sea bag, shaking hands with a counselor. I put my arm around his shoulder.

"Good luck, man," I said.

"Don't worry about me. I'll be fine. I'm dry for good. That's one thing I know. I'm done."

Tommy shifted his bag, waved and sauntered out to a waiting cab.

I walked back toward the lecture room with the counselor. "He's not going to make it," the counselor said softly.

The lecture was nearly concluded—the speaker was at the terminus of the Jellinek Chart now, with its three famous apodictic outcomes: death, insanity or imprisonment—so I just went back to my room and sat on the edge of the bed thinking about Tommy and John and the weight of the counselor's stark pronouncement. I didn't have any illusions about my old shipmate; there had been a sad desperation in his eyes and he had been practically licking his lips. No doubt that that cab went straight to the nearest dive. The only question was whether Tommy would make it back on a boat or catch a berth on skid row.

What preoccupied me was the realization of what I was up against and the change that was being asked of me—the commitment John had talked about on the patio. It was a commitment I didn't even understand. That, more than anything, frightened me. I kept thinking about the hunched figure walking toward the cab. Tommy had once told me that even on my best day and on his worst, I could never outwork him . . . and he was right. Shoveling coal onto a conveyor belt deep in the bowels of the ship, he would outlast me to the point of exhaustion. He was a tough, determined son-of-a-gun, but I could muster no more hope for him than the counselor had.

"He's not going to make it," was all he'd said. And that was all he had to say for me to ask myself for the first time, Would I?

5
Faith

You do not necessarily have to have faith in order to change, but it helps. A lot. Because it means you don't have to do it alone in a spiritual vacuum.

By faith I mean more than simple belief in yourself or confidence in your actions, though that is important and necessary. The faith I refer to is an elemental belief that there is a loving power greater than ourselves to whom we can appeal for strength and help, who answers our call and guides our steps, especially when we face or attempt difficult change. Change is both the hardest and most necessary thing life asks of us. For many of us—though not all—dealing with change would be nearly impossible without the concept of God in our lives. Yet so many of us try. I've certainly been there, with predictably drastic consequences.

For a long time I was a good, God-fearing atheist. I'd grown up steeped in the God business, but I'd outgrown him. God was an abstraction, an irrelevancy, a figment of the collective human imagination, our only way to cope with the knowledge of our own mortality. Yet for an atheist, I sure seemed to spend an awful lot of time thinking about God. I didn't believe he thought a lot about me though. God was many things to me, but he was not real, at least not in the sense that I could experience his existence in my life. I simply did not see how my existence could ever intersect with God's supposed one.

Faith is the bridge we build to God, our way of connecting to a greatness we can never hope to fully apprehend. Sometimes that bridge is just a thread, the slimmest connection, yet the power and presence of God never waver; only our faith does. It is to that power we must turn when the challenge of personal change seems impossible, when our very capacity to be happy is at stake.

Who hasn't despaired in the face of a great challenge? Sooner or later we find ourselves in circumstances in which our own strength is simply not enough. Every person I've told you about so far has faced that crisis point and reached deep within for personal strength—and found it—yet in every single instance only with faith in something even greater than their own determination could that person take the final, seemingly impossible steps forward. Real and permanent personal change, I have come to believe, for most people requires a leap of faith. Are there those Nietzschean supermen and women who are triumphs of their own will? All I know is that I am not one of them.

There are many different forms of faith—faith styles, if you like. For some, faith is intuitive; for others it is hard-won. For some it is most deeply experienced within; for others it is accessed through orthodoxy and the purity of doctrine. No matter what the style, I believe that true faith is the ultimate freedom, for it liberates us from bearing the full burden of our existence. It doesn't so much allow God into our lives as it allows us to recognize that divine presence.

The relationship between faith and change can be subtle or it can be huge. We published a story in *Guideposts* a few years ago that thrilled and fascinated me by the sheer audacity of the storyteller's faith, the kind of jump-off-the-cliff faith that I at times envy. Don't be put off. It isn't the sort of faith most of us have, but I think there is a great lesson contained within the story, a lesson that helps me with my own far less daring leaps of faith. It is the lesson of learning to listen to that small inner voice we all have. This is the startling story of Marty Via, whose spiritual journey was literally a thousand-mile road trip to a place he and his family had never heard of, except through a mysterious urging. Call it the audacity of faith.

Plans had never been Marty Via's strong point. They got in the way of his freedom. "For a long time I pretty much played the hand I got, and it wasn't much of one." Marty grew up poor on a farm and was the smallest of the Via boys, so he tried to make up for it with bluster and spunk. He went to church occasionally but made it a point not to listen to what the preacher had to say. Heck, it was enough just asking him to show up. Besides, Marty didn't listen to anyone anyway. Everybody knew that.

That caused problems with his teachers at school, and at eighteen Marty enlisted in the Army, which specializes in making people listen and telling them what to do, minus the option of saying no.

Marty was a discipline problem, to say the least, but he did get married, have a child, and manage to get an honorable discharge. Whatever salutary benefits army life may have conferred on Marty quickly dissipated. With a wife and child to care for, he took up construction work with all its roustabout trappings. He caroused until all hours with his buddies, many of whom were his age but not tied down by a wife and child. The rest were divorced or on their way there.

So was Marty. Before long, his wife had filed for divorce and for custody of their son. He was free. But what Marty always thought of as freedom now felt like a terrible trap. Doing the next thing that came along and following his own immediate desires regardless of the consequences to others suddenly felt like a burden, as if the weight of his own character were crushing him. He wanted to escape that person he was; he desperately wanted to change but didn't know how. Finally he found himself alone one day in an empty, dingy apartment. "I was burned out," he says. "Totally miserable. I longed for someone to give me advice, tell me what to do. I thought about my parents, that preacher when I was a little boy, my teachers, my drill sergeant, my boss, my ex-wife. The list went on. They all said the same thing: 'You don't listen, Marty!'"

Marty dropped to his hands and knees and did the one thing he had never tried, probably because he knew on some level that prayer was more about listening than asking.

"Lord!" he cried out, his voice sounding hollow against the thin walls of the pre-fab living room. "I realize I haven't done a very good job of handling my own life. I need your help. I'm ready to listen."

Whether it was a miracle or simply the desperation of a man who had run out of options, Marty did change. He read the Bible and joined a church where he met Dale, a single mom whose faith he admired. Marty and Dale married, and with her two school-aged children, Chris and Lindsay, they moved to Ohio.

Marty still worked construction, a model employee now. In a relatively short time he had been completely changed by faith. His life was what it always had been meant to be. Or so he thought.

One day on the job Marty was carrying an armful of steel pins across muddy ground when he lost his footing. His legs flew from under him and the pins came crashing down. He felt something give deep in his back and knew it was big trouble. He was laid up for weeks. His and Dale's savings evaporated overnight. Ever since Marty found God, he had been living on a kind of pink cloud. Now that cloud darkened and Marty was plagued by doubts. He had sustained himself for a long time on the story that life had dealt him a really crappy hand. Then he'd come to believe that the Lord had given him a different kind of hand. Now he wondered. For once in his life he had listened, yet still he saw himself sliding into despair, the hopeless inertia of a born loser. Was this simply his fate? To always have life slipping through his fingers?

Marty's pastor had an idea. Why didn't he help out with the church's benevolence mission, handing out clothes and household items to folks who were even worse off than he was? Marty took to it and one day the pastor said, "You have a talent for this, Marty, a spiritual knack." Had he ever considered the ministry?

True enough, Marty loved the work. But the idea of seminary—school—intimidated him, and he shrugged off the suggestion. When his back got better—if it got better—he'd go back to construction.

"You never know," the pastor said, and dropped it.

One Sunday in April Marty was driving his wife and kids to church when he was overcome by a powerful urging. No, it was more than an urging. It was as if his very will had been overridden by some inexplicable force.

Marty, get your house in order, he distinctly heard an inner voice address him. *I am calling you.*

Marty tried to shake it off as a trick of the mind, a mind that had been under a lot of stress lately. He pulled into the church parking lot. He could see people streaming inside. Again he heard the internal command: *Go home now. Get your house in order.* This voice wasn't beating around the bush, burning or otherwise. This voice meant business.

Marty sat frozen at the wheel. Dale turned to him with a quizzical look. A second later, she blurted out, "Marty, you're going to think I'm nuts, but I have the strangest feeling we're not supposed to go to services today."

Without a word, Marty jerked the wheel, turned the car around, dodging incoming parishioners, and headed home. He and Dale immediately went to their bedroom and knelt in silent prayer for a long time. Finally Marty said, "I distinctly heard the word *Georgia*."

Dale was trembling. "That's exactly what I heard. Georgia."

Georgia. What the heck did that mean?

As convinced as they were of the synchronous urgings, Marty and Dale were not so convinced they weren't crazy. They continued in prayer, hoping that somehow all of this madness that had suddenly seized them would be sorted out. After a while Marty shook his head and whispered, "Waycross."

"Way what?"

"Cross," replied Marty. "Waycross."

Dale found an atlas, found Georgia, and found Waycross, a smudge of a town tucked up against the Okefenokee Swamp.

Marty shook his head again in disbelief and thought, *A town on the edge of a swamp in Georgia? We've never even* been *to Georgia.*

That voice inside of him was having none of it. Each time Marty tried to seal his ears, the voice grew more insistent.

Dale and Marty trotted downstairs where the kids were watching TV. They explained the situation as generally as they could, and then asked Chris and Lindsay to each take a piece of paper and pencil, go to their separate rooms, and pray. If they felt anything revealed to them, anything at all, they should write it on the piece of paper.

Understandably Chris and Lindsay were puzzled by this odd request from their usually level-headed parents. But they did as asked and a little while later both emerged from their respective rooms looking more perplexed than ever. Chris handed Dale his paper first. "This is all I could get, Mom," he said.

There was a single word written down: "Way."

Lindsay unfolded her paper and thrust it at Marty. "It's not even a word," she moaned.

It was a simple cross.

Marty stared at the two and then at Dale. They had said nothing to the kids about Georgia or Waycross.

Marty prided himself on his practicality. Every reasonable instinct told him it was plain nuts to pack up his family and just light out for an unknown town in Georgia on the edge of a swamp. *Am I crazy?* he kept asking himself. Still, the more he prayed, the greater the sense he got that this was what faith was asking—no, *demanding*—of him. It was a test, a great test, and sometimes faith trumps sanity. Dale, too, felt challenged to act, as if urged to defy her rational mind and put her trust in something greater. But this was no small act of faith, like saying a prayer and believing it would be heard. This was a huge life change they were contemplating on the basis of something they couldn't explain to themselves or anyone else for that matter.

They rented a small moving van, left Ohio behind, and headed south with only a vague notion of how far Waycross was and how long it would take to get there. Marty drove, Dale sat up front with a map spread across her lap, and the two kids sat in back with the family cat. They drove straight through—eighteen hours—until they hit their mysterious destination, a sleepy and somewhat run-down town squatting beneath rows of pine trees. Marty scanned the empty storefronts and boarded-up houses and dropped his forehead to the van's steering wheel. What had he done?

After stopping at Piggly Wiggly for a few supplies, Marty drove the van to a campground on the edge of Okefenokee to spend the night. A park ranger looked inside the van, frowned, and said, "I'd keep that cat locked up if I were you. The gators love small critters like that. Perfect size."

There had still been patches of snow on the ground in Ohio, but here the heat and humidity were suffocating. Marty tossed and turned, spooked by the strange hoots and howls coming from the ancient swamp. He slept nary a wink. Had that ranger really said alligators?

In the morning they drove into town and arranged to rent a cheap house, blowing a big hole in their savings. But Marty wasn't going to sleep next to that swamp again. Then they scoured the town for work—convenience stores, the Piggly Wiggly, a lumber mill. Times were tough in Waycross. Dale and Marty both came up empty-handed.

Things did not get better and Marty slipped deeper into despair, like a man caught in the quicksand of his own conscience. Had he again done something completely reckless, as he had so often in his wild past—only this time, instead of chalking it up to being a wayward youth, he was trying to pin it on God? As if God would talk to *him*, anyway. And if he did, would God tell him to drag his family to some desolate swamp town in Georgia? Who was Marty kidding?

Every night he lay in bed struggling to listen, to hear God's voice again. Finally, one hot night when the humidity seemed to cover him like a sodden sheet, Marty silently cried out, "Our money is running out. There's nothing here for us! Lord, did I hear you wrong? Was I a fool to listen?"

Again, as he had that Sunday morning in Ohio, Marty heard a voice. It said, *"Workers I have many. Ministers I have few."*

Marty didn't know what to make of this. He was no minister. All he had ever done was work with his hands. He couldn't change now.

Suddenly Marty jumped out of bed, grabbed a pen and paper, and went to the kitchen. He sat at the table and waited. Before long his hand began to move. Words flowed from the pen. Marty didn't even stop to read them. He wrote until his eyelids drooped; then he went back to bed and fell asleep immediately.

In the morning, over coffee and a few cold powdered donuts from Piggly Wiggly that had been waiting to go stale in the refrigerator, he read to Dale what he had written. It was a detailed outline for a benevolence mission that would provide food and clothes to the needy. Beneath it was a list of congregations and their pastors. Dale grabbed the Waycross phone book and cross-checked the churches.

"How did you know all these names?" she demanded, flipping the phone book shut.

Marty scratched his head. "I can't tell you," he said. "I just wrote down what came to me."

Dale stared at him for a long time. These past few weeks had been terrifying, with their finances vaporizing and no prospects at all for income. She'd been nearly frantic with worry but had put up a good front for Marty and the kids. They mustn't see her panic. Something deep inside her kept saying, "Trust." And she kept trusting, though each day it got a little bit harder. And now this.

Marty and Dale made the rounds of the Waycross churches he had written down in the middle of the night, expecting at best to be gently rebuffed and at worst driven to the outskirts of town and told to stay there. Marty didn't sugarcoat his explanation. He told everyone about the urging, the strange interior voice that told him to uproot his family and drive to Waycross for no good reason other than that he was convinced it was what he was meant to do.

Marty got his share of bemused and skeptical looks. Yet no one shot him down completely, and some pastors grew quite interested. A couple of them arranged for Marty and Dale to have a tiny, dilapidated storefront downtown—no problem for

Marty since he'd been itching to do something with his hands. He got right to work fixing up the place. Still, no one came by, partly because they had nothing to provide. They were a benevolence mission with no benevolence to give. "Just keep trusting," Dale urged Marty after he'd run out of things to fix up.

One day a woman showed up with a sack of clothes in her arms, her head just poking above some faded flannel. "Heard about you folks," she said, dropping the sack on the floor with a grunt. "My kids have outgrown this stuff. Y'all are welcome to it."

Almost as soon as the woman left, a young mother trailing two disheveled kids wandered in. "Y'all must be new in town," she said. The clothes were a perfect fit for the children.

After that, Marty and Dale's storefront, which they christened Brighter Days Ministry, took off. Not that there haven't been tough times. But in the fifteen years since Marty and Dale heeded a call they didn't understand and were willing to undertake a change they never could have imagined, there has not been a day they doubted they did the right thing. For Marty Via, a man for whom listening did not come naturally, had heard something more clearly than many of us ever will—the voice of God.

We all have our Waycross moments—though perhaps not as over-the-top as Marty's—when our lives are inexplicably tugged in an uncharted direction. These instances can be small and seemingly inconsequential: a feeling about a trip we should or shouldn't take; an old friend we suddenly shoot an e-mail to or find on Facebook; a stranger we strike up a conversation with. A door in time we walk through.

We call these moments by many names: synchronicity (a concept made famous by psychologist Carl Jung), fate, destiny, or in Marty's case, the extraordinary voice of God. By whatever name we call them, we look back at these junctures in space and time and marvel at their improbable impact on our lives.

Sometimes they are monumental and revelatory: the sudden realization that if you don't do something and do it now you will always regret it, waking up at night years later wondering, *What if?* Or a decision that you know, right or wrong, is going to change the course of your life. Each time we face these proverbial forks in the road, we depend on faith to center and reassure us, to guide our steps. And sometimes we just know through some miraculous process that we have been handed a gift that will change everything.

I was introduced to my wife, Julee, by her dog, Rudy, a rather corpulent cocker spaniel. I was walking on West Seventy-second Street in Manhattan on a seemingly ordinary May evening when along came Rudy, trundling at a measured but determined pace, completely undeterred in his stately progress along the busy sidewalk by his fellow New Yorkers, who were using their two legs to try and get past him. On the other end of his leash was a dazzling blonde with massive green eyes. I could almost feel a breeze when she batted her lashes.

"That's the fattest cocker spaniel I've ever seen," I blurted out, thinking this might be a good way to strike up a conversation. I was met with an annoyed look for my efforts. Julee tried to keep moving, but Rudy suddenly became obstinate. He stopped, looked at me, woofed perfunctorily, and bulldozed his way over, dragging a scowling Julee behind him and nearly pulling her off her pumps. She was an actress and singer, I was soon to learn, rushing home from an audition to walk her dog.

We walked around the block together while I tried to smooth-talk my way out of my opening conversational salvo.

"Rudy has the most magnificent ears I've ever seen," I offered.

That got me another turn around the block and Rudy, in what I surmised to be an effort to impress me (or perhaps to help me impress his owner), tried to pick a fight with a much larger and younger dog, and I was able to help extricate him from the conflict. By the time I walked Julee and Rudy to their building, I felt I was coming close to redeeming myself. Julee showed lukewarm interest in my offer of Chinese food later that week, scribbled her phone number on a taxi receipt pulled from her purse almost as an afterthought, and disappeared into the elevator, Rudy giving me a final look over his shoulder as he slipped past the closing door. Upstairs on the twelfth floor, Julee let herself into her apartment, tossed Rudy a treat, and then dialed her mother in Iowa. "Mom," she said, "I just met the man I'm going to marry."

Me? I was just hoping to get to see her again. On the way home I ducked into a pet store. Usually you get the girl a gift. I got Rudy a little something, planning to drop it off with Julee's doorman in the morning. An inner voice told me it would be a good idea.

Sometimes God shouts, sometimes he whispers, and sometimes he sends a woof.

In Richard Stearns's case, it took a good deal of shouting and a woman who had broken off a college romance with him because in her heart of hearts she didn't believe that someone who refused to know and love God could ever truly know and love her.

Today Richard Stearns is president of World Vision, the global relief organization to which if you've never given anything, you should. World Vision has done as much to lift children out of the misery and cruel injustice of poverty as any organization in human history. They are not missionaries; they are simply committed to relieving suffering.

Had you told him a dozen years ago when he was a hard-charging corporate CEO that he would run such an organization, he might have thought you were talking about someone else. And had you told him some forty years ago as a Cornell undergraduate and hardened religious skeptic that an all-encompassing faith would lead him to the greatest personal and professional changes of his life, he would have thought you were making a bad joke. In fact, Richard Stearns was more than just skeptical of faith; he mocked the very idea of it.

His views had their genesis in his childhood. Richard's father drank. His parents argued violently. During one of their nastier blow-ups, it became hopelessly clear to ten-year-old Richard that his parents' marriage was coming apart before his very eyes. The money was gone, the bank was about to foreclose on their house, and there were other women.

Richard suddenly had a realization that no ten-year-old should ever have: His parents could do nothing for him. "They can't help me," he told himself almost matter-of-factly. "Not anymore."

That's when a kind of iron rod formed deep inside him, not so much a revelation now as a retrenchment. If you couldn't rely on your parents—your own flesh—then who could you trust and believe in?

Far from being frightened by this stark realization, Richard felt liberated, empowered by it. He didn't doubt his parents loved him even if they didn't quite know how to love him. But none of that mattered. The lesson was clear. Others would inevitably let him down, so why put faith or trust in anything other than himself? "I decided right then and there," Richard recalls, "I would never, ever let myself down." For Richard, there was only Richard. "It was the religion of self-reliance," he says.

Richard Stearns threw himself into the predictable role of the overachieving child of a broken, alcoholic home. Despite the fact that neither of his parents finished high school, Richard set his sights on the Ivy League. There was a plan for his life, and it was manifestly *his* plan, even though it was brought about by circumstances beyond his control.

By the time Richard Stearns set foot on the campus of Cornell University in Ithaca, New York, about fifty miles from Syracuse, where he had grown up, he was a force to be reckoned with: a hard-nosed know-it-all with a full scholarship and a lot to prove.

Richard was smart and tough, yes, but he was not a cynic. His years at Cornell filled him with a love of knowledge and a deep appreciation for the good that human beings can do. Yet he held fast to the notion that human beings were fully responsible for and to themselves, responsible for their triumphs and failures, their heartaches and joys. There was something deeply satisfying to Richard in knowing that he controlled his life, for good or bad. He was his own CEO.

The next step in his plan was the University of Pennsylvania's Wharton School of Business, another stop in the Ivy. But while finishing his senior year at Cornell, he was set up on a blind date with a freshman from California whose roommate called her the "Jesus Freak."

The date was practically a joke. Some of Richard's frat brothers were eager to see what might happen when the aspiring Nietzschean superman met the wide-eyed religious frosh, Renee. Richard didn't mind. He'd dated Christians before. His high school girlfriend's uncle sang with the Billy Graham Crusade. It didn't get much more religious than that. Besides, Renee was drop-dead, out-of-this-world *gorgeous*.

"God loves you and has a wonderful plan for your life," were virtually the first words out of her mouth when they met for the date. Oh boy . . .

"You're kidding," Richard said, trying to keep his eyes from rolling.

No, she wasn't, and she promptly produced a pamphlet from her purse in support of her position. Richard's first instinct was to excuse himself and not come back. But he was still a gentleman even if he wasn't a believer. For the next several hours Richard happily debated Renee over the contents of her pamphlet, with Richard blithely comparing the Resurrection to the Easter Bunny story. Renee was undeterred by his sarcasm and laid out the breadth of her beliefs. He didn't want to admit it, but he was impressed by her rigor, and even more impressed when he asked her what she wanted to do "when she grew up" and she said, "I'm going to be a lawyer and help the poor."

"That's what you should do, then," Richard urged, "because that's your plan."

"No, it's not my . . . ," Renee started to say, but stopped herself. By now she realized it was no use. Richard Stearns was too hard a case.

They maintained a long-distance relationship once Richard went off to Wharton. It was an odd attraction. They had clearly fallen in love, yet what separated them was perhaps the most fundamental difference two people can have, a disconnect so deep it can rarely be resolved. Richard wasn't simply agnostic or spiritually indifferent. His unbelief in God was as passionate as Renee's belief in God, and Richard's life was as predicated on that unbelief as Renee's was on her belief. Things were bound to come to a head.

They did, one weekend in November while Richard was visiting upstate. The whole issue of faith blew up between them, like the ugly emotional trench warfare he used to watch between his parents.

"I will never, ever turn into a Christian," Richard raged. "You had better accept that, Renee, and stop trying to change me. It will take a walking-on-water, so-called miracle for me to change. I'm sick of arguing about it. You have a choice to make: It's me or God!"

Had Richard truly understood Renee, he would have known that no such choice could possibly exist. And in fact Richard knew that what he said was more desperate act than genuine ultimatum. He just wanted Renee to shut up about God and marry him.

Yet nothing could have been worse to say to a woman like Renee. There was a hit song around then called "Walk Away Renee," and that is precisely what she did. It hurt worse than anything had ever hurt her, and she cried harder than she'd ever cried, but she did not for one instant think it wasn't the right—indeed the only—thing to do.

Richard, however, experienced no such certainty. He suffered pain without process, not really understanding the storm forming inside him. His emotions—those inconvenient little components of his nature—spun out of control. Back in Syracuse on break, he found himself compulsively reading about religion, like some jealous jilted lover trying to plumb the identity of the enemy suitor who had snatched his romantic prize. He read some fifty books, cover to cover, not just on Christianity but on all religions. He sat up all night debating himself. He talked to friends until they found excuses not to talk to him. Finally he called Renee in California, where she was spending time with her family.

"I've been reading up on the Easter Bunny business," he said.

Renee was not amused.

"Seriously," he continued hastily before she slammed the phone down, "I was wondering if you had any books you could recommend."

"How about the Bible?" she answered immediately.

In all his reading, Richard had not read the Bible. Maybe he sensed that it would necessitate a total realignment of everything he took as truth, and uncertainty was a terrible thing for a man like Richard Stearns. Still, a longing deeper even than his longing for Renee drew him in. Slowly, word by word, verse by verse, he consumed the Bible. And it nourished him like nothing in his life so far. He had always loved books, but no book had ever loved him. Knowledge gave way now to the beginnings of faith, a kind of uncoiling of something that was always within him, and Richard experienced a sensation he'd never known was missing from his life until that moment: happiness.

Maybe it was a miracle, just as Richard himself had predicted it would take. After all, profound personal change contains something of the miraculous. I don't need to tell you that Richard and Renee were gloriously married, had five kids, and lived happily ever after. Or almost.

Richard indeed became a highly successful CEO, and Renee battled for the poor as a lawyer. While Renee fought in the courts and the churches and the streets, Richard moved from one corporate role to another, burnishing his brilliant reputation at every stop. Everything he touched turned to gold. He started at Parker Brothers, the game makers, and then moved to Franklin Mint and finally to Lenox, the china giant, where he had a desk the size of a battleship. Not bad for a kid from the wrong side of the tracks in Syracuse, New York. And none of it, Richard now fully believed, was only by dint of his wits and work ethic. Richard saw a greater hand in life than his own. And that was just fine, he thought.

Then came a phone call from an old friend and Bible study partner, Bill Bryce. It was from Bill that Richard had first learned about World Vision back during a period when he was working and living in Massachusetts. Now he told Richard that Bob Seiple, the legendary president of World Vision, was leaving the organization. A search for a new president was underway.

Richard made it short and sweet. He wasn't interested. He wasn't available. And he wasn't qualified.

"Richard, I'm going to tell you where to send your résumé."

"Don't bother. I love my job."

Months passed, but not Bill's persistence. He was positively evangelical about the opportunity he saw for Richard. Finally, if only to put an end to the increasingly stressful matter, Richard agreed to fly out to Seattle to meet the World Vision board. Maybe if he told them no in person and firmly articulated his reasoning, the thing would come to an end.

On the day he was to fly to Seattle, Richard was wrapping up a meeting with a visiting CEO of a large British tableware company that was about to merge with its main competitor. The man, Keith, was in a position to offer Richard a job that would make him extremely wealthy. Now Richard's head was really spinning. Richard mentioned the meeting he was shortly to have concerning another position, being careful not to name the organization. He explained that he and his wife were Christians and had supported the work this organization did helping children in the poorest areas of the world. This prompted Keith to share a story.

Decades earlier he and his wife had been unable to have children and finally had adopted a little girl from India who they loved as their own until she died very suddenly at age ten. Keith and his wife were devastated and eventually their marriage crumbled. His business faltered too. Grief consumed everything in his life.

"Then I got this appeal from an organization called World Vision inviting me to sponsor a child for twenty pounds a month," he said. Keith asked the organization if he could possibly sponsor a ten-year-old girl from the same region his daughter had come from. Within two weeks World Vision sent him a picture of his new "daughter."

"Rich," he said, growing quite emotional, "somehow, by sponsoring that little girl, I was finally able to let go of all my grief. It changed everything. My life came back, thanks to World Vision. Have you heard of it?"

So Richard Stearns went out to Seattle and was named CEO of World Vision, a title he holds to this day. "I have never been happier in my life," Richard says. And to think of the resistance he put up! Why do we humans fight so hard against what is so right and so natural for us? Richard's journey was the culmination of a process of change that had been directed by his faith, and until he found that faith he had no direction and no love in his life. Like Marty Via, Richard questioned and resisted what was being asked of him. In the end he had no choice but to trust the direction in which his faith was moving him, on a journey he could only understand through trust.

These two examples I have given are particularly dramatic, even extreme, and may not be easy to relate to. Most people have a quieter faith, an almost organic spirituality, not the road-to-Damascus variety. Indisputable, however, is that faith is a game-changer. For many, as was the case with me, it is yet a struggle.

I did not have Richard Stearns's contempt for faith. On the contrary, faith seemed like a fine thing for people who needed it or could find it. What I was to discover in that rehab facility in Lapeer, Michigan, however, was that faith was not an option, not for me. Belief in a power greater than myself was the only thing that would save my life. More to the point: the absence of that belief was quickly killing me.

After two weeks of sober captivity in rehab I was feeling pretty good, even cocky. My weight was up, my skin tone returned from gray to pinkish white. The only setback had been a tooth I broke on a pork chop bone in the cafeteria. The tooth in question was an upper wisdom that I had somehow remained in possession of all these years. I was driven down the hill and across the street to a clinic where, with a minimum of Novocaine, an extremely large, girthful dentist performed the extraction using no more than his thumb and forefingers.

"The upper ones just pop right out!" he exclaimed, grunting. "Nothin' to it!"

To be sure, I'd had my share of indignities visited upon my person. Junkies and alcoholics always do. Once on a lake boat I tore a jagged gash in my arm that the cook sewed up with standard needle and thread, dousing the wound with rubbing alcohol and me with gin. Following the extraction I reflexively complained of pain and asked for something stronger than aspirin . . . maybe Percocet or Darvon, I hoped. Or even Tylenol with a number after it. Something fun.

"How long do you want to stay in that rehab?" the dentist wisecracked, tapping me on the elbow with his underutilized forceps. "Pain is part of healing. We can't live life without going through some pain. Sometimes I think alcoholics try to live life without feeling any pain . . . and that just brings on more pain, terrible pain, pain that will kill you. No, I think you'll do fine with aspirin. If it gets worse, call me. Could be infected."

I walked back up the hill to the rehab. It was a perfect, hot summer day, a day made for cold beer. I could have just walked away. There was absolutely no one who would have stopped me or even cared that much. I was here on my own volition. It was a choice, albeit something on the order of a last-chance choice. But I had met people here who had ping-ponged in and out of these facilities for years. It was their lifestyle. That scared me.

I fell to my knees at the top of the hill, flopped on my back, and then stretched out my arms and rolled. I rolled and rolled, faster and faster, seeing sky and dirt, sky and dirt swap places until I came to a rest across the street from the dentist's. He was looking at me strangely out the window while he worked on another patient. I waved to let him know I was okay, and then staggered very much like a drunk back up the hill, wondering if I'd done the whole thing just to feel a little high. Whatever—I felt strangely elated and detached from myself.

When I got back to my room, a familiar pair of cowboy boots was there to greet me.

"Hey, John."

"Hey, Eddie."

While I pulled off my shoes and got ready to take a shower before the afternoon AA meeting, John emptied the contents of the bag of goodies he always brought, my special care package—chocolate bars, gum, licorice, cigarettes, *Sports Illustrated.*

"Thanks, man," I said.

"No problem. Happy to do it."

Then with a swift, almost violent sweep of his right boot, John kicked my discarded shoes under the bed. I gave him a look.

"Next time you go to put them on, you'll have to get down on your knees to find them. It would be the perfect time to say a prayer. You won't have any excuses."

I thought I detected a flash in his one good eye—anger or zeal or something I hadn't seen before in him. John had been so gentle and understanding, giving me the reassurance and kindly persuasion I was desperate for. My old neighbor had been driving up from Birmingham every few days to check on me and keep me company, which was exceptionally decent of him. I felt as if I owed him the world. I also suspected he'd been huddling with my counselor, Don, probably about the trouble I'd been having with the whole God concept. Not that I rejected it, but I sensed my acceptance hadn't been terribly convincing.

"You talk a pretty good game, Edward," John said, sitting on the edge of the bed, swinging one leg back and forth. "At least that's what I hear."

That I knew about myself. I always talked a good game. I'd been the perfect rehab resident. I did all my assignments, demonstrated insight into my problems, empathized with others, shared articulately at the AA meetings, memorized the 12 Steps and traditions, read the Big Book, professed a desire to change, and said all the right things, not necessarily because I believed them but because I was supposed to and was motivated to do it right. I wanted to get straight A's in AA, so when I walked out the door of this place no one would say, "He's not going to make it."

But Don had been pressing me lately on the God thing, digging at my denial and resistance. Was I really ready to turn my will over to a loving power greater than myself to whom I could surrender my will and my life and admit that I was powerless over alcohol? That I couldn't manage my own life? Was I capable of that magnitude of surrender? Not provisionally, but completely? Not on my terms, but on absolute ones? I wanted to surrender, but I didn't want to give up.

"Not in an uncharming way," Don had observed, "you are incredibly willful."

Really, I tried not to be—willful, that is. I tried to let go, but even I knew that deep inside, something just wasn't breaking loose, some hidebound chunk of consciousness that was tenaciously moribund. If I stopped being me, who would I be? If I was an alcoholic, a committed substance abuser, would there be anything left if I stopped? I kept telling myself to "act as if." That the longer I acted as if I could be and stay sober, I'd eventually become the change I still somewhat only pretended to be. I didn't want to go back to the life that drove me here; I knew there was no going back, only going down further and further into an existential abyss. Yet the real and total commitment required of me to make that choice seemed elusive on anything other than a rational, intellectual level. Who wants to admit defeat, AA's Big Book asks. Who wants to say that he cannot manage his own life and has to call a Higher Power in to do the job? That last leap, to find a faith in something greater than myself, in something that shrank my will to the tiniest point in the universe, was impossibly frustrating, a source of despair I could scarcely admit.

John was looking at me with his eye.

"I'm trying, John; I'm doing my best. I get the steps. I know what my problem is. I think it's just going to take me a while to absorb the whole package, to really . . . integrate it into my life, you know? But I will. I feel like I owe you that."

"Don't do it for me, Edward. That won't work. You think I'm standing here in this backwater rehab for you? I'm not. Hell, no, I'm not. I'm here for me. I'm here because this is how I keep my sobriety. I'm not trying to get you sober; I'm trying to keep me that way. Your sobriety is up to you. It's your business. I like you, Eddie, and I love your parents. But in the great scheme of things it won't matter much to me if you drink yourself to death before you're thirty. So do this for yourself. Make it matter to *you*. I'll tell you one thing—I could not have gotten sober without getting God into my life. I don't think you can either."

I stared at the array of candy on the bed while John lit a cigarette and leaned against the wall. One thing that people didn't seem to care about around here was how much sugar you consumed. There was sugar everywhere you turned. What was it with sugar? I gulped nervously. I didn't feel like eating right now. I didn't feel anything but a great, dark, dizzying void opening up beneath me. For a second I had the sensation of falling. Was I going to faint? Was it my extraction site acting up? Suddenly a vision of the big wisecracking dentist pulling my tooth out with his fat fingers shot through my mind and I almost started howling with laughter at the dismal absurdity of it. I thought about rolling, rolling, rolling. . . .

"I can't stay for the meeting today," John said finally. "I've got a commitment back in Birmingham. I hear you've got a good speaker though. Look, I'll see you in a few days. Let me know if you need anything."

"Sure. Thanks."

Again the click of John's boots as he strode off down the hall. What must it be like, I wondered, to walk out of here and feel good? Not broken and defeated, not shamed and humiliated and dishonest, like Tommy.

I showered quickly and rushed to the common room for the meeting, my hair still dripping. Arriving late for a meeting was seriously frowned upon and generally taken as a gesture of defiance, conscious or otherwise. I settled into my usual chair by the window and joined in the group recitation of the AA preamble. At the speaker's table a few feet in front of me was a wisp of a woman I'd seen before, one of the few outsiders who seemed to come and go. That she was sick was clear and I suspected she had something people were just starting to talk about, a strange and frightening disease that seemed to eat away at its victims who were, from what I'd read, disproportionately hemophiliacs, gay men, and I.V.-drug users. The room quieted and the speaker pushed up the sleeves of her shirt to reveal arms that stuck out like a scarecrow's. The sleeves didn't stay up. She pushed them up again. Same deal. She seemed to disappear in her clothes.

"I'm Amanda and I'm a sober and grateful recovering alcoholic and drug addict," she started.

"Hi, Amanda!" the group said in that kindergarten way groups say things.

Her story, frankly, was not much different than any other I'd heard. In fact, what I was learning about addiction was how drearily predictable it was. The people were different but the stories, the inexorable strangulation of self that addiction universally occasions, were as utterly predictable as day and night. Yet with Amanda, a woman shadowed by death, the story was brought into high relief. She had every excuse to keep drinking and using. Why stop now? Why bother preserving a body that is devouring itself? Why care about anything at all?

Yet she did, with a courage and stubbornness that totally unnerved me. "I don't know how much time I got left," she said after ten minutes or so, appearing to tire.

"Take as long as you like," someone said.

"No," she said, smiling and pushing up her sleeves again. "I mean on this earth. The doctors say they're not sure what's wrong. They don't even agree on what to call this thing I got. I probably got it because I shot dope or slept with someone else who did. Probably both. I mean, I'm not going to sit here and try to tell you I'm a hemophiliac or some kind of Girl Scout. All I know is I get sicker and sicker. I'm not going to last much longer. Nobody does, not from this, but I was serving a death sentence anyway when I was out there. . . . "

Her voice trailed off and she wiped tears from her eyes with her skin-and-bones forearm. I leaned forward and gently pushed a box of Kleenex on the table toward her.

"But I get down on my knees and thank God for every sober day I got left," Amanda said. "All I can say is if I was to go out of this world all messed up and high, it would be like I hadn't ever really been alive at all, like I never existed. I don't really believe in hell, but I think hell is like never having been alive. So I'm going to die sober if it's the last thing I do."

There was an uncomfortable beat or two when everyone wondered if we were supposed to laugh or if Amanda had made an unfortunate gaffe. Finally Amanda broke into a huge, crooked, gap-toothed smile and the room exploded, as much in relief as anything, and pretty soon everyone was reaching for the Kleenex.

When the laughing and clapping and sniffling subsided, Amanda opened the meeting up to sharing, but I couldn't bring myself to say anything for once and I caught Don looking at me from the back of the room where the counselors sat. I went up afterward and shook Amanda's hand and told her how much her story meant to me; then I hurried back to my room for the half hour of "free time" before dinner.

I lay on my bed next to the mound of candy. Amanda's story had moved me and I couldn't help wondering what it was like to be living with a disease like she had. Along with surrender to a Higher Power, the disease model of alcoholism was another concept I was struggling with. I understood that if you treated addiction like a disease it often responded to treatment. Did that really mean it was a disease? Or was the clinical approach a cop-out, an excuse for a weakness of character? Was the belief in God more important than the existence of one? These were the ideas that, like clothes in a dryer, kept tumbling around in my head. It was difficult for me to accept that I had a fatal disease, like Amanda, or that there was a God who was able or willing to do anything about it. I wanted to accept it, yet I fought and fought not to.

I skipped dinner. What did I need dinner for, with all this candy? I lay still on the bed, staring at the ceiling while the light outside faded and only the glow of the clock radio pervaded the darkness. Every once in a while I would notice a number change. I would stare at the glowing digits, waiting for that instant of transformation, only to have it happen when I blinked or briefly looked away. Why couldn't I ever see it?

I was thinking about the looseness of Amanda's sleeve on her arm, that sad gesture of her pushing up the cuffs every few minutes, when I heard a sound. Someone was crying. Not just crying, but sobbing. Big heaving sobs. It was me.

6
Forgiveness

Forgiveness, of self or of another, may be the most transformative change any of us experiences. When we forgive, we release both ourselves and the person we forgive from resentment and anger. It's the ultimate act of letting go and moving on.

Letting go of anger and resentment, as corrosive to the soul as they are, is incredibly hard for most of us. Living with a resentment can become strangely comfortable, like an aching tooth you keep poking with your tongue. In a world filled with shades of gray, there's a reassuring moral clarity in believing we're the victim of someone's misdeed or bad intentions. Besides, why should we accept a wrong that has been done to us? An injustice? A misdeed that cries out for retribution?

But remember, the forgiver has the power. The offending action can't be undone, so forgiveness is the only way to release us from its dominance. That's why forgiving is a powerful act of personal liberation. It is the counteraction, the spiritual antidote to wrongful action. Most happy people know how to forgive. Most unhappy ones do not.

If you have ever forgiven something big, you know the experience is one of the most powerful and exhilarating a human can have. It is instant growth and change, because it clears out the negative drag of the past. With each person or act we refuse to pardon, a part of us dwells in that past, anchored to that bitterness, reliving the hurt again and again. The more unforgiving we are, the more ensnared we become. We spin our emotional wheels. Anyone who has clung to a resentment knows how exhausting it becomes. And in a fundamental way, it's illogically self-destructive: like drinking poison and expecting the other person to die. Change, I maintain, is impossible without forgiveness. Don't even attempt it.

If forgiveness is so purifying, why does it seem so difficult not only to forgive others, but especially to forgive ourselves? This last part is critical, since all forgiveness starts with forgiving the self, with having the capacity to accept our shortcomings and failings and move on.

My first introduction to the notion of self-forgiveness was as a little boy growing up Catholic in Philadelphia. For a while I lived next door to a kid named Armstrong. I don't remember what he did one day to make me so angry, but I was furious with him. I lay awake that night thinking of all the horrible things that could happen to him and praying they would. I had never experienced such burning hatred.

I woke up with an incredible guilt hangover. How could I think such horrible thoughts? How could such a good boy pray so perversely? Yes, Armstrong deserved to be punished for whatever it was he'd done to me. But the violence in my heart frightened me.

I saw Armstrong on the bus to St. Denis School that morning. I felt so terrible about my evil thoughts that I could hardly look at him. He acted as if nothing had happened. That made me angry all over again, followed by more guilt and self-loathing. All day, fantasies of revenge and retribution alternated with waves of shame and self-recrimination. Finally, after school, I raced across the playground to our parish church, where I knew the priests were hearing confession. I would reveal to a priest the terrible person I was and he would ask God to forgive my wretched soul. And maybe, just maybe, I would be okay again.

The one problem was I couldn't quite pinpoint the sin. My mind scrolled through the Ten Commandments. I knew what most of them meant. You shouldn't talk back to your parents; you'd better go to church on Sunday or have a darn good reason why you didn't; you shouldn't lie; you're not allowed to swear (and if you do, you have to confess it, including the exact word); never steal; never eat meat on Fridays . . . well that last one wasn't exactly a commandment but the nuns insisted it was as good as one. There was one commandment I wasn't quite sure of. Process of elimination decreed that was the one I had violated so grievously.

I waited my turn at the confessional until the little cross above the entrance was aglow, indicating I could go in. I pulled the curtain closed and knelt in the comforting dimness. I heard the priest slide the little door back from the screen we talked through. Theoretically he didn't know who I was, but the priests knew everything. And I knew who he was by the silhouetted profile—Father Morrissey, a tough Irishman I sometimes overhead my father refer to as "Big Jim." Still, I was determined to unburden myself and be forgiven. It was the only way I could go on with my seven-year-old life.

"Bless me, Father, for I have sinned. . . . "

I warmed up with a few minor infractions—disobeying my mother, talking in church, reading under the covers with a flashlight after I was supposed to be asleep. Then I took a deep breath and dropped the bomb, choking back a miserable sob so I could get it all out, even the strange word.

"Father, I am guilty of adultery. Please forgive me."

At the time I thought the priest was having a retching fit, though I realize now how valiantly he was trying to stifle his laughter. It took him several moments to compose himself. The small dark place where I knelt suddenly felt like a coffin, a coffin for my soul that was going straight into the fires of hell. Clearly I would not be forgiven for this.

Finally Father Morrissey spoke. "Tell me, son, what it is you think you've done."

Surprised, I haltingly enumerated the bloody impulses I'd harbored against Armstrong. I was completely honest in my recitation. I could barely whisper when I was through. Hearing myself say out loud what I wanted to happen to Armstrong was a searing self-indictment. Even more than the sin itself—whatever it was—that knowledge was utterly devastating. All along I had been fooling myself about who I really was. I was not a good boy. I was not worthy at all. I was a fraud, and now God knew it.

I could discern that Father had removed his glasses and was rubbing his eyes.

"And why do you think what you have done is adultery?"

I explained the process of elimination by which I had arrived at my conclusion.

"I hate to break the news to you," he said gently, with the remnant of a brogue, "but you are not an adulterer, and I hope to God you never are. But you did sin. It was the sin of wrath, of hatred, the greatest of all sins. What is the opposite of hatred?"

"Love."

"Whenever we hate, whomever we hate, we also hate God. You cannot hate and still love God. It is impossible. And you cannot hate yourself for your sins. God does not hate you; he only hates the sin. The sin is not you. This is your penance, then. You must love Armstrong or you will never forgive him. If you love and forgive your enemies, you will love and forgive yourself. It is easy for God to forgive us because of his great love for us. But not so easy for us to forgive ourselves. That is what you must do: love Armstrong and forgive yourself. Go in peace."

I immediately went home and looked up the word *adultery*. The concept was a bit fuzzy, but I pretty much got the picture. I'd been a little off on that one.

I lay in bed that night thinking about the rest of what Father Morrissey had told me. It was the most unusual penance I had ever received. Usually there was a formula: X number of Hail Marys for the souls in purgatory, X number of Our Fathers for those who did not know Christ. Maybe put a nickel in the poor box and hug your mom. What had been asked of me was extraordinary.

I couldn't grasp the idea of loving Armstrong, but I resolved to be nice to him no matter what. It would be hard and I would have to work at it, and that was good. I would pay for my sin. But the other part of Father Morrissey's penance was a mystery. I had never considered the notion of loving myself. I knew others loved me and I loved them, but I never for a minute thought about whether I loved myself or even whether it was necessary. You were who you were and you lived with it. Right? This idea of loving myself was a very new one and would take some getting used to. A lifetime, as it turned out.

When we change, we are seemingly rejecting something in ourselves. All the people whose stories I've told had to reject a character trait or habit that had become bound up in who they assumed they were—skepticism, arrogance, poor self-image, fear of the unknown, self-doubt, materialism, pridefulness. Change required that they forgive themselves for these traits and move on. Personal change begins with self-forgiveness, and self-forgiveness depends on our capacity to love ourselves.

In fact, we don't necessarily reject an aspect of ourselves when we change; we often transform it. Richard Stearns's passion not to believe in God became his passion for helping the poor in God's name. Richard needed to believe in something, even if it was a negative. For so many of us, change involves turning character flaws into character strengths. An overly controlling person can curb that tendency and channel it to become a strong mentor or manager, for instance. We can work to shape our shortcomings into strengths.

Forgiveness is an act of love, as Father Morrissey tried to explain to me, whether directed toward self or toward others. If someone has said an unkind or untrue thing about me, or has hurt me in some way, the only way to free myself from that pain is to forgive the person, which is an act of love. It is an assertion of freedom—I *choose* to forgive—that is powerful and transformative. It defines us as humans. Indeed our very capacity to love at all requires us to forgive the people in our lives who may have hurt us—to forgive our parents, our children, our partners, our friends, our enemies.

In my years at *Guideposts*, the most breathtaking stories I've worked on are the stories of forgiveness, and of those, maybe none was more astonishing than that of Jeanne White.

Most of us remember the story of Ryan White, the boy who brought AIDS into our national consciousness in 1985, arousing fear and bigotry yet also challenging our better angels of tolerance and compassion. His life up to that point, in many ways, could not have been more ordinary. He was a boy from Kokomo, Indiana, a town with a population of fifty thousand, not a bad sized town for the Midwest. Delco was a big employer locally. That's where his dad worked, and his mom too. Ryan's parents were divorced. Both their families had lived in Kokomo for generations.

Ryan differed from other kids, though, in one significant medical way. He was a hemophiliac, which meant he lacked a clotting component in his blood. He bruised easier than a ripe peach, and any cut, even a minor one, could cause a dangerous loss of blood. Imagine what it would be like to nick yourself shaving and not be able to stop the bleeding for hours. That's what Ryan faced every day, and he wasn't even old enough to shave yet. Still, none of this prevented Ryan from being a fairly active, normal boy at Western Middle School—thanks in large part to Factor VIII.

Factor VIII is a blood product that can be a godsend for a kid with hemophilia. In fact, when Factor VIII was first developed it was heralded as a lifesaver, especially for children prone to falls and accidents (and what kid isn't?). A constituent clotting factor made from the blood of thousands of anonymous donors from all over the country, it is administered intravenously. Ryan got a lot of Factor VIII growing up.

Unbeknownst to the manufacturers of Factor VIII, lurking in some batches was HIV, the organism that causes AIDS, a then newly recognized fatal disease of the human immune system. Once the virus began its full-blown onslaught on the immune system, the patient died in a matter of months—or perhaps a year or so. There was no cure and barely any treatment regimens. It was terrifying, and clusters of cases were also appearing in intravenous drug users and homosexual men, especially in cities such as Miami, New York, San Francisco and New Orleans.

Ryan's mom, Jeanne, and his granddad had worried about Ryan's susceptibility, but doctors were reassuring about the odds: AIDS was spreading much faster among gay men and I. V. drug users. When it struck hemophiliacs they were mostly older patients who had been on Factor VIII for a long time, and even then it struck rarely by comparison to other at-risk groups. Besides, the government was moving quickly to make the blood supply safe.

Then, in the summer of 1984, Ryan felt ill—nothing his doctors could pinpoint, just a lingering malaise with weakness and weight loss. His vitality waned. Then, after a series of rare illnesses and conditions throughout autumn, including nearly dying of a form of pneumonia children don't usually get, Ryan was diagnosed with AIDS in December, a few days after his thirteenth birthday.

Her son's hemophilia had been tough for Jeanne but she had leaned on a lifetime of strong faith in the difficult times. This was devastating. AIDS was a death sentence. She didn't want to tell Ryan about it until after Christmas. Ryan loved Christmas. His doctor, though, said he couldn't be sure Ryan would even live that long.

What shocked Jeanne nearly as deeply as the diagnosis itself was something she could never have imagined. Her first inkling came when she overheard a nurse say, "I don't care what they claim about not being able to catch it; I'm not going in that boy's room. No way!" It wasn't so much the words that shook Jeanne but the irrational fear in the nurse's voice. If this was how a medical professional responded, what about the rest of Kokomo?

But Kokomo was where Jeanne had been born and raised, and where her friends were. Kokomo was the center of her family's life and of Ryan's life. Kokomo was home. Surely this great town would rally.

The brave saga of Ryan White has been told in movies and books: how parents wouldn't let their children attend school with Ryan and ostracized him; how Jeanne had to get a court order for him to return to classes, only to have him be made to use his own private bathroom and eat off of disposable dishware; how kids ran screaming from him when he walked down the halls; how death threats were made and a bullet was fired through the front window of the Whites' home.

The final heartbreaking straw came in church one Easter during the greeting of peace. Ryan sat in a rear pew so his coughing wouldn't disturb the services. Jeanne watched as the traditional handshake was exchanged all around while Ryan held his hand out weakly for someone to grasp. No one did.

That, more than the hate mail and the harassment and even the bullet, convinced Jeanne they would have to move. Kokomo had hardened its heart against one of its own.

Meanwhile Ryan had defied doctors' expectations and survived illness after illness. His plight drew worldwide media attention and the support of celebrities including Phil Donahue, Elton John, NFL star Howie Long, Senators Orrin Hatch and Edward Kennedy, Paul Newman, John Cougar Mellencamp, and Bruce Springsteen. He was also given the Norman Vincent Peale Award for Positive Thinking. Dr. Peale had no problem shaking Ryan's hand.

Yet all the prayers, acclaim and star power could not stave off the inevitable. In early April of 1990, Ryan White died holding a lighted plastic angel that had been with him through-out his terrible illness—Ryan's angel. He was eighteen.

"Ryan's miracle was that he changed the way people see AIDS in this country," Jeanne White told me as we sat in her cozy living room in Cicero, Indiana, just a stone's throw down the road from Kokomo. She'd recently written a book about her journey with her son, a book so honest and human that I talked my editor-in-chief at *Guideposts*, Van Varner, into letting me spend a few days in Indiana to meet with her about a possible article.

Three years had passed since her son died. Outwardly Jeanne White's life appeared to be returning to normal, or at least to an even keel. As she explained to me while she got us coffee, she had cared for Ryan all his life, every day, first with hemophilia and then through the horrors of AIDS and the drama and controversy, even the hate, that would explode around it. I suspected that losing a child who had required such constant care was perhaps harder even than losing a healthy child, as your life became so consumed with caregiving. Was it?

"I miss him every time I take a breath," she told me, bringing the coffee. "But the work I'm doing now with our foundation raising public awareness about AIDS keeps him close to me. He didn't want hatred and division. He preached tolerance and understanding. The disease was the enemy, not the people who had it. It's what he wanted and what he tried to do all the way to the end."

For the next several hours I listened to Jeanne recount Ryan's life and all that they had gone through as mother and son. The story itself wasn't new to me. I'd read Ryan's book, which he wrote with Ann Marie Cunningham, and watched the movie *The Ryan White Story*, with Lukas Haas as Ryan. I'd also reread Jeanne's book on the plane from New York to Indianapolis. But to hear it from Jeanne herself was a revelation.

I heard the deep tide of emotion that ran through Jeanne's telling, the rawness of a mother reliving the life and death of her son. It was not uncommon to experience such rawness in preparing a personal story for *Guideposts*, but I still hadn't gotten quite comfortable with it, even after several years as an editor. Many of the first-person stories we tell in *Guideposts* deal with the deepest and most profound emotions and spiritual truths of the narrator, and the process of uncovering them can be painful for both the subject and the interviewer. "You ask questions nobody else asks," is a frequent response in a *Guideposts* interview. And it can make you feel bad drilling so deep into a person's emotional core, their spiritual persona, as if you were venturing into places no one else would go, sometimes not even the interviewees themselves. But it is utterly necessary if you are to help a narrator find the heart of her story.

For reasons that were just beginning to haunt me, talking throughout the day and into the evening with Jeanne was making me very unsettled. Yet I pressed on. I wanted to know if she had forgiven the town of Kokomo and if so, how. After all, the alienation of her hometown had been almost as painful as her son's death, and in some ways more shocking, as if a family member had turned on you in your greatest hour of need in the ugliest of ways.

"I was born in Kokomo," Jeanne said, wiping a tear before it could escape down her cheek. "My mom was too. Her biggest fear was that I would marry someone who would take me away from Kokomo. You weren't ever supposed to leave Kokomo. Kokomo took care of you. It was home. It was love. Then Ryan got AIDS."

Jeanne rose and took a framed photo off the mantel; Ryan's seventh-grade portrait from Western Middle School, the school that would try to bar him from classes. It showed a painfully thin, undersized boy with a smile that made you forget all that frailty. There was something about his eyes, the penetrating stare, that was far too deep and wise for a thirteen-year-old.

She took hold of my hand. "Ryan taught me to forgive," she said. He had told her that people were afraid, and fear makes people do bad things. "Ryan said that however misinformed and misguided people were, they believed they were just protecting their children and families. He understood that. Ryan didn't like it but he understood it. I had a harder time."

In Cicero, Jeanne found a new church, and after Ryan's death she dug deep into her faith to try and find peace. "Jesus taught us what it was like to be hated, and he met hatred with love. That was the great lesson. Every act of God's love is an act of forgiveness. Early in his illness Ryan said Jesus had come to him. 'What did Jesus look like, honey?' I asked him. 'Well, he certainly didn't look anything like that picture I got hanging in my room!' Ryan said Jesus told him he would take care of him no matter what. He never mentioned that incident again, but I know it explained the bravery Ryan faced AIDS with. After he died, I thought a lot about that. Ryan didn't have time to be bitter. I didn't either."

The death of a loved one is change—huge change—for death is indeed the great transformer for both the living and the dead. Ryan's illness and the circumstances accompanying it might have made Jeanne White retreat from life. Bitterness and anger could have kept her trapped, unable to move past the grief of losing her son and the love of her hometown. Yet Ryan's example freed her. The act of forgiveness turned her son's death into a reason to go on living with passion and purpose. Change was not a part of life in Kokomo at that time— one reason Ryan posed such a threat, for his illness challenged accepted mores. "Nothing," said Jeanne as she ushered me to the door well after dark, "has ever changed me more than Ryan. That little boy changed my life forever."

I got back to my hotel late that night. It was a strange hotel and I had no one to blame for staying there except my own eccentricities. When I travel on business, I try to avoid the typical sterile, cookie-cutter business hotel—the corporate ones with a phone in the bathroom just in case you have to take a conference call at a crucial moment. The hotel I was staying in had once been part of the Indianapolis railway station, its ambiance harking back to those days of yore when trains, with all their attendant mystique, were the primary form of long-distance travel. As kids in Philly, we used to hop freight trains all over Delaware County, never knowing where we'd end up or how to explain to our moms why we'd be five hours late for dinner. But it was fun.

My hotel room was actually a converted section of an old train car. It had all sounded so quirky and charmingly odd when I read the description in the Mobil Travel Guide. But in reality my accommodations were dark, cramped and discomfiting. It made me quite anxious for some reason to spend much time in them. The mall the hotel was attached to, however, was closed, so I couldn't roam around until I got sleepy. Instead I lay on my bed—it was a terribly hot night, as I recall, and the air-conditioning labored to keep me cool—and thought about something. What was it like for a mother to lose a little boy? What must that feel like? And does it ever stop feeling that way? These were questions I had never asked my own mother, though she knew their answers.

My family was resolutely East Coast, so when my father accepted a job transfer from Philadelphia to the Detroit area in 1961, our relatives were alarmed, as if we were striking out for the frontier in a covered wagon, dodging tomahawks en route. Actually, my father had turned down several earlier opportunities to transfer to locations less far-flung. It was because of Bobby that we stayed put.

Bobby was my brother with Down syndrome, three years my senior but never much older mentally than a four-year-old. The only reason my father finally accepted the Michigan transfer was because he had found a good, progressive Catholic day school for Bobby to attend called St. Barbara's. The previous locations to which Dad had been offered transfers didn't have special-ed schools to his liking, so he turned them down at the expense of his career advancement. That was typical: Bobby came first. Bobby, as everyone said, was the apple of Dad's eye, and there was no doubt my father saw this son as a special blessing from God; indeed, a gift.

After Mom delivered Bobby, her third child, the doctors knew soon enough that he was "mongoloid," in the odd expression of the day, and the priests swooped in to offer to take him to a place where he could be "properly" cared for. "This is where the church will serve you," a monsignor told my father. "We have orders of nuns who serve children with these needs. It's their calling from God, and God is calling your son to their loving care."

Not according to my father.

My parents, who were obedient, practicing Catholics in every possible way, could not conceive of this. Bobby would live at home with them, with us, a full member of our family, loved unconditionally like any other child. And there was to be no further discussion, not even with these well-meaning priests.

None.

My mom was pregnant again not too long after, and it was quite a surprise. But she miscarried. Then, at age forty, Mom was pregnant once more. Again the priests were alarmed. Mom was old by the childbearing standards of the day. She'd already had a Down baby and a miscarriage. There was a procedure called a D and C that was not strictly an abortion, and Catholic women who got them early in pregnancy under certain circumstances were not necessarily viewed as committing a sin. But that was not what my mother wanted. She wanted the baby. That baby would be me.

Bobby and I were as close as two brothers could be. Maybe his limited verbal skills forced us to communicate on a deeper or more intuitive level. Early on I trained Bobby, who was mulishly strong, to liberate me from my playpen. Mom was puzzled to discover me mysteriously at large in the house until she finally figured out what the game was. Later, when Bobby and I were both a little older and would go roaming around the neighborhood, I was his protector. Bobby was part of the regular crew on our block, but if outsiders ridiculed or taunted him I would launch myself at them like one of the Furies. Plenty of kids scared me, but as soon as they said something about Bobby, that fear would take flight. Not that I didn't get my butt kicked, and on more than one occasion it was Bobby who delivered me from a beating.

He was the gentlest soul and it was a terrible thing to see him cry. I don't think there was anything sadder. We were at the shore one summer and Bobby sustained a huge sun blister on the very top of his arm after a too-long day at the beach. It must have hurt something fierce. That night, from my bedroom window, I watched him sit on the back porch crying. We'd all had such a good time at the beach that afternoon, and I'd enlisted everyone to help me construct one of my monumental sandcastles, like Pharaoh enslaving the Israelites. I guess I'd overdone it. Again. I'd never felt so heartbroken. He was in pain, and it was my fault for keeping him in the sun too long, but that was not the worst thing. Bobby was crying so hard because he couldn't understand what had happened or why he hurt so much, and that is what broke my heart. I'd failed him.

Yet I was no saint; my brotherly love was often and sorely tested, and never more so than through an incident with my beloved turtles, Sarge and George.

One afternoon, shortly after I started attending St. Denis for full days, Bobby, who only went in the mornings, thought he would do me a great favor and change the water in the bowl where I kept my little green turtles. They'd come from the corner pet store up the street in Oakmont.

I arrived home later that day and went directly to feed my turtles. But Sarge and George weren't hungry. In fact they would never be hungry again. Bobby had unknowingly filled their turtle bowl with boiling hot tap water. My poor turtles could not even escape to their little island with the plastic palm tree, for he had submerged it.

Just then Bobby and Mom walked into the room. "You stupid—" I started to scream, but caught myself. Bobby's pale blue eyes clouded with pain. He had no idea what he had done, and I didn't want him to know, because it would hurt him more deeply and more lastingly than it would ever hurt me.

Mom sent Bobby outside to play. I think she was as close to hitting me as she would ever come. Instead she grabbed my shoulders and said in a voice of deadly conviction: "Just remember, God put us here to help him, Eddie, to protect him. Remember that."

On Friday the twenty-second of March 1963, the Michigan cold was almost inescapable. Winter wasn't going anywhere yet. I was sitting in Mr. Schaffer's drafty fourth-grade class at Meadow Lake School when the lesson was interrupted by a knock at the door. Mr. Schaffer disappeared into the hallway. Instantly someone tossed an eraser and knocked over someone else's books. Mr. Schaffer came back in looking grim. Now we were going to get it. His eyes fell on me and my heart tipped over. He motioned for me to follow him outside, where I was perplexed to find Mrs. Arnold, one of our neighbors, standing nervously beside the principal. "Eddie," the principal said, "Mrs. Arnold is going to take you home."

Nothing more was said. I was both scared and curious. I stared out the car window at the stark trees along unpaved Walnut Lake Road and the unbroken snow stretching endlessly into the bare woods. We'd lived in a fairly urban environment in Philly—trolley cars and busy sidewalks—but Michigan was different. We'd moved into one of the new suburban subdivisions being carved out of farmland and woods, and ours was one of the newer ones, Balmoral Orchards, with an artificial lake and curving streets and sociable cul-de-sacs where no homes had been built yet. No one doubted they were coming though. The streets had already been anglophilically named and were just waiting for people to say they lived on them: Cambridge, Hedgewood, Kensington, Broughton, Priory. This was the outskirts of Birmingham, and it was the mailing address you wanted.

We turned onto our street, Pebbleshire, and immediately my pulse raced when I saw an alarming flurry of activity around our house. Several police cars were parked outside, as well as a couple of vans bearing logos I knew as those of our local TV stations. I even recognized some of the reporters milling around, drinking coffee and trying to stay warm. They all looked me over carefully, as if sniffing me with their eyes. I was whisked from Mrs. Arnold's car and taken inside, where my parents sat at the kitchen table talking to detectives. My sister, Mary Lou, was there too, in her Marion High uniform, looking distraught. My brother Joe was back East attending military college. I don't remember who it was who told me Bobby was missing.

Missing how? I wondered. In the house? I knew all his hiding places. I could find him in two minutes. I listened more to the conversation. Apparently Bobby, now twelve, had taken a walk up Pebbleshire, as was his wont before the school bus picked him up for his afternoon session at St. Barbara's. A construction crew on lunch break who knew him had said hello and he'd cadged a sandwich off one of them. That he would take food from strangers surprised my parents but apparently it was a regular occurence, according to the detectives who had interviewed the workers. Then he'd continued up the street in that shuffling gait of his, his rubber overboots flapping, their buckles jingling a little in the wind. It was the last anyone saw of him. He'd just disappeared into the frozen gray Michigan afternoon, the sun a faint glow behind the snow-laden sky.

The police had found a puzzling set of footprints at the subdivision pump house, an open area across from the fake lake, but they led in circles and went nowhere. State police were checking every square inch of the lake, which had been solidly iced-over for weeks. I'd played hockey on it just a few days before and now it was covered by an undisturbed blanket of snow. Still, that was the first place they looked, and the next day they would cover it again on horseback.

I listened to my mother at the table, face buried in her hands, go over and over every trivial detail of the morning, tearing every moment apart fiber by fiber. Was Bobby usually allowed to go out on his own? Yes. Did he ever threaten to run away? No, interrupted my dad firmly—never, he was an obedient child. I could almost imagine Dad glancing my way when he said it. My mom did cast me a quick look and I could see her eyes melt with relief that at least I was accounted for. For the first time I felt something break loose inside of me, a rush of panic and fear and anguish and guilt, emotions I had no idea how to negotiate. I wanted to crawl into my mother's arms and protect her from these questions because each one must have made her doubt her every action.

It made no sense to me, my brother missing. We'd play games where we hid from each other. He could never find me unless I wanted him to, and I could always find him. Why couldn't I find him now? Why couldn't I tell them where he was?

I don't know if it was that night or the next that my parents appeared on one or more of the local evening-news broadcasts, pleading for the return of Bobby, or if he could hear them, to please let them know. It was a shock seeing my parents on television, as if two separate realities had suddenly merged. My mother was trying to keep her voice steady. Dad was stoic and stiff. Bobby had memorized his address, and that information, along with our phone number, was usually with him, they said. The anchor then cut in with a description of what Bobby was wearing and flashed his school picture on the screen, Bobby looking unfamiliar in a plaid sport coat and crooked clip-on bow tie. Who would recognize him from that?

My brother's baffling disappearance was front-page news in the Detroit papers and reporters stayed camped in our yard. One of the articles said my parents had voluntarily submitted to a lie-detector test and had passed. The FBI toured our house, covering everything with fingerprint dust. They talked to me. They asked if Bobby ever told me about any secret friends or told me anything I wasn't supposed to tell my parents. I said he didn't talk all that well and, besides, he told me everything he could. He didn't have any secrets. Except, maybe, the sandwiches.

What about the night before he disappeared? they asked. Was he sad? Did my parents punish him? No, we played. I rode on his back and called him Bobasus because Mr. Schaffer was teaching us Greek mythology and we just learned about Pegasus.

Days went by, then weeks, with no sign, no clue of the lost little retarded boy, except for a few false sightings and the usual collection of nuts who claimed they had information. One woman was taken seriously, however. She lived down the street and claimed she'd seen Bobby talking to a man in a brown car, a person she had seen cruising the neighborhood previously. She said the man had red bushy hair and a mustache and Bobby got in the car with him. The woman was something of a recluse—possibly an alcoholic, I surmised much later in life—but the police would not discount her information completely, even though her husband eventually made them stop questioning her. They had searched every square foot of our neighborhood and the surrounding area, deep into the woods. They had nothing else to go on. So a sketch by a forensic artist of a bushy-haired man was quietly circulated.

Media interest gradually faded. At one point my father, through some business connections he had involving Dick Clark, persuaded Annette Funicello, who had been Bobby's favorite Mouseketeer, to tape an appeal that was shown on the news. To this day it is one of the most surreal and disturbing memories of my life. She'd graduated from the Mouseketeers by that point, but I kept wondering as I watched her if she shouldn't have worn her Mouseketeer ears just so she would be more recognizable to Bobby if he was watching. That made sense to my nine-year-old thinking, yet the whole thing seemed so bizarre and sad and desperate, such a confusing merging of the real and unreal.

As the weeks drew on, like a long painful silence, time for us stood still, as if some clock had stopped on the day of Bobby's disappearance. Every Sunday that Lenten season, his name was read out on the prayer list at church and the antiphonic response was an increasingly disheartening "let us pray." And every night I lay in bed, the winter wind rattling the siding outside my window, begging God to find my brother and wondering why he wouldn't. Was it something I had done? Was that fair? If there was a kidnapper, was he waiting for me? Was I next? Did God even care?

And even if he didn't care about me, or if the prayers of a nine-year-old just weren't big enough, how could he turn his back on my parents? Their faith was as deep as anyone's could be. My mother had not stopped praying since the hour her little boy went missing. Her hair had gone completely white. I think she must have stopped sleeping so she could keep praying. And if she did sleep, I could only imagine the nightmares that would have haunted that sleep.

I have no idea how my parents maintained their sanity, especially after several false alarms that their son had been found safe as far away as California. My father had taken to following men in brown cars with bushy red hair and reporting their actions and whereabouts to the detective in charge of the investigation, Chief Dehnke, who was as obsessed with Bobby's disappearance as my parents yet knew how dangerous it could be for my father to be tailing would-be kidnappers or, more likely, perfectly innocent citizens who would not take kindly to such scrutiny. He gently tried to persuade my father to desist.

At one point the case was referred to Peter Hurkos, a Dutch housepainter who, after a concussion resulting from a fall off a roof, was reputed to have gained psychic powers that had been of use to police around the world, including in the ongoing search for the Boston Strangler. But the information the erstwhile housepainter provided was of no use, as was the information provided by countless other seers and often well-intentioned psychics who came out of the woodwork, several of whom briefly became suspects themselves when they wrote rambling letters to us.

Finally the tenacious Michigan winter gave way to a spring thaw, and once again police scoured the area, thinking the uncovered ground might yield something, anything, to account for the disappearance of Bobby Grinnan. They sent divers into the lake. And still there was no sign whatsoever of my brother. "At least," one investigator told a newspaper reporter, "we know he's not in that lake."

On a day in mid-April when the sun was warm but a stubborn hint of winter laced the stiff spring breeze, a teenage girl named Margaret from a neighborhood family we didn't know went for a walk. When she came to the lake she looked out over the wind-rippled water. Squinting into the sun she saw what looked like a bundle bobbing on the surface. Something about it seemed out of place to her. Shading her eyes, she walked up to the shore for a closer look. The bundle wasn't very far from land. She stared for a minute; then she turned for home, running.

That April week, the week after Easter, we didn't have school, and that afternoon I'd gone with friends to a movie—*Son of Flubber*, starring Fred MacMurray as an absent-minded college professor who invents a powerful substance that, among other mysterious and disturbing properties, can influence the weather and help his school's football team vanquish their evil foes on the gridiron. I don't know whose idea the movie was— or at least our going to it was—but I remember being bored and uneasy until a friend of my mother's from church came into the theater, put her arm around me, and led me outside to her car. She was crying, or had been, and I was trying not to.

This was the moment I knew had been coming, a moment of stark reckoning that I'd dreaded more and more as the period of my brother's disappearance bled on. The inevitability of this moment frightened me as much as the outcome it held. What would happen when we were finally delivered from this cruel limbo, when this dam of angst finally burst? Whether Bobby was alive or dead, how would we understand what had happened? How would I feel? My emotions, which I'd tried to keep submerged these past weeks, felt like some monster about to leap out of the closet at me. Once again I stared out the window of the car at the leafless trees racing by. Only this time I was really scared.

It was almost the same scene, as if a set had been rolled back in place: police cars, news vans, milling neighbors. I was whisked inside again. The house was crowded—Chief Dehnke, our pastor, Father Walling, family friends, cops and men I didn't know. But not my father. He must have been on his way.

My mother sat at the table, crying in a way I had never seen anyone cry before, so frightening it made me want to escape to someplace as far away as anyone could go, transported by some magical Flubber-like substance to the other side of the universe. I was hugged and squeezed and pulled and finally I was by Mom's side and felt her arm, as if it had a mind of its own, wrap tightly around my waist. Moments later my father walked in.

He was talking about another brown car and another man with bushy hair he'd seen, someone else the police might want to follow up on—he'd gotten the license plate—when suddenly he stopped and gave in to the reality of the scene, that last thread of desperate hope slipping from his fingers.

"Joe," my mother said, "they found Bobby."

He was silent at first. Only his shoulders moved, quaking; then came the terrible choking sounds and I saw my father cry for the first time ever, sobbing uncontrollably, standing alone in some terrible hell of solitude among all these people, experiencing something so painful and so personal that at that moment no soul on earth could possibly know what it felt like, until Mary Lou finally rushed forward and wrapped her arms around him as if he were a child.

I remember coming downstairs the next morning trying to act cheerful. I don't know why I felt it was my duty to put a happy face on this tragedy—denial, probably—but Mary Lou snapped at me with an anger that I'd never seen in her before and I was overwhelmed with shame. I went back upstairs and stayed in my room for a long time until my mother came and talked to me. She said that the days ahead were going to be hard, especially for Dad, but that everything would be all right and I needed to be strong. She needed me to be strong. Still I felt I'd committed some sin that could never be reversed. How could I act happy when Bobby, the brother I was supposed to protect, was dead?

After the autopsy Bobby's body was sent to Philadelphia by train while we followed in the car. We drove because Dad had a phobia about flying; it made him incredibly anxious to think of his son's body on an airplane. The ride was unbearably silent. No one talked about how Bobby's body could have gotten in that frozen lake. The speedometer rarely fell below ninety and the only moments of relief I felt were when we zoomed through the old Allegheny railroad tunnels the Pennsylvania Turnpike wound through, the all-too-temporary darkness like a comforting blanket, or maybe a shroud of Flubber.

I'd been to wakes when we'd lived in Philly. Not that they were happy affairs, but there was always some fine talk about what a full life she had led or how he had gone out doing the thing he loved or how someone had died a beautiful death. There was always some positive punctuation that was more for the living than for the dead, that eased the grieving so that people could go on—not so much with acceptance of a loved one's death but with acceptance of their own frail mortality.

There was none of that this time. The wake, with its closed casket, was jammed with grim and weeping friends and relatives—the Gallaghers and Rossiters, the O'Malleys and Dooners and Lowes and Kenneys and Donohues—all fighting to say something to comfort my parents and no one knowing what to say except how could this have happened to such a beautiful innocent child, retarded no less, one of God's special children. For me it was all a blur of pain and confusion, a stew of tears and the shock of raw emotion. I had never seen such mourning. I didn't know what to do.

Then came a moment, one of those moments in life that spread like a stain through your psyche, when I saw my father across from me on the other side of the casket. Everyone except my parents seemed to be smoking, so there was a bluish haze in the air and a suffocating stuffiness. My father's eyes met mine across the void and I was seized by a thought, a thought as ugly and as unjust as a demon, a thought no son should ever have about his father: *He wishes it would have been me instead.*

Maybe it was being trapped in the strange converted train hotel in Indianapolis after talking to Jeanne White that triggered the flood of memories about Bobby, my family and the journey back to Philadelphia, racing through the turnpike tunnels seemingly trying to keep pace with the train that carried my brother's body. Talking to Jeanne had certainly made me think about what my mom had gone through; what we all had. I didn't catch a wink of sleep that night. I sat up trying to remember everything.

By the time we returned to Michigan after the funeral there were buds on the trees and the winter chill had been drained from the air. There was controversy too. The Oakland County DA was anxious to close the investigation of Bobby's disappearance and death. He was a politician and he didn't want to have an open case on the books, especially the possible abduction and murder of a child. It made voters uncomfortable. The autopsy had not been very helpful and there were questions in the press about a rush to judgment. Politics won out, though, and my brother's death was classified an accidental drowning. Chief Dehnke, widely considered one of the smartest detectives in the state, quietly resigned in protest and for a time my father continued to take down license-plate numbers of brown cars.

My parents gave Margaret, the young woman who had found Bobby, a little gold cross on a chain with the promise that they would be forever grateful to her and keep her in their prayers. They sent a note to Annette Funicello thanking her for her help, and she sent a nice note back.

There was one thing that bothered people, though, and especially me. When the police pulled Bobby from the lake, he was wearing the clothes he had worn on the day he disappeared some six weeks earlier, down to his rubber boots. Except that the boots were on the wrong feet.

Try as she might, my mother couldn't remember if she had put his boots on for him that last cold morning or if he had done it himself. He was perfectly capable of pulling his boots on the correct feet, though, and she certainly wouldn't have gotten it wrong either. The circle of footprints in the snow at the pump house were not made by misshod feet. No such footprints were found that day, and in the end no one could ever explain how Bobby's boots came to be on the wrong feet.

"You still think about those boots, don't you?" said my counselor, Don, toward the end of my stay at Lapeer.

It had taken a while at the rehab to start talking about Bobby and all that had happened. Not that I hadn't talked about Bobby before, but mostly to myself. And I never wanted to be a whiner. Then came that night in my room after Amanda's unflinching qualification and something told me if I didn't start talking I would never escape the oblivion I was falling into, that I might as well walk right out of the rehab and into the nearest bar.

"Yeah," I said, "more as a symbol as anything else. To know the answer wouldn't solve anything."

"You understand Bobby's death wasn't your fault," Don said softly. "It might not have been anyone's fault. But it certainly wasn't yours. And no father, no matter how grief-stricken, would ever wish to exchange the life of one child for another. Fathers don't think that way. But you didn't know that. You were nine years old and trying to take everything on yourself. And now you have to let that all go or you will never stay sober; you will never change. And you can't let it go by yourself. You're not strong enough. No one is. You have to hand it all over to a power greater than yourself."

"I guess I've been walking around for twenty years with my boots on the wrong feet," I said.

This made Don laugh. "Maybe you have, Edward. Maybe it's time you cut yourself a break. You can't control the past."

The night I heard Amanda speak, something inside me had broken loose. A flood of feeling engulfed me. Not good feelings. Not bad feelings. Just *feeling*. Like I was suddenly alive and connected to something more than my own pain.

Maybe that something was divine and maybe it could change me if I let it; maybe it could deliver me from the murderous guilt and crushing responsibility I felt for something that had happened so long ago and for so much that had happened in later years. Because what I felt worse about was the person I had become.

"That morning you came down the stairs trying to seem happy," Don told me, "was just you trying to rescue everyone, trying to make everything better. Instead you just made yourself feel worse."

I don't believe in demons, at least not the ones conjured up by Hollywood directors. But I believe a thought can be demonic, by which I mean it can overwhelm the machinery of our intellects and eat away at our souls. A thought can possess us rather than our possessing it. That is what had happened to me, perhaps, when I stood staring across my brother's casket at my father in his boundless sorrow.

Yet that was not why I was an alcoholic. An alcoholic is an alcoholic because he is an alcoholic. People with perfectly wonderful childhoods can turn into miserable drunks. Drunks drink because they are drunks, and habitual inebriation has transmogrified into the disease of physical addiction. A first-year grad student can turn a cage full of teetotaling lab mice into raging dipsomaniacs in about two weeks.

"No one ever put down the bottle trying to figure out the past," Don said, "but it helps to know who we are and honestly acknowledge that. I think what scared you most back then were the emotions. You had never seen the people you loved stripped so bare. And it is scary. But we can learn to live without fearing our hearts."

Recovery is about moving forward and forgiveness was the saber I would have to wield to cut away the past—forgiveness of self, forgiveness of others. *Forgiveness*. It wasn't so much an action as a process, Don warned me in our last session, one that demanded vigilance and commitment. Staying sober would be a continual conscious act of letting go, a concept that daunted me until Don said this: "This is life or death, Edward, and there is no turning back. You may have another ten, a hundred, even a thousand drunks or drug binges left in you, though I don't think so. You could live on the streets for years. People like that come in and out of here all the time. But with each drink and drug, you will die a little bit more and happiness will slip further and further away until it will be unrecoverable. The point of no return. And you are closer than you think, my friend."

The first thing they do when you go into most rehabs is take a picture of you and the last thing they do is take another one, then lay them side by side. It is foolish to think that after a mere twenty-eight days of treatment most clinical alcoholics are very far down the road of recovery. In fact, no serious or lasting change in a person's life can ever take hold that quickly, and the odds are stacked against addicts. But the doppelgänger photos are a little exercise in the power of change that works quite well and gives great hope. I looked at mine and felt a strange shiver of relief.

My parents were waiting for me in the car about halfway across the parking lot. Dad honked and I waved, walking slowly with my duffel bag slung over my shoulder. So strange to be getting in a car with them, thinking about that one ride all over again. Cars have such great power over our lives, I kept thinking, over our memories. But I wanted to go home.

I didn't think I was cured; I didn't think I was healed or whole again or anything like that. In fact, I was scared out of my wits. But I thought I had a chance. I thought I might make it. It felt like I might have my boots on the right feet at last. Now if I could only remember to kick them under the bed at night.

7

Acceptance

hange is good. Except when it's not.

What's that supposed to mean? It means that change is what we make of it. And that has much to do with acceptance.

Of the nine change factors we examine in this book, acceptance may be the most elusive. On the surface acceptance seems passive—the antithesis of change. Acceptance, however, is not to be confused with acquiescence or apathy. Acceptance is dynamic. It is a choice.

How many times have you found yourself in a situation you hate but can't change? Where, no matter what you do, you have no material effect on your circumstances? You can give in or give up, but that's not acceptance. That's quitting. Acceptance is the power to change yourself in order to adapt to an immutable reality.

We do this in many ways, including

- curbing our expectations;
- controlling our reactions;

- being painfully, even brutally honest with ourselves about a situation;
- letting go of a need for control by turning away from magical thinking and fantasy; or
- giving the situation over completely to a power greater than ourselves.

The act of acceptance is liberating. We feel victorious rather than defeated. True acceptance frees us from a doomed struggle and allows us to conform mentally and spiritually to life events we have no power over, may not understand and cannot change.

I have a friend I'll call Dan whose wife left him several years ago, after a decade of marriage. It really doesn't matter why she left—it wasn't anything particular he did. He begged her for an explanation but all she could offer was a blunt, "I don't want to be married to you anymore."

Was there another man?

"No," she said, truthfully.

"Don't you love me anymore?"

"No," she admitted, "not like I used to. I'm sorry, but that's why I'm leaving."

Try as he might, Dan could get no more clarity or closure than this: I loved you once but not anymore, or at least not enough to stay married to you. People *fall* in love, but it seems they often drift out of it.

The loss of love is one of the most wrenching feelings a human being can experience. We all know people who never recover from this kind of heartbreak. The world is full of broken hearts. In fact, few of us haven't had our hearts broken at some point in our lives.

My first heartbreak was at the hands not of a woman but at the paws of a cat.

I found her off of Walnut Lake Road while I was riding my bike through a field one hot summer day. She had a thick golden coat striated with fluffy white fur and was crouched under a bush when I spotted her. I dropped my bike and, almost trancelike, as if under some fairy-tale spell, walked over and stared at her until she blinked. My heart raced.

"You're mine," I said, scooping her up and riding home with her under my arm.

She was the most beautiful thing I had ever laid eyes on. I could not believe I had found her. That she had somehow been given to me. I had never felt a feeling like this, some deep and undiscovered part of myself. I gazed at her while she delicately ate a can of tuna my mother scooped into a dish. I was mesmerized by the way she walked and stretched and twitched her tail. When she napped I got down on the floor with her, counting her breaths, putting my finger out and feeling the air flow gently from her nostrils. I blew in her ear until it twitched. That night she curled up at the foot of my bed and slept there till morning, when she meowed and squinted her chartreuse eyes at the sunlight streaming through the window.

And all the while my mother said very little about the cat, whom by now I'd named Sunny.

A day later my father came home from a business trip, saw the cat, and immediately pulled my mother aside. A very quiet conversation ensued, punctuated by glances at me and Sunny. Finally my father came over.

"This is not our cat," he said. "It's not a stray. It's well taken care of and someone is missing it."

No, I tried to explain. She was mine. She was meant for me. I loved her. I'd never loved anything more in the world.

No amount of pleading could change my father's mind or unharden his heart. In the morning, he said, I would take the cat back to the field where I found her and let her go. "Her family will be happy to see her," he said. "They're probably worried sick about her being missing." And then he turned away, carrying his suitcase upstairs, limping slightly from a bad knee that would one day almost cripple him.

In the darkness of my bedroom that night I grappled hopelessly for a course of action. I could take Sunny and run away. She would not be taken from me. Escape was the only option. Except it wasn't. Not after what had happened. I knew that.

The next morning as Dad was leaving the house for work, he turned to me and said, "Remember what we talked about."

I nodded and looked away. I wasn't going to give him the satisfaction of an answer.

I watched his car disappear down the street thinking that his heart must be made of stone. Then I put Sunny in a big A&P shopping bag—she didn't seem to mind—and went out to the garage where my bike leaned against a moldy old trampoline Bobby and I used to jump on till he fell and chipped a tooth and the thing got put away for good. I felt something behind me, a rush of movement, and before I could turn my mother's arms were there, wrapped around me.

I rode as slowly as the bike and gravity would allow down Pebbleshire Road toward the field, about half a mile away, the A&P bag with the cat resting rather precariously on the handlebars, her whiskers poking out. Occasionally she emitted an alarmed meow, but I was sobbing so hard I barely noticed. I kept stopping and wiping my eyes, and then pedaling again, wobbling along trying to understand this feeling that was as new and strange and powerful as the infatuation that had overwhelmed me for Sunny in the first place. This utter sickness in the pit of my being.

I rode up the trail in the field to the spot where I judged I'd found her. I didn't even get off my bike. I just tilted the bag till she leapt out. She gave a quick and probably indifferent look at the strange kid who had briefly abducted her from whatever life she had been leading, and then disappeared into the brush, her tail swishing. I whipped my bike around and rode as fast and as hard and as far as I could before turning for home.

This all happened just a few months after Bobby died, and I wasn't old enough to connect any of the emotional dots. I moped and pouted. I cried myself to sleep. Sometimes I would ride through the field looking for her, but I never got a glimpse of that magnificent cat again. I spent most of my time missing her and was certain I would feel that way for the rest of my life. Would I ever accept this loss?

Then one evening later that summer Dad took me out to a house in the country, where a litter of puppies in a chicken-wire pen danced and squirmed and yipped. There was an older couple standing off to the side watching. I walked slowly toward the pen, my eyes growing wide and my heart racing. "Pick out any one you want," my father said.

The ink was barely dry on the divorce decree when Dan's ex-wife got engaged and moved across the country. There really couldn't have been any more emphatic end to the relationship. She'd moved on in every conceivable sense.

But not Dan. The cold finality of the divorce did nothing to relieve his torment. No legal document could do that. He was inconsolable. It was almost impossible to have a conversation with him without it deviating into a discussion about his ex-wife and why she had left. Why, why, why? One night we were talking about a trade the Yankees had made for a new pitcher, and that's all it took to set him off.

"Look," I tried to reason, "you're asking a question you can't answer and probably never will. No one can. She probably can't even say for sure herself. And the more you torture yourself with this question the more obsessed you become. You have to accept this and move on. Let go, Dan."

"I can't," he said. "I will never understand. I refuse to understand!"

"You don't have to understand. You just have to accept."

Dan was impervious to reason or reassurance. Julee and I set him up with a few women we knew, but the relationships never took. One of our friends told us she just couldn't keep listening to him go on about his ex and the divorce. "I know the guy is hurting, but it's been more than a year. Get over it."

Getting over things is not so easy sometimes, and the loss of love, especially when you still love, can feel impossible to accept, like a wound so deep it will never heal. Yet human beings have remarkable powers of resurgence, and the heart is a durable thing, both vulnerable and resilient. You don't have to become a prisoner of your own pain. Entombing in your heart the hurt that someone has caused you is a surrender of the power you have over your life and your feelings. It rejects reality rather than accepts it. When we refuse to accept reality, only unhappiness can result.

It's been a few years now, and Dan is beginning to find some sense of acceptance and embrace the reality of his life. He has a girlfriend and the relationship seems to be going somewhere. Yet I know how much he still thinks about the divorce, about the moment when his wife said, "I simply don't love you anymore," and how impossible that was for him to believe, let alone accept, without a long, hard struggle. I knew all too well from my own experience. More about that a little later.

Sometimes acceptance is not so much a process but a moment. That was true for my friend and mentor, Van Varner, whom I've mentioned in an earlier chapter, and whose friendship was one of the great gifts of my life. It may have helped save my life, but that, too, comes later.

Van—Uncle Van to the incredible array of people who loved him—was a wonder of a personality. There was so much of him to know. A Kentucky gentleman if ever there was one and a passionate New York transplant, he had qualities that never ceased to reveal themselves and amaze. One of the most dramatic (and indomitable) was his lifelong sense of adventure. It seemed he had been everywhere and had seen everything. No continent lacked his footprint, no sea his wake. There was rarely a place you had been that he hadn't been before you. He was as tough as he was courtly. In his seventies he made it up to the Inca fortress city Machu Picchu, lung-bustingly high in the Peruvian Andes. I did that in my twenties—one of the few places I'd been able to boast I'd been that he hadn't—and it was no picnic.

When he was in his sixties Van found himself in Australia, and not for the first time. But this trip he was determined to climb legendary Ayers Rock, also known by its Aboriginal name, Uluru, which means "island mountain." Aussies usually just call it "The Rock."

The Rock lies deep in the outback, some two hundred miles from the nearest speck of civilization, Alice Springs. Over 1,100 feet high, it is the second-largest monolith in the world and bulges like a great blister out of a vast, flat, primeval seabed, a solid mass of red sandstone two miles long and one-and-a-half miles wide. To the Aborigines Uluru is holy ground, and to anyone who has ever seen it looming from the desolate earth amid ten thousand square miles of emptiness, it can only instill a sense of awe and wonderment.

So why, at a relatively advanced age, did Van think he should climb it?

"It's a symbol," he said one night when we were having dinner. Van had an interesting relationship with food. I don't think it really mattered to him very much, which may have been why he ate quickly and often spoke with his mouth full, in a singular betrayal of his otherwise impeccable Southern manners, as if eating shouldn't get in the way of good talking. Van loved having a dinner partner; he loved making friends with the host, the waiter, fellow diners, busboys, anyone who caught his attention.

"Aussies take great pride in saying they climbed it," he continued, talking through a piece of bread. "I wanted to send postcards home announcing I'd climbed it too. I wanted to accomplish it."

The Rock is not a technical climb by any means, just a straight, steep shot to the top, the equivalent of a one hundred-story building. Handholds and chains help the adventurer on the dodgier parts. Most of the deaths that occur are due to heart attacks rather than falls.

Van was by no means a fitness nut. In fact, he was amused by my addiction to the gym. His principal mode of exercise was walking his dog Clay in Central Park. Still, he could be stubborn to the point of willfulness, and when he set out to accomplish something he rarely allowed anything to stand between himself and his ends.

He started out alone in the early morning, before the heat could take its toll.

"It was exhilarating," he told me as the waiter put down our main courses. "The air was still and the silence felt almost sacred. The only sounds I heard were my feet on the rock, step after step after step."

Soon the sun rose and so did the wind, and the way grew steeper. Now the sound Van heard was his own labored breathing. He stopped more frequently, not so much to enjoy the view but to catch his breath and mop the sweat from his brow. Others, later starters, were overtaking him. Van looked at me across the table, and shook his head, sputtering in exasperation, and then took a big sloppy gulp from his glass.

"I began to doubt that I could do it. 'Are you a quitter?' I actually demanded of myself out loud." He thought about the postcards he wanted to send, how badly he wanted to boast of his climb. "Then I would set out once more, slower than before and rasping for air. My knee hurt. Everything hurt. God, it was hard!"

Three-quarters of the way up Van stopped again. This time for good. He could go no farther. His body could not keep pace with his will.

As the busboy cleared our dishes Van said very quietly, "I realized getting to the top was, for me, hopeless. I'd gone as far as I could go and I knew it."

I couldn't quite believe what I was hearing. Would Van go all that way just to fail? Wasn't there going to be some miraculously supplied transfusion of strength and energy? I waited for Van's miraculous ending to his story. But no, he didn't get any farther toward the goal he'd dreamed of. Yet there was something else, according to Van, a sort of revelation. A strange new feeling overcame him. He gazed out at the vast, sweeping view of the outback, a view both fearsome and inspiring. This rock had been formed five hundred million years earlier, an almost incomprehensible age.

"I was suddenly quite amazed at myself," Van said. "It was fine. I'd done my best but at my age I wasn't going any higher. I didn't have to. I could completely accept that. There are limits. I had found mine and it wasn't so bad. In fact, I felt blessed because three-quarters of the way up Ayers Rock, I was seeing one of the most magnificent vistas anyplace on God's earth, and it made me very happy."

The bill landed on the table and Van snatched it up, holding it to his chest playfully, as if there were any chance he would actually have allowed me to pay. But I would have, gladly, for that story and to discover one of his little secrets to happiness. For Van was above all a happy—if complicated—person.

Van did send those postcards after all, proudly denoting in pen the spot three-quarters of the way up where he turned his back on Uluru's summit, and we were all mightily impressed.

Acceptance was his success that day, and his blessing.

We are asked to accept many things in life that we try to resist and even reject. Sometimes these are people. And sometimes those people are your family.

If there's one thing you can't change, it's your family. You're born with the genes, the name, the history. Family is all about acceptance. It is the first way we feel accepted in the world. Infants recognize family members almost instinctually, their mothers automatically. By and large, families are the rich soil God provides for us to grow in. The more love, the richer the soil.

In some families, though, that soil can seem barren and even poisonous. Not all families are good, and dysfunctional ones can be as destructive as good families are nurturing. Nothing damages a person's life more than coming from a troubled family because you never completely leave that family, and you can carry the pain with you forever.

Patty Rose felt that way about her family, or more specifically about her father, until a call she never wanted to accept came one day.

He was a hard man, critical and controlling, and as soon as she was old enough, Patty had moved away as far as she could and saw as little of him as possible. Not that she didn't think about him. She did, but almost always with anger and bitterness. She could never care much about such a man, or even pity him. And never could she love him. He had taken care of that.

She had built a life of her own, marrying a man the opposite of her father, a man who was kind and loving to her and their daughter. It was as if Patty were trying to create the life she had wished for growing up. The family she built with Dennis was her sanctuary from her father and the memories that couldn't quite be buried.

Patty's dad was a Marine and never let anyone forget it. The first song she learned as a toddler was not "Happy Birthday" or "Jesus Loves Me" but "The Marines' Hymn," and she had better sing it out or she'd have to do it again and again until she did.

"He ran our house like a military barracks," she says. "Everything by the book, and the book was whatever he said it was." He fought with Patty's mom constantly; their bickering was the disheartening soundtrack to her childhood. At night she would cover her head with her pillow to drown out their angry voices. Anger seemed to be at the center of everything.

She remembers at Christmas having to hang the tree ornaments just so, though invariably her father would tear them all down and rehang them so that there was exactly the same spacing between them. "Can't you ever do anything right?" he'd shout.

But it was what he didn't say that scarred Patty the deepest. "If I could have heard him say just one 'I love you, Patty,' it would have made all the difference. But I never did. I prayed and I prayed but I never heard those words."

She simply could not understand why her father was so hard and unloving. Why? What had made him that way? He was like a man packed in armor who thought his family was the enemy. On practically the day she turned eighteen, Patty told her father she never wanted to see him again and left for good. A few years later, so did her mom.

Then came that call one cool winter day from the manager of the trailer park where her now-aged father lived, about five hundred miles away in Southern California. He'd given Patty as the person to contact in case of emergency. "Mrs. Rose," the manager said now, "there's something seriously wrong with your father and, you know, he ain't got nobody. Would you mind coming down here and checking on him?"

It had been a long time since Patty had seen her father, and she only wished it could have been longer. Part of her wanted to slam that phone down, cut him off once and for all, as payback for all that hurt. Yet as she held the receiver, squeezing it until her knuckles whitened, a chill rippled though her. Her arm froze. He was her father, a terrible one, yes, but he was family, like it or not. He was in trouble and there was no one else to help him. But why her, after all he'd done—or, more precisely, hadn't done?

Some flicker of mercy deep within her, a mercy she didn't want to feel, stopped her from just hanging up. "I'll be there tomorrow," she heard herself promise.

All during the long drive, her heart burned with resentment, and by the time she reached the shoddy old trailer park where her father lived she was ready to have it out with him. How dare he expect her to help him now! Who was he to ask anything of her? What, was she supposed to stand there and belt out "The Marines' Hymn" one more time?

Her hand shook with both fear and anger as she knocked on his door. No answer. She knocked harder—it felt good, even the pain in her knuckles—and then let herself in with the key the manager had given her.

At first she didn't think it was him. He sat on the sofa, bent and frail, no longer the rock-hard Marine whose image had been burned into her memory. But in his rheumy eyes was a look of confused recognition.

"Dad?"

He stared at the floor. Everything was in disarray—papers stacked up everywhere, food rotting on the countertop, a small table overturned. The stench was so bad she had to step outside for a breath. When she came back in her father was crying.

He probably hadn't showered in weeks and God only knew how long it had been since he'd eaten anything. Patty's heart sank. Now what?

He's family, Patty kept telling herself. *He's my father.*

Well, he certainly couldn't stay in that rat trap of a trailer. She packed a few of his things, cleaned him up a bit, and took him home with her. It wouldn't be permanent, just until she could get him to a VA hospital and find out what was wrong with him. Then he would be someone else's problem and she could go back to the life she had made. *Maybe all he needs is some decent nutrition*, she told herself. A nagging voice said it was more than that.

It was. Patty's dad had Alzheimer's. "At this stage your father can no longer live on his own," the doctor advised her. "He's going to need some assistance."

As the reality of the diagnosis seeped in, her mind recoiled. Wasn't there some drug that would make him better? Some new therapy?

No, the doctor said, that's not how it goes with Alzheimer's. As the prognosis was laid out, Patty thought of a sandcastle being slowly devoured by the tide.

"It's okay, Patty, we'll manage," Dennis said when she brought her dad home from the hospital. "I'll help you. We're not going to abandon him."

He abandoned me, she thought, remembering the love her father had always so stubbornly withheld.

It wasn't the practical task of caregiving that ground her down—the cooking and the cleaning, having to watch him so he didn't wander off or hurt himself; it was the emotional price that caregiving demanded. How can you take care of someone when you refuse to care *about* him?

One night she was reciting to Dennis her familiar litany of accusations and grievances against her father. "He ruined my childhood. He was angry, bitter and hateful!"

Angry, bitter, hateful. The words rang in her head like a bell. Was she talking about her father or herself? And really, was there a difference? Wasn't it all just the same anger and bitterness and hate, passed down like some toxic family heirloom?

It was an insight that shook Patty to her soul. That night, when she prayed, she asked for help and forgiveness, for understanding and acceptance, for all those gifts she would need if she was ever to find peace in her life.

What can be crueler than a disease that steals our memories? In Patty's father's case it also revealed long-hidden experiences and feelings he'd warded off with his emotional armor. As his capacity for short-term recall evaporated, it was as if a curtain had been pulled back on his life and the ghosts of his deeper memories arose.

He had seen his closest friends die in battle and now he described to Patty what that felt like and how there is no fear like the fear you feel in war. That was the real enemy—fear. Anger was like fear turned inside out. It protected you from being afraid.

In disjointed ramblings he talked of his own childhood, which took Patty aback. She had never thought of her father as a child; only as a stern, unfeeling adult. She discovered that his father had committed suicide, a primal loss he could never explain or get over. Now, when he finally spoke of it, his voice sounded just like a child's, Patty thought: vulnerable, pitiable, innocent. For the first time she allowed herself to consider that the pressures that had formed her father into the man he was had crushed his soul. She'd only seen and despised the results. Underneath he was as human as she, and she was his daughter.

With that understanding came something like forgiveness or at least a letting go of the past, of the hurt and bitter disappointment of a childhood she could never change, of the love she would never have. She could not excuse her father's cruelty, but she could accept who he was and what had happened between them. That acceptance would unchain her from her own stark memories. She was no longer afraid of him. Without that fear, her anger faded.

Leaning over slowly as her father rambled on one day, Patty reached her arms around him and pulled him close to her. She held on like that for a long time, crying softly into his shoulder, and thinking, *You are my father and there is not much time left.*

One night Patty brought her father his dinner tray. He had been speaking very little lately, and most of the sentences he formed made little sense, his mind lost in the haze of Alzheimer's, a haze that is like some briny fog of the sea that thickens at night. Outside the sun was setting, its dying rays slanting through the blinds, casting shadows like slots in the floor.

Patty's father's hand reached out and grasped hers. The words came slowly. "Thank you for taking care of me," he said quite clearly. "I love you, Patty."

I love you. How many times and in how many ways are those words said every day? Love is the ultimate acceptance. Love distills life to its essence. Love disobeys the laws of physics because it can be everywhere at once and move through time, faster than the speed of light. It is our emotional gravity. But it also prepares us for and allows us to let go. Patty never could have let go of her lifelong bitterness for her father if she hadn't learned to accept the father he was and love him nevertheless. Sometimes, for the imperative of acceptance, we must let go of the things and people we love.

We love many things besides ourselves and one another. We love ideas and beauty, we love countries and hometowns, we love our pets and our animals, we love colors and flavors, songs and poems and prayers. We love God. We even love our favorite sports teams.

I did a *Guideposts* story once with a man who loved a team: a veteran baseball player named Tommy Herr who played for the St. Louis Cardinals. It was a story that taught me a lot about acceptance and how one finds the strength to move on, because I, too, had struggled not long before in my life with acceptance after the loss of a relationship.

Back when I started at the magazine and was doing a lot of the sports stories, I'd get letters from readers telling me what a decent, upstanding man Tommy was, a solid Christian who led the clubhouse Bible study, and a devoted husband and father. Which was all fine and good but didn't interest me any more than the fact that he was an all-star second baseman with a little pop in his bat. Where was the conflict that animates a good story?

I found it one day scanning the sports pages: a quarter-column item from the Associated Press announcing a surprise trade that sent Herr to the Minnesota Twins for a slugging right fielder named Tom Brunansky and cash. The wire writer noted that the second baseman seemed in shock and appeared to have trouble talking about the trade.

Maybe he'll talk to me, I thought.

I called the Twins PR guy, who said the team was flying to Detroit the next day for a three-game set with the Tigers, and maybe Tommy would be willing to talk then. Perfect. I could hop on a plane and meet Tommy at the park for our interview.

I got to Tiger Stadium early. Tommy was late. I hung out in the Twins locker room, watching Kirby Puckett run a raucous poker game. I tried to catch a glimpse of a couple of legendary pitchers, Bert Blyleven and Steve Carlton, but they must have been getting treatments in the trainer's room. I watched power-hitting Kent Hrbek sit in front of his locker, holding a bat and talking to a younger player about the Tiger bullpen. Still no Tommy.

If you've ever been in a professional-sports locker room you know that it is a kind of sanctuary for the players. Even with my giant all-access press pass dangling from my neck I felt like an interloper. There was still no sign of Tommy so I decided to head up the tunnel and onto the field and wait for him there before it was time for the visitors to take batting practice.

Anyone who has had the preternatural pleasure of walking onto a major-league ball field knows it's like walking into another dimension, a place where time stands still, measured only in innings and outs and runs and hits. The grass is greener and more vivid than any color you have ever seen, and the infield dirt so smooth it almost seems painted on, framed by perfect white baselines demarcating the indelible diamond configuration. It took my breath away.

Especially this field where I had seen my first of so many professional baseball games. The huge old stadium was empty, draped in the lengthening shadows of a lovely spring day. Soon the lights on the massive towers looming above the stands would come on and the stage would be set.

Like most red-blooded American men I had long since accepted the fact that I would not be hitting the winning home run with two outs in the bottom of the ninth in the seventh game of the World Series. Millions of boys dream of that and precious few get the chance. I've always believed that those who do don't really know how lucky they are. Only the rest of us, for whom it will always be a dream, understand.

Here then was my chance to at least set foot on the sacred diamond, to stand where Ruth and Mantle and Kaline and

Aaron had stood. I took my stance in the right-hand batter's box, scanning the outfield. *Why not?* I thought.

I took off for first, made the turn for second, running hard and hoping my loafers weren't kicking up too much dirt. I headed for third, rounded the bag, and turned on the speed. Should I slide? No, what if I broke my leg? Instead I jumped on home plate and then stumbled nearly headfirst into the batting cage. It wasn't the World Series but it felt exhilarating. It felt like a dream.

A burst of applause, accompanied by hoots and whistles, came from somewhere up in the second deck. *Oh no, I just made a complete jerk of myself.* It was a bunch of vendors readying their wares and having a good laugh at my insanity. I waved foolishly and staggered toward the visitors' dugout, where none other than Tommy Herr stood looking at me quizzically, a couple of bats tucked under his thick left arm.

I made a breathless introduction, and then asked if he had ever heard of *Guideposts*. He hadn't, so I explained that we would do a recorded interview that I would use as the basis for a first-person article under his byline that I would send to him for changes and approval before publication. He either wasn't listening or didn't care, so I plowed on.

We sat at the end of the dugout and talked a little about his background growing up a shy but athletically gifted kid in Lancaster, Pennsylvania. Right out of high school, he signed with the Cards. He had a wife, Kim, and two boys, Aaron and Jordan, and they still called Lancaster home. That gave me an opening to bring up the difficult subject I'd come to discuss.

How was his family handling the trade?

Tommy's mouth tightened and he tapped his bat on the dugout steps.

"Jordan's too young but Aaron started crying. He wanted to know why I wasn't a Cardinal anymore."

Tommy's body language told me he was still struggling with that question himself, perhaps even more than his seven-year-old son, so I dove right in. What did it feel like to be traded?

"I'm still not sure," he said, shaking his head. "I'm trying to process it."

I took him through that night. The Cards had dropped a home game to the New York Mets, though Tommy had managed a hit off Mets ace Ron Darling. In fact, despite the Redbirds' slow start that April, the second baseman was hot, riding a nine-game hitting streak. At thirty-two, he was at his peak as a player. Not a big slugger but a guy who could get on base. And his fielding was nearly perfect.

That fateful night he was standing in front of his locker brooding on the loss, half out of his uniform, when someone tapped him on the shoulder.

"Whitey wants to see you."

Whitey was Whitey Herzog, the legendary manager of the Cards, for whom Tommy had played his entire major-league career, and one of the shrewdest minds in baseball. Not everyone liked Whitey but everyone respected him. Tommy Herr loved Whitey Herzog. The manager was like a second father to him.

Tommy made his way to the skipper's cramped office, which was tucked behind a row of lockers. As soon as he wedged himself through the doorway he knew something was up. General manager Dal Maxvill was standing beside Whitey, who was seated at his perpetually cluttered desk. The manager looked both weary and harried.

"Take a seat, Tommy," Whitey said, running his hand across the snow-white brush cut that had spawned his nickname. Dal closed the office door.

Suddenly Tommy had the awful realization of what was going on. His stomach tightened and his jaw clenched. He felt like a man ascending the scaffold. He couldn't quite accept that it was actually happening. No, not this. Not him.

Whitey delivered the obligatory preamble: that Tommy had been a great player for the club and was a true professional, one of the best players he'd ever managed or coached, a guy who still had many good years left.

"You've given everything we've asked of you, Tommy," Maxvill interrupted, speeding the conversation along. "But you know we need more power in the lineup. We've traded you to the Twins for Tom Brunansky."

Tommy stared in shock at Whitey, who folded his arms and glanced quickly down at the chaotic desktop. Behind him hung some framed photos of star Cardinals players—Ozzie Smith, Willie McGee, Tommy Herr. Tommy wondered if Whitey would have to take his picture down.

Tommy thought about his friends on the team, the Bible study group, the clubhouse guys players become so attached to . . . *How do I say good-bye to all this?* he wondered. *How do I tell Kim and the boys?* They were planning to come to St. Louis for the summer once school let out.

Dal was droning on: " . . . the Twins, of course, will contact your agent about your contract . . . "

Tommy kept trying to redefine the word *trade*. He wanted it to mean something different. He wanted to be asked his opinion of such a wild idea as sending him to another team. But his contract did not include a no-trade clause. Tommy never thought he would need it.

"I think you understand our position." Dal was wrapping up. "The Twins want you to report for tomorrow night's game in Minneapolis against the Indians. Good luck, Tommy."

Dal wasn't a bad guy. Baseball was a business. Tommy understood that. Everyone did. Still, he never saw this coming—or had never allowed himself to—and it hurt, really hurt.

Tommy kept bouncing the bat handle against the dugout steps staring out at some spot beyond the centerfield scoreboard. "Kim told me it was all part of God's plan for us," he said quietly. "I always thought I would retire as a Cardinal. I guess I'm having trouble with the change of plans."

It was strange to hear a guy only a couple years younger than me talk about retirement, but a ballplayer's career is short. A decade in the bigs is an amazing run for most. Tommy pursed his lips and creased his brow. This was hard for him and I felt bad putting him through it. Maybe it was too soon. Maybe the wound was still too fresh. But on a certain level I knew how he felt—we all do—and that made me want to know more.

"I know I'm going to be all right," he continued. "The Twins are a good organization. They've got some real quality players. It's just that the uniform feels strange and I don't really know anyone yet. I'm still kind of lost." Then he laughed. "It would help if I got a hit."

He'd been talking a lot to Kim. When a player is traded, his whole family is traded. Kim would have to say good-bye to all the players' wives she had become close to in St. Louis. "I think she's handling it a bit better than me though."

The stands were starting to fill up, and it was time for Tommy to take some batting practice and get ready for the game. I said good-bye and then watched him crack singles up the middle, kicking up a rooster tail of dirt before slicing through that lush, gorgeous outfield. I was properly impressed by the power and fluidity of a major-league swing up close. Then I wandered back out through the clubhouse, found my seat over the third-base dugout, and grabbed a hot dog. I could only stay for a couple of innings before heading to the airport and back to New York but I was there long enough to see Tommy's first at-bat. He smacked a sharp line drive off Frank Tanana past a diving Lou Whitaker that was cut off by center fielder Chet Lemon before it could roll to the wall for extra bases. Tommy had gotten his first hit as a Twin.

I didn't know if I had enough for a story. Tommy still seemed so shell-shocked, and without some sort of turnaround I couldn't really put a piece together. I knew how long these hurts could take to heal. But he was a ballplayer after all, and it comes with the territory. So I called him a few days later with a few follow-up questions, hoping to get something more. He sounded better and seemed more eager to talk this time.

"I was complaining to Kim late the other night about how I was having trouble accepting being traded even though I knew there was absolutely nothing I could do about it. Trades happen. And she pointed me to the Bible story about Joseph. I got right out of bed and read it. Wow!"

I was trying to take notes and remember the story at the same time.

"Joseph was traded into slavery by his brothers for twenty shekels. He lost everything, including something he wore proudly, his many-colored coat, just like I lost the Cardinal uniform I wore so proudly . . . maybe *too* proudly. He was devastated, and with far more reason to be than me! Yet he accepted his fate and eventually triumphed."

There was certainly a stronger tone in Tommy's voice now, a conviction absent from our conversation at Tiger Stadium. Not resignation but acceptance.

"We don't always control what happens to us," he said, "or what other people do. I keep reminding myself of that. We control our reaction. I can't let this break me. It is what it is and I can live with it. In fact, I can move forward with it, and I'm feeling pretty good about that."

I had my story, and it was the cover of the September issue. But I'd also connected—more powerfully than Tommy Herr would ever know—with feelings I'd struggled with myself, some of the same emotional upheaval I had fought nearly to the death just a couple years earlier when I returned to New York from Michigan: the unresolved (or at least I considered it so) situation of the woman who had left me because of my drinking and whose love I was still quite convinced I could win back, despite the strong and unambiguous advice of friends, counselors and family to the contrary. It was an outcome I prayed for every day.

I was only out of the rehab in Lapeer a short while when my parents drove me to Detroit Metro for my flight back to New York, where I knew I had to return. There was no future for me in Michigan, despite a couple of small, well-meaning job offers ("We can find something for you short-term until you get back on your feet"). No, I needed to be back in New York. The city's siren song was too strong. I knew it wouldn't be easy. Maybe it was suicidal. But to recast a phrase: If I could stay sober there, I could stay sober anywhere.

I hugged my mom at the gate and shook my father's hand. He wished me luck. I'd discovered a lot about my father these past months, not that he himself had disclosed much. My mother confided that his father, my paternal grandfather, who died long before I was born, was probably an alcoholic. Generally you are not "probably" an alcoholic, so I felt confident concluding he was.

He'd lost his money and his comfortable job in the Depression and apparently did most of his subsequent career networking from barstools. My father would be sent out by my grandmother at night to search the local dives and bring him home, and then had to drop out of college himself to help support the family. Many years later when my father earned a degree from attending Wharton business school at night, my mother kept his diploma proudly.

Standing at the gate I was tempted to hug him to let him know everything was all right, that I didn't plan on being a genetic rerun of the nightmare with his father. It didn't fail to register with me that once my problems were out in the open, my father suddenly seemed to know more about me than he ever had. It was as if I had come into focus for him at long last, through a window of recognition neither of us wished. I took a half-step toward him; then I stopped, as if I'd encountered some psychic border guarding the frontier. No, a handshake would do.

I wish I had hugged him, for it would be the last time I ever saw him.

New York was kind of a heyday for AA in the early-to-mid eighties, if that doesn't sound too sacrilegious. Cocaine, disco, Wall Street, and the prevailing sybaritic ethos of the times had accelerated many people's demise into full-blown alcoholism and drug addiction ("Cocaine was God's way of telling me I had too much disposable income," I heard one recovering stockbroker quip), with the result that people were coming into the program earlier and younger, and meetings, which were 24–7, sometimes accommodated standing room only. Folks were hitting bottom left and right, and seeking help.

John Cavanaugh had gotten hold of a Manhattan meeting schedule and gave it to me as a going-away present, along with a pocket-sized address book. "Get as many phone numbers at meetings as you can," he said, "and call them. The phone can keep you straight."

Walking up to strangers milling around church basements and asking for their phone numbers was not exactly my style. In fact, I would have been the first to tell you that I was not a joiner. It didn't take me long to understand that that's what just about everybody who comes into a 12-step program says at first—"I'm not a joiner; I can do this my own way"—a universal excuse to avoid accepting yourself as who and what you are, and what you need.

I also quickly learned that these people didn't stay sober for long either. And I was good and scared at the prospect of picking up a drink.

Still, getting myself to a meeting, saying my name and that I was an alcoholic, counting my consecutive sober days out loud, sharing a bit of my story, and sticking around to talk to people afterward—all that was daunting. It hammered my ego. On some days it was terrifying. I would often think that this would be a lot easier with a drink or two in me.

That was the point, of course: to face life without alcohol as a lubricant or a crutch. Moreover, the Higher Power question still hung over my head. At my most honest, I could not say that I felt God in my life or, especially, in my heart. God was still a concept to me rather than a real and living presence. I prayed. I believed. But I did not always feel.

Maybe, I deduced, if I could get comfortable connecting with other alcoholics, through those people I would discover a true connection to God. In community I would find communion.

The alternative was everywhere I looked, slumped in doorways or passed out on subway cars. I was deceiving myself to think I wasn't just a drink away from their fate. I'd already been there; it would be so easy to slip back. In fact, in certain harrowing moments, I felt I belonged there, deserved to be there, that somehow it was a fate I was a fool to think I could resist. I was cursed never to be able to navigate life without drink. I'd inevitably be destroyed by alcohol and drugs; there was no middle ground for me. It was when these thoughts plagued me that I yearned for the presence of a Higher Power, some divine force, some light, that would intervene between me and oblivion. I prayed, not knowing to whom or to what, and not really caring. Just praying. There was a phrase I'd heard: "Act as if." That's what I did. I acted as if I had faith and hoped I would find it or it would find me.

I got a sponsor, someone with enough quality sobriety whom I could check in with every day and talk about what I was feeling—anger, elation, sadness, fear, desire, boredom. And I felt them all, usually within the same half hour. I found a roommate, Bob Y., who was also in the program. I kept body and soul together by working in restaurants and picking up a bit of freelance writing.

And I spent most of my time thinking about Daria.

Throughout the parts of this book that have been my story I've kept her in the shadows. Writing autobiographically is a little like performing surgery on yourself, without anesthesia. But it would not be honest if I excluded Daria from my story, especially at this juncture, when her presence, or lack thereof, so often overwhelmed my consciousness. In fact, in her absence she became more of a presence in my life than ever. I did not know how to accept the reality of her leaving me. I would not accept it, especially in the way that it happened.

I met her at Yale, where we both lived in a graduate-school dorm that was architecturally dull but socially interesting insofar that it was filled with students from many disciplines. She was a literature major, working on her PhD. The moment I laid eyes on her walking across the dorm lobby toward the elevator on the first day of fall semester, I was fatally smitten. I followed her into the notoriously unreliable elevator.

"You don't actually live here, do you?" were the words that stumbled out of my mouth. She wisely waited to see what floor I punched before she pushed hers.

"I certainly do," she said as the elevator lurched into action. "Why?" Before I could think of anything else to say on that eternal elevator ride to the third floor, she was out the door—but not without a reasonably inviting "See you later!" over her shoulder. And see her I would.

I won't bore you with the usual love-struck paean except to say that I can imagine no beholder in whose eye she was not beautiful in every way. She was everything I could imagine in the woman I would want to be with forever, to live with and die with—wit, beauty, intelligence, depth, sensuality. Whether she was my ideal woman or simply my idealized one, it didn't matter to me. My feelings for her eclipsed everything.

Daria and I quickly became a couple, or maybe more of a single two-person entity. My drinking became an issue much more slowly and insidiously. For as much as I loved her, that love had no efficacious effect on the progression of my alcoholism. It was not the cure I had hoped. If I couldn't stop drinking for her, how could I ever stop? I disappeared for days at a time, sending her into a delirium of worry, or I would refuse to answer my door or my phone. I'd wake up at night with terrors that could only be quelled by a drink, and in the morning my hands would tremble when I stroked her cheek. All this time she was trying to work on her degree and I was struggling through mine.

She could not understand why love couldn't fix all this. So she loved more and endured more, and I only got worse. The more Daria loved me, the more I hated myself for being so undeserving of that love. I swore I would stop. I didn't. Not for her, not for me, not for anything. When I took a drink, the drink took me. Alcohol, even more than love, had become the most powerful force in my life.

Was it ego or the hubris of devotion that made her say, "I will never leave you, Edward, no matter what. I will never leave you." And what made me deceive myself into believing it so completely?

My family adored her; hers not so much me. Daria's parents were divorced and her mother had my number. She knew I would break her daughter's heart someday, or at least my drinking would, and she did everything to blunt that eventual blow. She was very wise and I knew it.

I don't know how many nights of alcoholic insomnia Daria sat through with me; how many days she spent trying to get me to eat something when I was so sick I could not even keep down a drink; how many hours she spent during my several hospitalizations, talking to doctors and nurses and therapists and rarely leaving my side. I remember one night watching her sleep in a chair while I sat on the side of my bed, swinging my legs and literally wringing my hands, counting the minutes until the nurse would deliver my next scheduled dose of sedative, praying maybe this one would knock me out until the worst of the withdrawal was over. I looked at Daria's face and thought, *How can you do this to her? What sort of monster are you? If you loved her, you would leave her. She doesn't deserve this.*

I'm painting a picture that feels like a Bosch canvas and maybe it is the reservoir of guilt I still harbor, the sins that I can never recant, that compels me to do this. So I must dispel any impression that Daria was a hopeless enabler and I a chronic basket case.

There were times, certainly more times than not in the beginning of our relationship, when I was reasonably sober and reasonably sane and everything was bliss, times that were the most incredibly happy moments of my life despite the cliff that, on at least some level, I knew I was headed over. It wasn't just that she made me feel that way herself; it was how deeply and profoundly that I loved her that gave me such joy. By loving her, I sometimes found myself able to love myself.

I remember one beautiful day the summer I took her back to Michigan to meet my family. The two of us were walking through Greenfield Village, one of those historical recreations of a bygone era, complete with Ye Olde Blacksmythe Shoppe and Ye Olde Carriage House. I was buying us some ice cream at Ye Olde Soda Parlour when the cashier, decked out in Victorian bustle, said we looked like the perfect couple. I wanted to believe it.

After three years together in New Haven we moved to New York, neither of us with any solid job prospects. I'd finished my degree, an MFA, but she was still grappling with her dissertation. Daria did some runway modeling and print work—she was tall and beautiful—sufficiently intermittent employment to give her time for her studies. I landed a very strange job as part of a team of ghostwriters that constituted the "workshop" of a successful suspense novelist who spent most of his time lunching at "21" while we cranked out his crackling prose following an outline his agent provided after making us all sign non-disclosure documents and work-made-for-hire agreements. It was whorish work, and that's what I felt like.

New York was a treacherous new place to drink. It was one thing to drift on and off the bum in a town like New Haven, a sometimes dangerous but relatively confined space with ivy walls to hide behind when necessary. New York was the alcoholic big leagues, and getting lost in an alcoholic episode was tempting fate in a way I never had.

Maybe it was the reality of New York that changed Daria. A great city can do that. Or maybe at last it was just the grim reality of me. But she walked out of my life as suddenly as she had walked into that elevator the first time I saw her.

It was Christmas. She went out of town to visit her mother while I spent a few days alone—never a great idea at the time—at the apartment we were quasi-subletting from an acquaintance of a friend of hers. The plan was for us to meet in Detroit and spend Christmas with my family. I kissed her good-bye knowing it was a promise that I wouldn't drink. I'd been dry since Thanksgiving.

I don't know when I started and I don't remember what happened. When I came more or less to my senses, it was the day after Christmas and the answering machine was full of frantic, angry messages, none of which I could bear to listen to in full. The borrowed apartment was a disaster. It looked like someone had gone stark raving mad, but really it was the result of the slow accretion of alcoholic disorder over the five days or so I'd been binging: chaos in slow motion.

And that was it. Daria called my family. My brother, Joe, flew to New York to retrieve me and I'll never forget his disapproving scowl as I gulped a vodka and soda on the 8:00 AM flight back to Detroit. There I spent a few incredibly awkward days with my parents trying not to look at the still-wrapped presents under the tree with our names on the sparkly tags—Daria and Edward. No one seemed to want to talk about anything.

I spent the dreariest New Year's Eve of my life going to five o'clock Mass with my folks, and then having dinner at a Bill Knapp's Restaurant where I was the youngest diner by about half a century. The next day I beat a hasty retreat back to New York and convinced a friend in Hoboken to let me move in with him. He eventually invited me to leave and I ended up splitting my time between the Victor and the baseball field, the events I recounted in Chapter I.

Now, once again I had returned to New York, after rehab, with several solid months of sobriety under my belt, daily meetings, a sponsor, a roommate in the program, and enough income that I bobbed above the poverty line. I dated, went to movies, caught an occasional ballgame. Life was good. Really, it was.

Except for my thoughts of Daria. I had not spoken to her or seen her. Most of the, oh, couple of hundred letters I had written in the year and a half since I'd said good-bye to her for what I thought would only be a few days had all been stamped return to sender—rejected, I suspected, by her mother (Daria's home address being the only one I had for her).

All inquiries I made, whether with friends or even my own family, were met with stony silence, as if everyone had signed a blood pact. No one would even say her name to me. No one said anything. I couldn't find her in any phone book in any city, here or abroad, that I thought she might have a reason to be (remember it was still PG—pre-Google). She had completely escaped from my life.

"It isn't fair," I complained to my sponsor.

"It's not about being fair," he said.

"I want to find her. I'm sober now, and I deserve a last conversation, at least, some closure. Something I can hold onto."

"Obviously she wants no contact with you whatsoever. What more closure do you need?"

"More than this. I can't accept this. This is not life; this is limbo. It was supposed to be forever."

"For you, my friend, forever is a day at a time. My suggestion is to put the focus on yourself instead of her, work the steps, help another drunk, keep it simple . . . "

"Yeah, yeah, yeah."

"You're acting like a willful alcoholic. Seeing her would be the worst thing you could do. I'm not saying you would drink, but it would damage you; it would set you back."

"I know. I can't help it. There's nothing more pathetic than an alcoholic with a broken heart, is there?"

"Nope."

Yet deep down I always knew if I really concentrated my cunning on finding her I could. And I did. I don't remember how, exactly, but one day I found myself on the phone with the registrar at Johns Hopkins University in Baltimore who, after some sly cajoling, confirmed that Daria was enrolled in graduate school. Her class schedule would be easy to figure out.

I told no one. I guarded that forbidden knowledge like hidden gold. Then one perfect spring morning when the pollen was awful I walked to Penn Station from the Upper West Side and bought a train ticket.

It was rush hour and I had a few minutes to kill. I grabbed a newspaper but tried not to let it brush up against the new shirt I was wearing. I didn't want to risk looking smudged and seedy. I'd already lacerated my face earlier because I had shaved so vigorously, and I had a tiny wad of Kleenex stuck to the spot to stanch the bleeding. I passed a shoeshine stand and decided to stop. It seemed important that my shoes be shiny when I saw her, so I climbed onto the high seat and watched the commuters swarm by, remembering my mendicancy at the Hoboken train station and marveling at how things had changed, how I didn't feel like a different species from the humanity all around me. Maybe things would change more. The shine guy popped his rag and I was off to my train.

I chose a nearly empty car where I could have two seats to myself and watched the landscape sweep by, evolving from urban to exurban to rural and back to urban. We were pulling into Philadelphia. I thought of my dad. He was buried here.

He'd died not long after that handshake, killed by a massive coronary while swimming laps in the slow lane at his health club. He'd had several heart attacks in his fifties and a host of other health problems subsequently, including that crippling arthritic knee, but retirement had agreed with him and, frankly, he lived longer than a lot of people expected, including his doctors. My mother was standing near the pool yelling, "Joe! Joe! Get your face out of the water!" She knew he hated to get his face wet and always swam with his chin raised.

She didn't realize he was dead until a lifeguard pulled him from the pool and administered CPR. But the effort was in vain and eventually the lifeguard stepped back, sweating and breathing hard. By now a crowd had gathered—at that time of day mostly older folks, in dripping swimsuits and bathing caps. They stayed with Mom until my brother and his wife, Toni, showed up.

We buried him here in Philly next to his son, and as the train pulled out of the station I said a prayer and thought about how they had both been found floating in water and now they rested side by side.

I'd never been to Baltimore that I could remember and didn't plan to see much of it now. I briefly considered getting another shoe shine—I was growing more nervous by the minute—but grabbed a cab from Penn Station and headed for campus, asking to be let out along Charles Street at the Gatehouse next to the Baltimore Museum of Art so I could walk off some of the kinetic energy rocketing through me. I resisted buying a pack of cigarettes and smoking one because Daria hated it when I smoked (so did I). Still, my heart was doing a drum solo.

I wound my way through the lovely campus full of quality faux-Georgian architecture, sneezing from the pollen, stopping every so often to apply eyedrops, and hoping I didn't look like some bloodshot wino. Lush magnolias bloomed and shed their thick petals along a fairy-tale walkway. A bell tolled noon.

It was not too late to call this off. I mean, it wasn't like she was expecting me.

No, I'd come this far. Maybe she'd been testing me all along.

I checked a campus map posted under glass, located the building her department was in, and made my way to it. I thought I might have to hang around for a few hours until I ran into her, maybe even spend the night in Baltimore and try again the next day, but as I ascended the steps to the entrance I looked up, and there she was.

She had seen me before I saw her. She stopped and my eyes met hers—those same cerulean eyes—and an almost palpable vibration passed between us.

At least she didn't scream.

My mouth was too dry to speak, so she broke the ice.

"Hello there."

"Can we talk?" I finally managed to croak.

"Suuure," she said, elongating the word cautiously.

We walked to an open area crisscrossed by a stream of students, the Keyser Quadrangle, Daria explained, flicking her hand.

"I was sorry to hear about your dad," she said.

Well, she had been in touch with somebody.

We sat on a bench near a flowering azalea bush, a discreet distance separating us. She withdrew her sunglasses from her bag, but then seemed to think better of putting them on.

"My allergies are killing me," I stated, by way of small talk, and stared at an orphaned bike leaning tenuously against an oak tree across the path.

"I bet."

I asked her about her studies. She'd made a slight shift in her academic concentration. She didn't inquire much about me. I was beginning to fear if I didn't get to the point she'd get up and walk away.

"I feel like John Hinckley," I said, and that made her laugh a little. She understood the reference. The three of us—by which I mean Daria, Jodie Foster and I—were all at Yale when

Foster's campus stalker, John Hinckley, went down to DC and shot President Reagan.

"Don't," she said. "Don't feel that way." She leaned over slightly to tap my hand in mock reproach but I quickly withdrew it and rubbed my eye. I realized I still had the Kleenex pellet affixed to my cheek. I removed it, hoping I wouldn't start bleeding again.

"Are you happy?" I asked.

"I'm getting there."

"I've stopped drinking."

"Good. Good for you." I listened for a note of condescension, disbelief, relief, something. All she seemed to be implying was that not drinking was a good thing for me but had nothing whatsoever to do with her or her present life.

"Are you writing?" she wanted to know.

"I dropped you a few lines."

"That's not writing."

"How would you know?" I demanded, thinking of all those unopened letters stamped return to sender.

"You know what I mean. Don't give up on your writing, Edward," she said, and for the first time there was just a hint of intimacy in her voice, a fleeting sense that we were more than just two old pals having a conversation.

"Even if it destroys me?"

"It won't, if you're honest," she said, and then looked away.

"Are you seeing anyone?" I asked. I was ashamed of the question as soon as the words were out of my mouth and she didn't answer because it didn't matter.

"Look, Edward," she started to say, sighing.

"You said you'd never leave me."

"I meant it when I said it."

"And now?"

Silence interrupted by more silence. We sat for an eternity, saying nothing.

"I'm going to have to go soon," Daria said, tapping her sunglasses on her knee.

"I know. Me too. I'm sorry I did this. I'm sorry about everything."

"Stop," she said and leaned over again to put her hand on my arm, more for emphasis than out of affection, I was sure. I thought of the years we'd spent together and the utter familiarity of our flesh, yet now I wasn't at all certain I could survive her touch, so I stood.

"All right, then," I said, and all at once I felt overpowered by the aching, voluptuous void that was my love for her and, I believed, always would be. "Just tell me . . . if there is any chance, not today or tomorrow or next year . . . it's not a matter of time . . . is there any chance we might someday . . . possibly . . . I mean, I don't know if I can live without that hope . . . "

I would have never finished the sentence if she hadn't cut me off, albeit gently.

"No," she said, shaking her head. "No. You can't let yourself think that. It's impossible."

If I could have brought myself to jump on the bike leaning against the tree I would have, and I would have ridden as hard and as far as I could. If I could have brought myself to take her in my arms and kiss her, I would have. Instead I stood there wondering if I should shake her hand or what, warning myself not to cry or snivel or do anything else to embarrass myself more than I already had. Was it love or was it madness that made me do this? It was a fine line, to be sure. I sensed myself riveted in space and time. Impossible. That word. It came down to that single, infinitely final word. How could I ever accept that word?

Daria slipped on her sunglasses as a concluding gesture. It worked.

"Good-bye," I said, not moving.

"Bye," she said, moving, and then turning and walking in the other direction.

I watched her for a second and then started walking away myself, edging through the throng on the Quad. I only looked back once.

I wandered around campus for a bit before I became alarmed that I might somehow bump into her, which would be intolerably awkward and anticlimactic. Daylight was fading. I straggled through the campus neighborhood until the area grew sketchy in terms of personal safety. What would it matter if I was bludgeoned and mugged and left for dead? Baltimore was a good enough place for Poe to die.

Suddenly ravenous—I had eaten nothing all day—I slipped into a Chinese restaurant and was served some atrocious dish that I doused with hot sauce until I couldn't taste anything but the blistering burn. I was tired now, having exhausted my reserves of adrenaline. I thought about getting a room for the night but decided the loneliness would be unbearable.

I emerged from the restaurant thoroughly lost and disoriented. Cabs refused to stop for me until I figured out that the conventional signal of an unengaged cab was the opposite down here: an illuminated roof light meant the cab was engaged. One finally stopped and took me back to Penn Station, where I barely made the last train to New York.

This time the train was more crowded and I was not able to enjoy the solitude of an unoccupied row until we pulled out of Philly. I found myself staring out the window into the darkened landscape thinking about love, how close it can be to madness, how it can be as selfish as it is selfless. Maybe the fruit of the tree in Eden was not the fruit of knowledge but of love and all of the confusion and pain that comes with it. Perhaps the sacrificed bliss of Adam and Eve had been the bliss of indifference.

This trip had finalized my relationship with Daria, a relationship that I had destroyed. The question was, could I accept the results of my own actions?

As I stared at the docks of Newark flashing by with huge container ships unloading their cargo, I was seized by the realization that I had not thought of drinking this whole rollercoaster of a day. It seemed impossible. Yet it was true. How could that be? In the midst of what I'd just put myself through, not once had I even thought about a drink. That struck me as a miracle, one I needed to be more grateful for than anything.

The train slid into a tunnel and again I was under the river, heading for the lights.

8
Resilience

Change is challenging. All challenges come with setbacks. What dieter doesn't fall prey to the occasional forbidden calories? Who hasn't burrowed under the covers and slept in instead of showing up for that exercise class you committed to? And remember that person you said you'd no longer lose your temper with? All of a sudden, you're yelling at him again.

So we falter and we fall. Yet we do not have to fail. Resilience is the power we are given to bounce back from life's inevitable setbacks and resume our change journey with renewed energy, focus, and knowledge . . . however bruising. As usual, Mark Twain said it best: "Failure is success if we learn from it" (and as a failed publisher, failed miner and failed inventor who became the greatest literary figure in American history, he should know). I don't know anyone who enjoys failure or setbacks. But it's precisely those times when we get stronger and learn the most about ourselves.

Just now, for instance, I caught myself with a pen in my mouth. I wasn't gnawing at it as in the past, but I was tempting myself; I was ready to go to work on it and do more damage to my already eroded teeth.

As you know, I've been trying to break myself of my pen-chewing habit. Overall I've had more success than failure, but I've had my relapses. Now, though, I'm aware of them. Before, I just did it without thinking or caring. Now when I do the reflexive pen-in-mouth thing, I'm much more likely to catch myself before I start chewing. That's progress! Resilience helps me see it that way.

My relapses have also shown me when I'm most vulnerable to regressing: when I'm thinking hard or when I'm writing and am stuck on where an idea should go. So frustration is involved, and concentration, and cogitation. Those are clues I can use to prevent myself from backsliding, and also to know myself better.

I had a friend, Tammy, who wanted to break a habit she was ashamed of—swearing. Giving up swearing in this day and age may sound quaint to some, but for her it was a real issue.

Tammy was not a casual curser by any means. It took provocation. In fact, she only swore when she was really upset, often with herself, and then she would let fly! The first time it happened in my presence, she was looking frantically for something in her bag until she finally realized she'd forgotten it at home. The F bomb exploded from her mouth.

"I'm so sorry," she said immediately, blushing.

Actually I was trying not to laugh, because of all the people I knew who might detonate an F bomb, she seemed to be the least likely. Tammy was a reserved, humble, gentle person if ever I knew one. To hear that word come flying out of her was a shock, a little as if Mr. Rogers had begun cursing wildly at the camera over some minor production gaffe.

"I'm sorry," she said every time it happened, and I would reassure her that she didn't swear a fraction as much as some people I knew. I myself was known to have an occasional vocabulary failure.

"Don't worry about it, Tammy," I'd say. "No big deal."

"But it is. I wouldn't let my kids say those words, and I don't like it when I hear other people say them. I wasn't raised to curse, so I shouldn't do it. I'm going to swear off swearing."

That would seem to be an easy thing for a committed person like Tammy, yet she struggled. And each time she backslid, she'd beat herself up for it.

"It's so frustrating! Every time I think I've got it beat something happens—a car cuts me off in traffic, I can't find my cell when it's ringing, or *something*—and I'm right back where I started!"

But Tammy's setbacks only made her more determined and resourceful. She kept what she called a cursing diary—a record of her lapses, the circumstances that led to them, and how they made her feel. "Each relapse is a lesson," she told me.

One day we were talking when she spilled some coffee on her pants. *Uh-oh*, I thought.

There was a pause; then Tammy broke into a smile. "Oh well," she said. "It'll come out."

"Congratulations," I said with a chuckle.

My friend Tammy pretty much cured herself of the cursing habit, though she claims she still has some work to do because she occasionally curses in her head rather than out loud. "That's still swearing," she maintains.

Whatever. I for one am very impressed with her change, and how she used her setbacks and her diary to eventually attain her goal of being someone who didn't curse. Had she not been so resilient in the face of her many setbacks, she would not have been successful.

Of course, not all change starts with us. More often, it comes to us—unexpected, unsought and sometimes even undesired. Think of the huge change in the lives of the people of Haiti in the aftermath of the 2010 earthquake or of the US Gulf Coast following the oil spill that same year. Many of us have faced shifting circumstances we never imagined or wanted, none more so than in the 2008 economic upheaval that rocked the United States and the world. Unemployment, foreclosure, and bankruptcy struck people who never dreamed it could happen to them. In tough times, resilience is crucial, and it was in just such times that James Schwenk and his family, of Myerstown, Pennsylvania, were put to the test.

James's life could not have been going more smoothly than if he had drawn it up himself. In fact, it was almost as if he had. James came from a family of scholars and teachers and was himself a professor of religious history and a C. S. Lewis specialist at the Evangelical Theological Seminary, a small, idyllic college tucked away in the rolling green hills of southeastern Pennsylvania.

James had held this position for ten years, and if ever a job was a calling, this was it. The fact that he could support his wife and two kids doing what he felt led to do made it seem more of a blessing than a career. If James was certain of anything, it was that he was exactly where he was meant to be in life doing exactly what he was meant to do.

Until that spring day when the dean of faculty called him into his office. James was not alarmed; he assumed the dean wanted to discuss curriculum matters for the upcoming semester, and he came prepared with some lesson plans to go over. In fact, he dove right in, enthusiastic about his teaching as ever.

But the dean stopped him before he could really get going. James looked up from his plans and saw a look of consternation on his colleague's face. He sunk back in his chair as the dean leaned forward.

"James," said the dean, "you are aware of the financial challenges this seminary faces in these times."

"Of course," James answered, his mind already spinning out scenarios. Would classes be cut? Would his schedule change? Would he have to take on extra duties?

The dean continued, measuring his words like level teaspoons of flour.

"The situation is dire and we find ourselves having to make decisions no one wants to make. Yet make them we must. As of the first of next month your full-time position will be eliminated. I'm sorry."

Shock has a way of stretching time, of giving it a kind of elasticity that allows us to absorb information we might not want to know. The deadly silence that followed the dean's pronouncement felt like an eternity to James.

Slowly, as he sat before the dean, the walls of his life began to slide in. He and his family were about to move into a new home. His wife, Lore, had just lost her job as a receptionist, a development that had already occasioned some painful financial belt-tightening. Still, they'd thought they could manage on James's salary—which was now going to vanish. Their kids, Tyler and Heather, were closing in on college age. In this economy, though, they couldn't even find summer jobs.

How would James manage? If he couldn't even hang on to the job he was perfect for, what prospects did he have?

James's eyes scanned the wood-paneled, book-lined office. Academia had always seemed so safe and insular, as if cordoned off from the chaos of the outside world. Yet now it felt false and feeble . . .

" . . . you are a good teacher," the dean was saying, "and your students will miss you. I wish we could keep you on . . . you are young. Your future is not over . . . "

The words sounded weirdly eulogistic, as if his career were being lowered into a grave. This couldn't be happening. Ten years he'd taught here!

"If there is anything we can do," the dean wrapped up, "please don't hesitate to ask." Then he thrust out his hand and James shook it.

"I understand," James said, though he didn't.

That night James and Lore sat at their kitchen table pondering their options, if that's what they could be called. Lore was an office worker, and office workers were being laid off and outsourced. James had done construction in his twenties; he loved outdoor labor and working with his hands, but who was building in this economy? They had some savings but those wouldn't last forever, especially with a new house to pay for. In a matter of a few weeks they'd gone from a two-income family to a no-income family. It was all James could do to resist the panic welling up within. What more basic fear is there than the fear of not being able to care for your family? This was change he had not seen coming.

He and Lore held hands for a long time and prayed. "We'll get through this, James," Lore whispered, though neither could have said how.

Bills quickly ate away at their savings as James and Lore tried to juggle one obligation against the other. Soon school let out and Tyler and Heather joined their parents in the job hunt. With four of them looking, someone was bound to land something. James had always been a man of faith and had never doubted that his life followed a greater plan. Now, as his situation unraveled, he was struggling to see the greater scope of that plan. The more he prayed for guidance, the more lost he felt. Yet he couldn't accept that his faith had betrayed him. Then he would have nothing.

One morning Tyler asked James to drive him to a job interview at the Pennsylvania Renaissance Faire—a touristy re-creation of a sixteenth-century English village. The employees of the fair all dressed in period costume and performed their duties in character, speaking in a kind of mock Elizabethan dialect.

Tyler had caught the acting bug in his senior year of high school and was psyched about his prospects of landing a job. "I'm perfect, Dad," he said on the way over. "I bring a lot to the table."

James couldn't help but smile at his son's enthusiasm. If only it were that easy for an unemployed religious-history professor.

While Tyler sat hunched over his application in the crowded waiting room, James scanned the others filling out applications, checking their cell phones and crib sheets for former employers and references. It was all so familiar and dreary. James wandered over to a window and looked out at the recreated Tudor architecture housing the concession stand. The historian in him suppressed a smirk. Did the Elizabethans really have corn dogs on a stick? No, the people of that era led difficult lives of toil and struggle and relied on faith and determination to meet their challenges. Their lives were uncertain; war, hunger and disease were ever-present. Yet they persisted. They prevailed.

The more he looked out at the fairgrounds, despite their historical lapses and concessions to the modern world, the more alive and comforted he felt. What was it about history that was so reassuring to him, so energizing? Could the Elizabethans ever have guessed that we would be creating amusement parks dedicated to their lifestyle half-a-millennium later? Yet here it was, and it spoke to people. It spoke to James.

If history has taught us anything, James thought, it has taught us the resiliency of human beings and the upward nature of their journey. The history of our race is living proof that men and women persevere and prevail.

All of a sudden James strode over to the reception desk and asked for an application and an appointment with an interviewer. Tyler wasn't the only one who brought a lot to the table.

"I think I would make a good greeter or guide," James told his interviewer. "I actually know a lot about this stuff."

"That's good," the interviewer responded noncommittally, glancing up and down at James's application and undoubtedly noting that he had lost a good job and had a family to support. "But there's more money in maintenance, and more job security too, because we keep a skeleton crew on even when the park is closed for winter," she said. "You'd still be in costume and character when the park is in season," she continued.

James's heart sank a little, but then he rallied. Would it be so hard to wear tights and spout, "Hark! Yon Dumpster needs to be empty-eth!"? In fact, it might be fun.

"Maintenance it is," he agreed.

"Fine. We'll check your references and let you know."

James spent that afternoon painting a bedroom in the new house. The effort was therapeutic, and he was lulled by the soft, transformative swish of the roller and the wash of new color.

The future, James thought, can be scary because it is fundamentally unknowable. We can only *predict* what will happen to us. The past is there to be examined and learned from; it is fixed in time and its events are immutable. History is a blueprint. Yet something connects past to present to future.

That something, he thought, was faith, a spiritual gravity that anchors all events in the supreme presence of a divine power. God is as present in the future as he is in the past and in the present, present in the moment and every division of the moment, present everywhere, even in the very color of the paint James was putting on the wall. For James, the great lesson of history was to trust that presence, especially when it is hardest to trust and what lies before us is unknowable. Resilience, the capacity to recover from and triumph over life's travails, begins with faith and a determined human heart.

James and Tyler started their jobs at the Faire on the same day, soon to be joined by Lore and Heather. It was a magical summer, the four of them working together and having so much fun at it. James was impressed by how much the other employees knew about the historical period they were recreating. Sitting around on coffee break and discussing Elizabethan dance and the political intrigue of the day were not all that unlike chatting in the faculty lounge. It gave James a sense that if he kept working hard and moving forward, he would overcome his setbacks and he and his family would be all right. The tide of fear that had threatened to consume him at the kitchen table that night with Lore gradually receded.

Eventually James returned to teaching part-time, though he still kept his job at the Faire. His family is not out of the woods yet, but they have survived the worst.

The two examples of resilience I've told you about so far are easy to relate to: overcoming a nagging bad habit and facing the uncertainty of tough times. But one of the greatest demonstrations of resilience and personal change that I ever saw was in a man who overcame one of the great unconquered plagues—mental illness.

Imagine a man once quite successful, even famous, walking the streets wearing rags and raving like a lunatic, shunned by the very people who once admired him. Meet Lionel Aldridge.

The first time Lionel Aldridge remembers hearing the voices was one utterly ordinary morning in 1974 while standing before the mirror shaving. It wasn't quite a voice, more like something in the penumbra between thought and word—critical, accusatory, belittling: *You don't work very hard, do you? Everybody knows you don't care about your job.*

Lionel didn't think much of it at first. Maybe he was just having a bad morning, or had had a bad night's sleep. Besides, he worked very hard and cared very much, having parlayed an All-Pro career with the two-time Super Bowl champion Green Bay Packers into the role of an NFL commentator and local sports anchor in Milwaukee. He was a fixture in city life along the shore of Lake Michigan, hosting charity events and working with young athletes. What did the voice mean, he didn't work very hard? That was nuts!

The voices would come and go. Lionel could be driving home from work to his wife, Viki, and two adorable girls when clear as a bell, as if it came right from the backseat, a voice would demand, *Why don't you take better care of your family?* Soon the voices seemed to follow him everywhere. And they knew everything about him. They told him people didn't think much of him and were out to bring him down, to punish and humiliate him for all his detestable character flaws. He told no one about the voices. Who could he tell? People might think he was crazy.

"As a pro athlete," Lionel explained when I flew out to meet with him about doing a story for *Guideposts* many years later, "I was trained not to complain, to suck it up. I played for Vince Lombardi, after all, and we were tough. Packer tough." Lionel let out a low, knowing laugh, as if bemused by the notion that one can simply man-up against mental illness the way one might play through a strained groin or bruised quad.

We sat in his small, sparsely furnished basement apartment near downtown Milwaukee, drinking sodas from the can. We had just returned from a walk along the waterfront, where an obstreperous wind whipping off the lake had made our shirts balloon up like the Michelin Man. We'd retreated to Lionel's place because it was easier to talk there.

He was a big man. Defensive ends in the NFL usually are, and fast. Almost two decades removed from his playing days Lionel still had physical definition, despite the side effects of the medication he was on, which included weight gain and bloat.

The voices had made him edgy and moody, and since no one but Lionel knew about them, people wrote him off as simply being "difficult."

"Yes," Lionel said, shaking his head, "I was definitely difficult."

Before long Lionel caught himself talking back to the voices, defending himself against their bald accusations, arguing with them, sometimes in public. Rumors swirled that he was using drugs. Nothing could have been further from the truth, but Lionel was in no position to explain himself. The attention made it worse. Everywhere he went he felt watched and studied. That's just what the voices told him.

Viki grew so alarmed that she and the girls moved out, terrified by Lionel's rants and outbursts.

"One night," Lionel recalled, "I was attending a Bucks basketball game with a friend. I totally froze as we moved in front of the crowd toward our courtside VIP seats. 'What's wrong with you?' my buddy demanded, trying to move me along. 'These people,' I explained, 'they know everything I'm thinking.'"

Untreated, his illness only worsened, metastasizing throughout his mind. The camera lens zooming in on him during his weekend sports show became a glistening, all-seeing eye that could plumb his soul, a soul the voices said was corrupt and damned to hell. He was convinced viewers knew his thoughts.

Viki divorced him and the station fired him. His friends stayed away. Now it was just him and the voices. One night they commanded him to start driving.

Despite his troubles, he liked Milwaukee; it had been his home for a long time and Lionel knew he needed a home, now more than ever.

"I don't want to leave," he wailed. "Don't make me!" But the voices were insistent.

Thus began a twisted odyssey. He threw some clothes in the trunk of his car, along with an old Bible from his playing days that meant little to him back then and even less to him now, but for reasons he still couldn't explain, he took it. On his finger he wore one of his jewel-encrusted Super Bowl rings.

"I had no map and no plan. I just filled up on gas and started driving."

He crisscrossed the country via a wilderness of interstates. Initially he slept in hotels, then motels, then flophouses. Chicago, Kansas City, Dallas, Sacramento, Portland, Las Vegas. His funds evaporated and his credit cards were canceled. He started living in his car, occasionally washing dishes for food and gas. In Florida he ditched the car for a hundred dollars and hit the streets, a crazy man with a crazy ring that no one gave a second thought to. He talked back to the voices freely now as he wandered from job to job, shelter to shelter. People would stare at him and occasionally try to help. That only fueled his delusions of persecution. What did they *really* want from him?

"One morning I woke up in a little field off the interstate and the ring was gone," Lionel said. "Just gone." This memory made him stand and pace across his living room, his long strides covering the modest distance quickly. "I don't know if I lost it or someone stole it, though it's hard to imagine someone taking it off of me even in the state I was in."

It was as if the storm of his illness had deprived him of the last link to a life that had once been full of promise and opportunity, and with it the last remnant of sanity. He sat down in the weed-choked grass and wept into his hands.

At this point, he was in Utah, where he had played college ball. It was summer and the sun bore down on him from a cloudless sky. Perhaps he had come back here to recapture some vestigial memory of glory. He didn't know. Now he stripped to the waist with his arms outstretched, crying out to the cars and trucks screaming down the interstate: "Help me! I'll accept help from anyone!"

Some shouted back at him from their vehicles. A few threw things. Mostly they just drove by, oblivious to Lionel's private apocalypse.

He stayed that way until dusk; then he huddled beside a bridge, exhausted and tired, his arms aching. From his satchel he pulled out his old Bible.

"I was not a terribly religious man, at least not in the organized, traditional sense," Lionel explained to me. "But for some reason I couldn't let go of that Bible. I was reading through Paul when a passage leapt out: *Earnestly seek the higher gifts.* I'd been taught that these gifts were spiritual, given to lift us up from the poverty of our lives. I still had moments when

I could dimly perceive reality. A core part of me knew that I must get well."

In that demented chorus of voices that pursued Lionel around the country, could he find the single loving one to deliver him and lift him up?

He started listening for it—a voice that said that he was loved and always would be, fully and unconditionally. A voice that embraced rather than condemned, and that could lead him back to sanity. He knew it was there, an ember of clarity that still somehow burned within his tortured consciousness.

He drifted back to Milwaukee, becoming a fixture again, though this time as a street person. A picture appeared of him in the paper standing in front of a building that said "Rescue Mission," along with an article about his sad downfall.

"I was wearing a dirty white T-shirt under a threadbare wool overcoat I probably fished out of a Dumpster, and some kind of crazy knit hat. Man, I can't tell you where I got that hat!" Lionel laughed at the memory, clapping his hands. Those big hands coming together made an explosive sound and I jumped a little in my seat, suddenly reminded that he was still very big and, not that long before, very crazy. "After the article about me, people started reaching out. Not that I reached back. At least not right away. I saw most people as part of some intricate plot to hurt me. I was just so lost at that point. All people scared me."

How sad, I thought, for a man of his size and strength to be so fearful of his fellow humans.

It became painfully clear to the people of Milwaukee that Lionel was not simply a difficult personality. He was sick, and they understood that he needed help, desperately, even if he did not grasp that fact himself. Mental illnesses often come with their own built-in systems of denial. Resistance to treatment is part of the symptomatology. Yet how could they let a genuine Green Bay Packer hero, a man who played his guts out for Vince Lombardi, who left it all on Lambeau Field every frozen Sunday, simply drift into oblivion before their very eyes?

After repeated interventions, Lionel started getting help through a community-based mental-health service. He was diagnosed with paranoid schizophrenia, which typically strikes earlier in life, in adolescence and early adulthood. Perhaps it was the discipline and regimentation of playing Green Bay Packers football under Lombardi that had managed to delay the onset of Lionel's symptoms. Who knows, he wondered, maybe Lombardi had scared the bejesus out of the voices. In any event, the etiology of schizophrenia, along with many other mental disorders, is still largely a mystery to medical science, and there's no telling why Lionel's onset came so late.

"The doctors hit on some drugs that helped me," said Lionel. "They explained that the voices and the delusions were symptoms of the disease."

In retrospect Lionel could clearly see the nightmare his life as an untreated schizophrenic had become. And what a nightmare it was to wake from: like seeing a crazy man on the street and suddenly realizing you were looking in the mirror, as he told me. He had to face the lost years of his life, the friends and family he had pushed away, the bridges he had burned while he was sick. He had to work hard to understand that schizophrenia was every bit the organic disorder that diabetes or arthritis was, and that it wasn't his fault he had fallen prey to a disease that caused him to act the way he did any more than it would be fair to blame a person with a cold for sneezing. But like many people with mental illness, Lionel discovered the disease itself tells you that you are a bad person, that you are indeed to blame. And that information came through those carping, accusatory interlocutors who seemed to find him everywhere and knew more about him than he knew himself. Every bad thing he had ever done . . . man, the voices were on it.

He had his setbacks. Like so many people with mental-health problems, once he started feeling better on the medicine he stopped taking it.

"It made me fat and sluggish," said Lionel. "And I figured I didn't need it anymore."

Each time that decision led to disaster. After one episode that landed Lionel back in the hospital, he demanded that his doctor show him one patient who had gotten better.

"Well," the doctor said, "many people do recover, partially and even fully in some cases."

"No," Lionel interrupted, "I want to actually meet someone who's beat it."

The doctor shuffled his papers, uncomfortable. Most people who recover or are getting better rarely divulge that information or want to talk about it, he told him. "There's such stigma attached, Lionel."

Lionel was angry for a moment; then a light went on. And a voice. But this was not one of *those* voices. This was that loving voice Lionel tried to hear amongst the bitter chorus. This voice told him what he must do to get well.

"If I get out of here, Doc, I'm not going to be afraid of anything. And I'm going to talk about my problems to anyone who wants to listen. I'm going to talk about the disease of mental illness. That's what people like me need to hear to get better. Someone like me."

This was why *Guideposts* had sent me out to Milwaukee: Lionel had indeed become a spokesperson for mental illness. He had founded an organization that educated patients, their families, and their communities, and he spoke all over the country on behalf of the mentally ill. He'd done what that one voice told him, bravely and honestly, and it was awe-inspiring to me. He still struggled, I thought. "I have to take my meds," he confided. And there were fleeting moments during the course of our afternoon together when I sensed he might be beating back those cruel voices, but I didn't ask. It had been tough enough dragging him back through those lost and painful years, and I knew enough about remembering the painful past to know I didn't want to push him to that degree.

He told me a story I'll never forget about going to a café for dinner shortly after he got out of the hospital. He stood at the door convinced that every patron inside was saying disparaging things about him. He wanted to run home and lock himself in his apartment. "Then I told myself, 'No, you have got to do this!' So I figured, hey, maybe they're all saying *good* things about me like, 'Hey, there's Lionel Aldridge, used to play for the Packers. Man, could he hit hard! Then he had some problems. Look how good he's doing now!'"

"And if people really were saying bad things about me, I would just have to forgive them. Forgiveness made what they said harmless; it didn't matter whether it was real or imagined."

"Funny thing was, when I finally sat down to order my dinner, I suddenly realized these folks were talking about everything in the world *except* me!"

He let loose with a huge laugh, a laugh you had to be as big as him to make, and then clapped those big hands again. This time I laughed with him.

After I said good-bye to Lionel and thanked him for his time and generosity, I wandered back to the lakeshore and sat on a park bench. The wind had died down and it was sunset, the rays from the west glinting off the gray waters of Lake Michigan. I felt an intimacy with these Great Lakes, having grown up on them and sailed them. The year after my brother died, my dad had taken Mom and me on a ship that crossed from Muskegon to Milwaukee, about ninety miles. At 18 knots or so it was a four-hour crossing. I spent most of the time hanging over one of the stern rails, staring into the water, and breathing in the diesel fumes from the engine room below. I kept wondering what it would be like to jump. No one would know. Butterflies took wing in my belly, the idea scaring and exciting me all at once. What would it feel like to be airborne and then strike the water far below? Would I be sucked under by the prop wash or would I quickly disappear in the wake of the ship, a speck in the water before anyone knew I was gone? Suddenly I jumped back from the rail and found myself rattling off several Hail Marys for protection. I found my parents as fast as I could.

Lionel told me many memorable things that day, but one particular thing he said stayed with me long after his story was published in *Guideposts*. He said that day by the highway in Utah, with the cars screaming past and feeling as if the sun would devour him, he had committed suicide. "For a long time I had the idea—or the delusion, rather—that I had killed myself but was still somehow alive."

Lionel had no idea how profoundly I understood what he meant.

Back in New York after my hopeless trip to Baltimore to woo back Daria, I vowed to put the past behind me and move forward as a sober person and functioning, productive human being. I accepted that Daria was out of my life forever . . . well, at least for the foreseeable forever.

"No," my sponsor corrected me. "She is out of your life forever, period, a day at a time . . . dummy!"

Life felt good sober, even a day at a time, and I could sense myself getting stronger, even a bit cocky. I made friends and collected a few "sponsees" of my own, people who were newer in the program than I was and whom I helped guide and advise by sharing my experience, strength, and hope, not necessarily to keep them sober but to keep myself sober by helping another drunk—the very core precept of AA that John Cavanaugh had once tried to explain to me. It was, as I was reminded, a selfish program, for everything one did was to maintain one's own sobriety. Still, I'd never known a more generous and accepting bunch of people in my life than those who now embraced me.

In fact, there were days when I felt like I was the Aristotle of AA, dispensing wisdom and setting a fine, sober example for newcomers. But other days . . . nothing made sense. I felt like the town fool in a Flannery O'Connor story. On those days, I didn't even know why I was bothering to get sober, and the program was incomprehensible. Getting sober, I learned, was a roller coaster, both exhilarating and disorienting, and the trick was to hold on tight and not get hurled from the car and thrown into the midway.

I did service, first making coffee and buying cookies for a meeting, and then rising to be its treasurer. There were certainly moments when the urge to drink came over me like some sea creature breaking the waves from the dark deep, but now I had the tools and the support system to deal with these attacks. I knew how to protect my sobriety. I even remembered to pray . . . sometimes. And where once, in the beginning, I felt very uneasy with the prayer circle at the end of meetings—too much like church—now I was pretty comfortable with it, especially if we stuck with the Serenity Prayer instead of the Our Father, and especially if it gave me the opportunity to hold hands with an attractive woman, for there was no shortage of opportunities to meet the opposite sex. I once told my sponsor that sometimes the only thing that got me to a meeting was the women. He just laughed and said, "Whatever works."

I was starting to feel comfortable with myself as a sober person and not like some loser who had to hang around church basements on Saturday nights. Yes, maybe I was going to make it after all, I started to believe, unlike my old shipmate Tommy back in Lapeer.

One night over dinner I looked at my sponsor and said, "I have to pinch myself sometimes. I'm doing something that seemed so impossible to me for so long." My voice started to crack and I gulped my emotions back. No need to start blubbering here in a restaurant—a public place, for crying out loud. "This seems like a dream sometimes and I'm afraid I'll just wake up on some flight deck in a psych ward again."

My sponsor studied me for a long time. Even in AA, most people don't make it, and it is virtually irresistible not to wonder who will and who won't, especially when those who don't will likely end up dying as a result. Someone told me that the average life expectancy of an alcoholic who leaves the program and returns to drinking is less than five years.

Finally my sponsor took a sip of coffee and spoke. "Edward, sobriety is a gift, a gift that lasts for just one day. Each and every day we have to want that gift again. That's how we stay sober. If you ever wake up not wanting that gift, you are as close to having that next drink as you'll ever be. The drink is the end of a slip, not the beginning. You have to want the gift more than the drink every day."

I dated women both inside and outside the program. It was strongly advised not to start a serious relationship in early sobriety, so I dated a lot of women. Some drank; a few even used drugs socially. A couple were fairly wild, including a woman I dated for a while whom my sponsor took a dim view of. To me it didn't matter. My sobriety was about me and nobody else, and I certainly wasn't out to convert anyone. If I went to a bar, I ordered a soda. If I went to a party and there was drinking, I made sure to know where the non-alcoholic mixers were kept. If there were drugs, I avoided them. And I was always surprised by the number of people I met who were trying to get sober. New York was teeming with sobriety-seekers.

I'd been working in restaurants and doing some freelance writing of little note, and nothing of my own writing, of course.

I didn't know if I was ready for that—or if I ever would be—and that troubled me. A lot. Would giving up drinking mean that I gave up my writing? Was that exchange worth it? Was it writing that had driven me to this? I knew I was still in no shape to make decisions on such matters, but still the thoughts bothered me. If I wasn't a writer, what was I? A drunk, even a sober one? Who starts out in life aspiring to be a sober, recovering alcoholic?

Soon I found permanent employment, writing marketing and advertising material for a historic Danish trading company that distributed, among other things, Danish hams, high-end German printing presses, and bindery equipment throughout North America. I had a great boss named Jenny who was VP of sales and marketing, an American who actually knew something about sobriety, though she wasn't in (and didn't need) the program herself. We got along famously, which was good, because I had difficulty relating to the Danish overlords, who were all nice, if slightly insular family men named Hans, and to a dyspeptic German named Wolf who looked after the German interests, usually in a heightened state of suspicion that could morph into paranoia at any moment. He absolutely could not comprehend my abstemiousness; it just didn't penetrate his Teutonic worldview. "Vat," he would demand, "are you sick? When vill you get better? Then I can give you some schnapps. You vill drink schnapps with me; then we vill see about you!"

The spring after I started, there came an exciting announcement: We would all be making a pilgrimage to Drupa, a spectacular worldwide printing and technology expo held every four years in Düsseldorf, Germany. Afterward, I would travel on my own to global headquarters in Copenhagen to research and eventually revise a definitive history of the company in English, to be distributed wherever the Danes did business, which was pretty much everywhere, including Antarctica.

I'd done some foreign travel, spending time in Haiti and all over the Caribbean, as well as throughout South America and Mexico. I'd always thought Europe was too staid and civilized, so this would be my first trip. I was especially thrilled at the prospect of visiting Copenhagen, the city of Søren Kierkegaard, Niels Bohr and Hans Christian Andersen . . . three giants of philosophy, quantum theory and fairy tales. There was something about that trinity that fascinated me.

The expo went well and I diligently cranked out press releases about the equipment my company exhibited, marveling at how far I'd come since sitting in the Victor in Hoboken, hunched over a glass of flat beer trying to stop my hands from shaking enough so I could manage to light a cigarette butt someone had left in the ashtray. Sobriety was a miracle, I kept reminding myself. A gift.

I took a train to Copenhagen rather than flying because I wanted to see the countryside, to get a sense of the land. And I'd done a strange thing: When I left my hotel in Düsseldorf I'd confiscated all the Lilliputian bottles of liquor from the minibar and stashed them in my luggage. The company was paying for them anyway, so it seemed a shame to let them go to waste. What if I met people on the train and wanted to offer them a drink just to be convivial? The idea didn't seem absurd to me.

A beautiful if chilly May afternoon greeted me when I disembarked from my train and finally found my way out of the cavernous, fuliginous Central Station, over which loomed the most monstrous clock I'd ever seen mounted high above the main concourse, an almost overbearing reminder of time. Who would dare be late with a clock like that staring down at you?

By cab I made my way the short distance to my hotel, the Kong Frederik, one of Copenhagen's finest and most storied, a jewel from the previous century. I was shown to my room by a bellman decked out in a preposterously Napoleonic uniform and I tipped him numerous kroner as a result. The room was elegant but small, and had a bit of trouble accommodating my big American luggage. It, too, had a well-appointed minibar.

I finished acquainting myself with the amenities of my room; then I showered and headed out for dinner. I made my way on foot to the waterfront, one of the prettiest in the world, and found an outdoor cafe along one of the slips. The waiter brought me a carafe of water. Would I like to order something to drink?

No, thank you, water will be fine for now.

It was an altogether lovely moment, one of those stilling-of-time moments when you feel as if you are sitting inside a picture. The sinking sun washed the old wharf-side buildings in luminous still-life tones, with splashes of moving color here and there. Single-mast schooners bobbed in their moorings a few yards away, the water lapping at their hulls. The air smelled faintly of dock tar and fish. The waiter served the couple sitting at the table next to me two tall glasses of beer—Carlsberg, no doubt, the proud local brew. Carlsberg signs were all over this city. The amber nectar glistened in the sunlight. Gulls wheeled and squealed just above our heads. A breeze ruffled the tablecloth and I caught my napkin before it went aloft.

I couldn't tear my eyes away from the two glasses. Their shape was curved, almost feminine and fertile, convex at the middle, and I was mesmerized by the gilded hue of the liquid they bore and the inch-thick froth that crowned them. The couple raised the glasses and clinked them in a toast, and for an instant the spell was broken. The glasses came back down, depleted by half. I could almost feel the fluid coursing down my throat, like a liquefied shaft of sunlight, cold and satisfying with a bittersweet barley aftertaste, a hint of the harvest, and then a familiar glow enveloping my mind, a swelling bliss right behind the eyes, a dimensional shift. The feeling rippled through me, a soft spasm of pleasure, and every muscle in my body eased. The waiter returned to my table. Was I ready to order?

"A Carlsberg, please," I could not stop myself from saying.

I awoke in my room at the Kong Frederik the next morning with the merest shimmer of a hangover, which was odd considering how little I'd actually drunk. I'd dispatched the first Carlsberg apace and then nursed a second one with my dinner, leaving an inch or so in the glass, an assertion of control and mastery and perspective. No need to drink all of it. No need at all. After dinner I'd taken a nice walk through the area around my hotel; it was bustling and I had a sense that something was going on, and stopped for another partial beer to watch the flow of people. I felt only slightly lightheaded but altogether different somehow . . . not drunk but transformed. Into what, I didn't know. It had been more than two years since I'd had my last drink.

As I dressed for my morning meetings, everything seemed slightly imbued. With what, I wasn't sure. Shapes and colors were heightened. I felt vaguely anxious but not quite panic-stricken by what I'd done. I was okay, right? Did this prove I could drink again? Or was this a slip I would never repeat—and never tell anyone about? A secret, solitary lapse, a fall from grace for which no one would ever be wiser, like a tree toppling unobserved in the forest? Could I simply pretend that nothing had happened?

I took a cab to my company's headquarters, a stately old building in the center of the business district, where I was given a tour and met with some of my counterparts, including the company historian, who showed me to a room where they enshrined the company's considerable legacy, and who bid me to make myself at home and to call on him if I had any questions at all.

I spent the day thumbing through books and documents tracing the company's proud heritage back more than a century to its origins as a Far East trading company and its strategic alliance with the King of Siam. Great stuff for the book. Still, my mind kept drifting back to that first voluptuous glass of beer at the waterside, as if I'd been reunited with some long-lost love. By mid-afternoon I was getting restless. I still had another whole day in Copenhagen to finish my research before I was scheduled to fly back to the States. So, pulling together my things and the numerous photocopies I'd made, I slipped out of the building.

The sun was still quite high in the sky. In fact, there would be about eighteen hours of daylight this time of year. The streets were filling with people. At headquarters I'd been informed that this was the beginning of the spring festival, when hordes of Scandinavians descend on the city to celebrate the end of the long dark winter with much reveling and debauchery. I thought it best to make my way back to the safety of my hotel.

I remember walking through the lobby and noticing the bar was crowded and raucous. There was magnetism to the throng; it called to me. I wanted to join them, to be just like them, having a drink and celebrating spring. What could be more pleasant? Or normal? And I wanted to be normal. It seemed like such a harmless human activity. What could come of it? I'd stopped at just a few the night before; I'd tamed my thirst, hadn't I? I remember thinking I had a choice. Just a quick one—one!—to honor this wonderful Danish tradition. No one would know. Perhaps I wasn't an alcoholic after all. Perhaps there was no such thing as alcoholism; it was just how one chose to conduct oneself. I would stop if things felt like they were getting out of hand. Or I would simply do what I wanted to do and surrender to wherever my actions took me. I felt an existential willfulness taking hold of me, a wildness I can't explain, as if the sober me were a cage some animal was being freed from. I wanted to know what the next drink would do. I told myself I had to know. This was a quest for the truth, and what was more important in life than that? As I turned and headed to the bar, I wondered if I should say a prayer. I almost did.

No one will know, I repeated to myself, wedging through the crowd and shouting out my order.

My memories of the events that followed that night are fragmented at best, like reflections in the shards of a shattered mirror. All I know is by the time the alcohol hit my stomach, my blood, and my brain, my world had already shifted on its precarious axis. I repaired to my room at one point and availed myself of some of the miniature bottles I'd hoarded. Later still I recall being swept along Strøget, Copenhagen's main pedestrian thoroughfare, by a swarm of revelers and staggering in and out of bars, buffeted through the crowd like a pinball. I found myself back at the waterfront sitting at a table full of strangers who tried to teach me a few phrases of Danish and laughed uproariously at my ridiculous linguistic ineptitude. I tried to engage a young woman in conversation but she soon turned away, saying, "I think you are very interesting but I wish you weren't so drunk," a disconcerting brush-off to be sure, considering how inebriated she was. I remember falling down and struggling back to my feet, only to fall again and almost tumble into the water, which, as you may recall, I have a propensity to do. I don't know how I got back to my hotel but have a vague recollection of being let into my room by a bemused bellman, who said, "Go to sleep" as I crawled around on the floor trying to gather up the tip I'd dropped. He was gone before I could give it to him.

I awoke with a poisonous hangover and a floodtide of guilt and anxiety, the rising horror of which I immediately addressed by choking down a miniature vodka mixed with sour orange juice from the minibar. My mouth was parched and my heart raced, my pulse pounding in my eyes and ears. I wondered if I was going to have a stroke. Finally, after another drink, probably two, my nerves steadied sufficiently to call

into headquarters with an unfortunate case of food poison-
ing. They were very apologetic and asked if I needed a doctor.
No, just rest, I assured them. I drank some more and went
back to sleep with the TV turned to CNN International and
the Do Not Disturb sign on my door, which I double locked.

Tivoli Gardens is one of the great and beautiful attractions of
Copenhagen, beloved by residents and tourists alike. It is both
amusement park and gardens, and full of nice little outdoor
cafés and bistros, one of which I found myself sitting in amidst
the cold, early-morning fog. The spring bacchanalia was over
and I could not have told you how many days had passed—well
over a week, at least—and since I hadn't been across the street to
the train station yet to buy an International Herald Tribune,
I could not have told you with certainty what day it was either.

I was drinking a large coffee with steamed milk, to which I'd
surreptitiously added a libational enhancement in the hopes
that my hands would stop shaking enough to hold a cigarette
to my lips and light it.

I was no longer in residence at the Kong Frederik, having been told my room was needed and I had overstayed my
reservation, though I suspected there may have been more to
it in terms of wanting me out. I'd relocated to the Sheraton,
inhabiting a small, self-consciously contemporary room, all
sleek and black and gray with pastel accents, more of a com-
partment than a room, on one of the higher floors. Now that
the weather had turned, the view was hazy and bleak.

For all intents and purposes I had pretty much disappeared
from the face of the earth. I canceled and rescheduled my
flight home a couple of times; even made an attempt to pack

and head for Kastrup Airport but couldn't. I was in no shape to move, much less travel. I holed up in my room with the phone unplugged.

By now people were probably wondering, some frantically, what had become of me. No one knew I'd relocated to the Sheraton. No one knew why I'd canceled my flights. No one knew anything. Only that I had vanished.

Which only deepened the virulent shame and self-hatred I was feeling, a condition for which the only reliable short-term palliative was more alcohol. So I sank deeper and deeper into myself, into a solipsistic wormhole, hoping to be delivered from my all-consuming angst by my own eventual destruction. Now, mostly, I kept to my room, venturing out to Central Station daily to draw money off my credit card and try to eat something and not vomit. I would sit and watch the crowds and be reminded of sitting in the Victor across from the Hoboken train station, only this time I was using an Amex Gold Card instead of panhandled change. That was about the only difference though. Inside it felt the same . . . worse, if possible. My circumstances had changed but I hadn't. *No, you haven't changed at all*, I told myself.

Finishing my coffee, I left Tivoli and headed for the station, picked up some newspapers, and began to make my rounds of the dingier bars, thinking that somehow this would soon end. It *had* to. I couldn't go on physically or mentally. Yet it was impossible to imagine getting myself together enough to board an airplane and face what awaited me in the States. There was no way. If only I could disappear from myself.

I knew I had to eat. There is a condition called alcoholic anorexia that afflicts severe alcoholics and usually caught up with me after a number of weeks of continuous drinking. The mere thought of food and even water would make me retch unless I had enough—but not too much—alcohol in me to stimulate my appetite. Too much drink, and I couldn't keep anything down. So there was only a small window of opportunity to nourish myself; if I wasn't careful I could go days without eating or even feeling hunger.

Which is why I now headed for the station, with its embracing shadows and oppressive clock. I could get something cheap to eat at one of the stalls; my room-service bill was becoming alarming. In fact, the hotel bill itself was staggering.

It was here outside the station a few days earlier that the man had approached me about the church. I'd been minding my own business; I wasn't aware that I looked like someone who needed help. In fact, I'd just cleaned myself up a bit in the hopes of not appearing seedy. An older, well-dressed gentleman—a complete stranger to me—came up and suggested I visit Grundtvig's Church, an expressionist architectural landmark I had read about, named after a famous Danish philosopher and teacher of whom I knew absolutely nothing.

"It's in Bispebjerg," he said, laying a hand gently on my arm. "You can take a bus, Number 66. You must see it while you are here."

I pulled back but did not want to hurt his feelings. There was nothing creepy about his entreaty. He seemed to be kind and well-intentioned—though did I really look that bad off? A bit puffy and bloodshot, perhaps, but it was early enough in the morning that I could stand upright.

"You'll find it there."

"Find what?" I wanted to know. What was he talking about? I was getting aggravated.

"Help," he answered. Then he went on his way.

For a moment I wondered if I had hallucinated the whole thing. Had I gotten to that stage already? When the DTs did strike, my hallucinations tended to be more auditory than visual, and they were mostly non-delusional—I was usually aware that they were not real and that my mind was playing tricks on me. This man was real; I was fairly sure of that. So I took his advice—what on earth did I have to lose at this point?— managed to get on the right bus, and went to the church in question, an enormous and impressive structure that gave the appearance of a cathedral, set back off the street to lend it even more scale—the largest Evangelical Lutheran church in Scandinavia. With its soaring, symmetrical sanctuary and wooden chairs instead of pews, I sat there feeling like a speck.

What struck me most, however, was the copious amount of light that filtered through the church. Churches, and especially cathedrals, were dim and candlelit in my experience; their gloominess and dark corners comforted me. Maybe it was the paucity of the winter sun so far north that caused the Danes to build a church like this, a church that seemed to capture the sun. The light streaming through the tall, fingerlike windows in the apse caused me to squint and bow my head. Was it something in my current brain chemistry that made me feel disoriented by the light? Or something else? Was this that help the man foretold? At once I began praying to the pervasive light, praying for deliverance, to be cleansed and forgiven, to have the shame and anger and guilt and despair removed from my mind and soul. If only I could be allowed to feel some sense of peace, some hope, I could go on. Yet the desire that was the strongest, the one for which I prayed most fervently, was to be delivered from my life, a life that felt very close to its miserable and deserved end in any event.

I must have gotten something to eat and drink at Central Station. Then I headed back to Tivoli and wandered on shaky legs through the friendly fog before going back to my hotel and passing out. I'm not sure how much time elapsed after that— maybe a day or two or more of blackout drinking—before I struggled to surface again, like a diver coming up for air.

It was dusk, the long slow gloaming of a Scandinavian spring evening. The room was a wreck, the phone still unplugged and sitting in the middle of the floor, and the window was open, the diaphanous standard-issue hotel curtains weaving languidly in the updraft. I didn't remember opening it.

Immediately I made myself a drink, not even sure if I could keep it down; the act was purely medicinal at this point. I went into the bathroom just in case and noticed that the toilet bowl was full of blood and bits of my stomach lining, and I vaguely recalled a violent attack of the dry heaves sometime earlier. God knows how long it had been since I'd eaten anything, though there were room-service plates all over with mostly untouched food. I hit the flushing mechanism with my foot and nearly fell over, caught my balance by grabbing the edge of the sink, and found myself staring at my ravaged visage in the mirror.

I saw an utterly depraved human being holding a glass and staring back at me, a degenerate doppelgänger who had thrown away what little he'd been able to recover of his life in the last two years, thrown it away as if it were garbage, a person who could never face his family or his friends or his roommate or his sponsor or even the people at the front desk downstairs.

I went and sat on the edge of the bed. I gulped from my glass and clenched my teeth until I felt that faint warm glow from the liquor, that inner illumination I'd been hopelessly chasing since my first slug of Old Grand-Dad more than twenty years earlier. The liquor stayed down, thank God. What made my brain respond like this? What disastrous misalignment of neural pathways could account for this behavior? Or was it emotional, some tangle of feelings I could never unknot? I would never know the answer to those questions, unless through some jolt of insight at the last second, just before impact. Maybe then.

The wet breeze from the window felt good. I'd opened that window for a reason, and I knew what it was.

The claim by people who said they made a conscious decision to drink themselves to death had always struck me as fallacious. For an alcoholic, alcohol is life. Suicide is never the final option. Another drink is. Just one last cocktail before the end. In a way, that next drink was the only thing keeping me alive.

Great resolve would be required to overcome that primal urge. Another drink would help, so I poured one. My muscles relaxed. This wouldn't be so hard.

I thought of the utter wreckage I would leave behind. I thought of my mother, who had already lost one son, and felt myself cringe and squeeze shut my eyes. None of it would matter when it was over though. Death was the ultimate hard stop. It would end all remorse, all regrets, all guilt, all anxiety, all feelings. It would just be over and whatever I left behind would be for the living to deal with. Not me. And whatever the con-sequences, they certainly seemed preferable to my continued existence.

My decision to destroy myself once and for all was not an act of despair but an act of pure logic, the only rational outcome of the state my life had devolved to. Why be the living dead when you can just be dead? Why cause such pain when you can end it? My condition was terminal anyway; surely everyone knew that by now. My recovery had been a ridiculous charade. I'd faked my way through rehab. I'd never believed, not really, I understood now, in any of the AA Higher Power stuff—not in my heart, though I talked a good game to AA newcomers, assuring them there was a God who loved us, drunks though we were. But my sobriety was a fraud. I'd pretty much gone on with my life as before, just without drinking. I'd stumbled up the twelve AA steps, treating them like classroom assignments I had to get an A in. I'd tempted fate and played loose with the rules, doing everything my way. I'd ignored my sponsor's advice about relationships and kept secrets. I thought it all passed not only for being sober but also for being changed. And now look. I was back to being my true malignant self with a vengeance. No God could ever love me.

Far from being a selfish act, my suicide would be transcen-dently unselfish. It would liberate people from me. Eventually everyone would understand. It was my life to end, after all—my absolute right to seek the beckoning comfort of oblivion.

I kicked off my shoes, walked to the window, threw one leg over, and straddled the sill, leaning back against the jamb. My right leg dangled heavily over the void. I had no idea what lay some twenty floors below, but I knew I couldn't possibly survive it. My left foot rested gently on the carpet. I was in perfect equipoise. The room light was out, so no one could see me. Besides, I was in the back of the hotel over some kind of airshaft or something where there had been a fair amount of noisy construction going on. I was safe. I nestled my glass atop my belly, breathing a sigh. I had at last grown completely indifferent to myself.

Closing my eyes, I thought, *I could just stay here drinking until I pass out and let gravity decide.*

I don't know how long I remained in that state of, frankly, rather sublime equilibrium between life and death, daring death to prevail. I was utterly relaxed and may have even drifted off. All I know is that I was rudely aroused by an insistent knocking on my door. My heart nearly exploded out of my chest and I toppled to the floor, sloshing alcohol everywhere.

"Are you in there?" a man's voice demanded. "Can you hear me?"

It was imperative they not kick the door in; I couldn't bear that drama on top of everything else, so I lurched over to the door and opened it a crack, keeping the chain on, and peered out.

Two nearly identically dressed figures were in the hallway, a man and a woman, wearing no-nonsense dark suits. The man wore a tie and the woman's collar was open.

"Yes?" I said. "Is there a problem?"

"You tell us," the man said as he and his partner both pulled out identical leather holders containing extremely serious-looking badges. I squinted but couldn't make out what manner of law enforcement they represented.

Now the woman spoke.

"Interpol," she said, and then repeated herself deliberately as if speaking to a slow child. "We are from In-ter-pol."

Had I killed someone? God knows what I might have done in a blackout. Why would the international police be here at my door? No one could have seen me poised on the sill, I was sure of it. I calculated how long it would take to kick the door shut and make it to the open window. They made no attempt to enter the room, though, and simply asked if I was who I was supposed to be. I affirmed by nodding somewhat sluggishly.

"Can I help you in some way?" I said, trying not to slur or stammer.

They just stood there staring at me.

"We're just checking to see if you are alive," said the man finally.

"Apparently I am," I said, and tried to smile. It occurred to me that I'd had my Do Not Disturb sign on the door for several days at least. Had my prone form scared one of the housekeepers who may have ventured in?

The two continued to scrutinize me, as if unsure of how to proceed. But why Interpol? Why not just send up hotel security? I smiled once more, though it must have looked like some kind of horrible, spastic grimace. Eventually the male half spoke again.

"All right then," he said, stuffing his badge back in his pocket. "We're just checking."

"Thank you," I said. "Kind of you."

They turned and headed slowly down the hall.

"Look after yourself," the woman said over her shoulder. There was something in her look, something all too knowing, that unnerved me even more than I already was.

I sagged against the door, closing it with my body weight, and waited until I heard the distant telltale ding of the elevator before making a petrified beeline for the bathroom, slamming the door shut, and sitting on the edge of the tub, breathing so heavily I feared I might hyperventilate. I broke out in a cold, drenching paranoid sweat. Fear vibrated through me like an electrical current. Who were they? What did they want? Who sent them? Was it because I'd solicited a bellhop for some drugs? The questions pinballed through my brain. I was on the verge of hysteria.

How long I sat perched on the tub I couldn't tell you. Soon enough, though, the acute exigency of my need for alcohol, the precious supply of which was on the other side of the door, overcame my terror. I crept out into the room, praying I hadn't depleted the minibar, which would necessitate a call to room service and an agonizing wait. Or I could venture up to the cheesy penthouse disco, which I was pretty sure I'd visited somewhat recently and nearly as certain that for that reason they likely wouldn't let me in. Maybe they would bring a drink out to me . . . .

The light didn't register at first. I must have written it off to the ongoing annoyance of the midnight sun. Slowly, however, it dawned on me that the room was pervaded by an incredible brilliance pouring through the open window. My first thought was that I was about to go into a convulsion. I moved toward the source of the light but was literally driven back by the searing intensity of it. I could not keep my eyes open. Surely this was some kind of brain seizure, some kinetic disruption of the temporal lobes.

The light drove me back onto the bed. I sat down heavily, shielding my eyes with my forearm, trying to discern the source of this violent illumination. This was no gentle light. This was dominant. It was emphatic, almost brutal. It demanded my attention.

I thought of the light at Grundtvig's Church. This time I did not pray to it. I did not try to venerate it. It was incalculably more powerful. If anything, I resisted it, yet ever so slowly I felt myself give in to the light, in an act of involuntary surrender. All power was being drained from me. I was dying. This was the light of death.

Gradually there was a diminution of its intensity, and along with it a baffling calm welled within me, as if the very light was flowing in by particle and wave, filling the void it had hollowed out. I felt incredibly, indescribably at peace. If this was dying, I didn't want it to end. I wanted to die forever.

Gently now I was forced back onto the bed, supine, disoriented. Where was I? I wondered. Copenhagen, of course. In a hotel room in the city of Kierkegaard, of Niels Bohr and Hans Christian Andersen; in the city of existentialism and quantum mechanics and fairy tales; of anxiety and uncertainty and myth. This trinity struck me as important; each in its own singular way had uncovered truth: Kierkegaard's insight into the nature of man's relationship with God, with which I had so struggled; Bohr's uncovering of the paradoxical duality of matter; and Andersen's understanding of the transformative power of the human imagination. Each man, it seemed, had arrived at a moment Kierkegaard called "a leap of faith," a belief in the unseen, that which is both unknowable and omnipotent, be it the quantum essence of the laws of physics, the transcendent power of human beings to change, or the eternal existence of a knowable and all-knowing God. I felt both weak and strong all at once.

And with that I fell into a deep, restful sleep.

Construction activity and a cold breeze woke me. I rose and went to the window, leaning out, my gaze met by a handful of workmen just a few yards away. Attached to their scaffold were several huge work lights, which were on and extremely bright. The day was cloudy and drizzly and their work space didn't get much natural light in any event. I squinted at them and they looked back at the disheveled figure who was crazy enough to have his window open on a nasty day like this.

I slammed the window shut. And started laughing. Was it those work lights that had created the illumination I'd experienced, the hallucinatory perception of some divine cosmic light? Had that—a work light—been the true source of my epiphany? It was so maddeningly hard to keep track of night and day in this country. I fell back on the bed, laughing hysterically at the potential irony. No, that couldn't have been the source, could it?

But did it matter? Because that serenity that had overcome me just before I fell asleep lingered. I could still sense it within me, not fully expressed but there, hovering and humming. It was the manifested internalization of that epiphanic experience, real or otherwise, that mattered—and who cared if a work light was the culprit? It was my feeling of serenity, however tenuous, that was the real blessing and would be the seed of whatever change and growth might come next. Regardless of circumstances, what had happened had been real. I was different. I was absolutely certain of it. In fact, I had no choice but to believe it. I was no longer the same me I had been.

Now came another knock at the door, this one quite timid. The housekeeper.

"You want clean?" she asked, peering around the door. The room, and I, must have looked like some post-modern art experiment gone horribly wrong.

"Yes, please, but not now. I'll be leaving soon."

"I come back," she said, undisguisedly relieved.

I called the airline and began packing, hurling things into suitcases. My shoes—what had I done with my shoes? And of course it hit me: I knew exactly where to find them.

I wish I could say that I abjured all alcohol at that point; that I was struck sober like Paul struck by lightning on the road to Damascus. It didn't happen that way in Copenhagen. Alcoholism is a physical disease, and sudden cessation for a drinker on a long, foodless, dehydrating binge can be fatal. I tried to be moderate, nursing just a few drinks and forcing down some B-vitamins at the airport to ameliorate the effects on my ravaged central nervous system before boarding my nine-hour flight back to New York's Kennedy Airport. I'd long since lost my business-class seat through a series of erratically canceled reservations and was therefore claustrophobically relegated to a middle seat in steerage, not the ideal place for a dipsomaniac fending off severe withdrawal symptoms that included extreme agitation.

I was up and down constantly, pacing the aisle and hiding out in the bathroom. At one point I tried to buy a first-class ticket from a stewardess but was told it was not possible and that I would have to return to my seat immediately. Eventually the captain came back and had a little chat with me; then he was kind enough to find two adjoining vacant seats farther forward for me to hunker down in (and for him to keep a closer eye on me, I suspect).

My homecoming was much less agonizing and humiliating that I had projected, naturally. Within an hour of clearing customs I was sitting in a meeting with my sponsor and Bob Y., my roommate. I went to dinner with the two of them afterward, and again very carefully but scientifically moderated my booze intake, cutting back to just beer, hopeful that I would be completely and safely off in a day or two, though I have to tell you that there is no more unsettling experience than drinking in front of your AA sponsor, especially when he is paying for it.

I didn't sleep at all that night, not unexpected in withdrawal; it would be a few more days before I would sleep, I calculated, or even eat much, except a few Ensures if I could choke them down. Water was a problem—I threw it back up—but beer had a fair amount of water in it. The next morning, an unnecessarily hot and humid spring Saturday, my roommate and I were walking up Broadway on the Upper West Side, headed for a meeting, when I collapsed and went into a violent alcoholic seizure. I'd tried to cut down too fast. I came to in the emergency room at St. Luke's-Roosevelt Hospital, a Valium drip in my arm, bleeding from a number of deep cuts I'd incurred flopping around on the sidewalk like a landed fish, trying vainly to recite my Social Security number and address to an ER doctor. Unfortunately, I knew the drill well.

"Better," he said. "But you're in no shape for me to release you. Besides, Mr. Grinnan, we need to run some tests."

I knew what that meant but I knew it would be suicide to refuse admission. Here I'd be given sedatives to ease the withdrawal and hopefully forfend the DTs, which would land me on a psych ward for sure, something I definitely wanted no part of. Another stint on the flight deck and I'm not certain I would have survived with what little sanity I had left.

So I spent that long Memorial Day weekend arguing the doctors out of yet another spinal tap—they still thought I was too young to have alcoholic seizures, especially after having been clean for better than two years—and receiving a couple of MRIs instead as well as a steady and totally unexpected stream of visitors who appeared to actually care about and love me at a crossroads in my life when I felt so utterly unworthy and unlovable. Their love overwhelmed me.

Love. It was as if I'd forgotten what it felt like to be loved; how completely the feeling of being loved so eclipses everything else. There is no greater, more powerful feeling. For the first time in a very long time I could actually allow myself to accept it, like the light, to let it fill me and heal me. To embrace it as it was embracing me. I had never felt so unbelievably and undeservedly loved, so filled in empty places. I knew that somehow, in a way that I may never be able to fully comprehend let alone explain, that I had been blessed with the gift of resilience: a resilience that had brought me back from the brink of death; a resilience forged in the heat and light of a divine love; a resilience that was present in my life now for only one reason—so that I could change what seemed so hopeless to change. Staring out the window of my hospital room, I knew with an unquestionable certainty that somehow, miraculously, I was going to be all right. That I had, beyond all understanding, changed.

9

Love

A nd so we have come full circle, or almost—there are some loose ends to tie up, to be sure. To get there, we turn to love, the last change factor to be discussed in this book and the most encompassing, as the final indispensable step to personal transformation and happiness.

Why do I say this? Because love is the greatest power for change in the universe. It transforms us in ways we could never dream, makes the impossible possible, and allows us to break free from the prison of our own fears and doubts. We cannot be happy without love in our lives. When love is lacking or absent, we feel empty and purposeless, and even, I believe, more prone to self-destruct.

Which is where I was, my leg dangling over that airshaft and not caring what happened. I had reached the worst degree of despair—the despair of indifference. My life was loveless in a completely existential sense: I was devoid of love. Not romantic love or a general love of life, but of that primal metaphysical essence that allows us to understand and be ourselves: to be one with who we are.

Somehow, bathed in whatever that light was, I finally knew this: that within me there was a burning, indestructible core of life, and within that discovery I experienced a deep and profound happiness such as I had never known before, and an optimism and faith concerning my very fate as a human being. That faith was more than just faith in myself. It was faith in a power greater than myself, whose love could redeem me from sin and despair and eternal darkness. A loving power that could comfort and reassure me, a power upon which my very survival depended. Against all odds, and against all resistance that I had mounted, and perhaps against reason itself, I was changed by love—but not to something different. No, at its very essence, change is a process of self-discovery. I didn't become a different person. I had simply and finally become myself. Love does that. And when it does, it gives us the power to do the same for others—on levels quite unimaginable, in situations we never thought we'd experience, much less be equipped to handle.

I want to share with you an example of the power of love to change lives. A story about how a wife's love for her husband helped change not only her but also the way our country cares for its wounded servicemen and women and their families.

America has been at war for more than a decade, and we are not likely to see all our troops come home for some time. I have never served in the armed forces. I was a little too young for Vietnam and little too old for the Gulf War. My father was in the reserves during World War II, but all my uncles served and saw action. There was a tradition of service in my family that went back on my mother's side to Captain John Rossiter, who was said to have had something to do with the founding of the Continental Navy (he was aide-de-camp to fellow Irishman Commodore John Barry). Still, I often feel that war has never really impacted me all that directly.

I am extraordinarily proud to say that in the past decade *Guideposts* has worked closely with the US military, supporting our troops and their families not just by supplying free magazines, books and literature, but most important by telling their stories. One of the most moving moments in my tenure as editor-in-chief was delivering magazines to and visiting wounded soldiers at Walter Reed Army Medical Center. It wasn't until I looked into the eyes of a young woman who had had the lower part of one leg blown off in an IED attack while on patrol in Baghdad that I felt the war had finally touched my life in a visceral way. I remember what that soldier said: "Sir, if the country supports us, then my injury was worth it. It was an honor."

Of all the stories we've told in the magazine from soldiers and their family members—and we've told some pretty tough tales—Tonia Sargent's has left perhaps the most lasting impact on me. It brought the war home.

Nearly forty thousand men and women have been wounded in the wars in Iraq and Afghanistan, and in a way that is a hopeful number. Battlefield medicine today is so advanced that it is saving soldiers who, in any other war, would have died. That has also created great challenges for our military medical system and for military wives like Tonia, who was to discover a fighting strength she never knew she had until her husband, Kenny, was grievously injured in 2004.

"I was a typical Marine wife," she says. "Kenny and I were high-school sweethearts. We got married right after graduation. Kenny enlisted with the Marines and I took up teaching aerobics."

Aerobics was a portable skill, one Tonia could take with her as she and Kenny spent the next seventeen years raising their two girls and moving from base to base. She was teaching at a YMCA near Camp Pendleton when Kenny shipped out for Iraq. Like any military spouse, she was terribly worried about the mortal dangers her husband faced, a fear that was mitigated by the fierce pride she felt in his selfless valor. After all, this was why he had become a US Marine.

In many ways, Tonia thought she was almost as much a Marine as Kenny. The Corps was their entire life. That life was about to change.

When the call came from a military hospital in Baghdad, the details were sketchy. Her husband, Tonia was told, had been gravely wounded in a firefight in Najaf. A bullet had ricocheted off an armored personnel carrier and struck him in the head, penetrating under his right eye and exiting the left side of his skull. Medics were able to keep him alive—barely—long enough to evacuate him to Baghdad, where he was being stabilized before being transported to the National Naval Medical Center in Bethesda, Maryland.

Tonia's memories of the next few days are frantic, as if they'd been put in a blender. She remembers scrambling to find someone to take care of their daughters, Tasha and Alishia, while she prepared to fly east as soon as Kenny was brought back. His condition was still unclear, conveyed to her by patchy cell-phone calls from overworked doctors and nurses in Iraq, though she certainly understood Kenny had suffered brain damage—the signature wound of this war.

Finally she found herself in Bethesda, exhausted and distraught, and having to delay seeing her husband in order to fill out the complicated paperwork for financial hardship assistance so she could afford to stay at the rooming house provided for relatives of the wounded.

When she at last got to the intensive-care unit, she encountered a bank of monitors near the nurses' station. One, identified by Kenny's Social Security number, displayed an X-ray of a shattered skull. You didn't need to be a doctor to see the damage. Tonia took in a deep breath, almost a gasp, and asked for Kenny's room number.

"As I was starting down the hall," she recalls, "a doctor took my arm. 'Ma'am,' he said, 'why don't you sit with me first and I'll brief you on his injuries.'"

"I stared at this young man, incredulous. What could be more important right now for Kenny than my presence at his side? I wasn't angry, but I was firm: 'Doctor,' I said, 'I've been waiting five days since that call from Baghdad to see him and that's what I'm going to do. He needs me.'"

The doctor's hand fell away from her arm—he knew better than to oppose this kind of loving determination—and she entered Kenny's room. In fact, she entered a whole new world.

Tonia didn't recognize the man in the bed. His head and face were swollen and disfigured, marked with dried blood and rows of staples. He lay inert, attached to a massive bank of equipment and monitors and whirring, blinking devices that seemed far more animated than the figure in the bed, as if Kenny—if this was Kenny—were somehow more alive in the digital anatomy of the machines than in his own body.

By now the doctor and several nurses were standing behind her, observing silently. Approaching the bed, Tonia slipped the man's hand tenderly into hers and whispered, "Kenny, squeeze as hard as you can if you know who I am."

A moment of eternity passed, articulated only by the laboring of the medical machinery. He did not move his head or open his eyes or make any other motion. Then she felt it, faint at first, weak, and then stronger, until Kenny gripped her hand so firmly it was as if he never wanted to let go. She laid her head gently on her husband's chest, her tears dampening the sheet.

Love had prepared Tonia to be at Kenny's side in sickness and health; that was not hard. In fact, it was a privilege. Yet little had prepared her for the bureaucratic labyrinth of paperwork, and the endless legal and medical decisions she faced over the following weeks. Tonia worried that decisions she made now would affect Kenny's care far down the road, so she prayed for guidance whenever she felt the process was going to overwhelm her. God would grip her hand as firmly as Kenny had, she was certain.

More than anything, Tonia was vigilant about Kenny's care: "His injury left him with near-total amnesia in the beginning and he had difficulty just putting words together. Doctors and therapists worked hard with him. But there were so many patients on the ward, that the staff struggled just to keep up. Kenny was the center of my world, but I knew each and every patient was also the center of somebody's world, some wife or husband or family."

Every day Tonia got Kenny out of bed, washed him, steered him around the ward, and pointed out rooms with other Marines. No subject got him talking like his fellow jarheads.

"The week's highlight was Sunday phone calls from the fifteen men he commanded in Iraq. That, or me renting movies or talking about Tasha and Alishia."

Sometimes doctors had to take time out from attending to this procession of the maimed to escort politicians and other VIPs touring the wards (I cringed when I heard this, thinking of my own visit to Walter Reed). Tonia was moved to do a strange thing when they stopped by Kenny's bed: She collected as many business cards as she could. At the time she couldn't have told you why.

Tonia absorbed every aspect of her husband's medical care, even learning to perform some tasks when nurses weren't available. She developed a sufficient grasp of terminology to speak knowledgeably with his doctors, which helped her make decisions, and decisions were critical. Decisions affected their future. And she grew savvy enough to request a copy of every piece of paper that was added to Kenny's medical record, a record of slow but definite progress.

During quiet times, Tonia prayed with her husband and read to him from the Bible.

Kenny was transferred to a VA rehabilitation hospital in Palo Alto, California. Tonia was getting Kenny settled into his new room when a nurse came in and said matter-of-factly, "Visiting hours are from 1:00 PM to 7:00 PM."

Tonia was taken aback. "I'm sorry," she answered patiently, "I'm not a visitor. I'm Sgt. Sargent's wife. I've been at his bedside almost constantly for a month. He suffers amnesia. I assumed I'd be staying with him. I'm pretty used to sleeping in chairs by now."

The nurse was unmoved. She handed Tonia a sheet of paper. "Ma'am," she said, glancing over Kenny's chart, "here's a list of nearby hotels."

Tonia was stunned. Kenny needed her here, not in a hotel room, no matter how nearby. The nurse was not giving ground, though, and as Tonia left she tried not to look at Kenny, whose eyes widened with fear. This was a whole new environment for him, and now she was leaving.

She didn't sleep that night. Maybe she had been foolish to think that an aerobics teacher with no college education could take on this massive medical establishment. She prayed but the only answer she seemed to get was, *Tonia, stay strong*.

But how?

She returned the next day—during visiting hours—to find Kenny still looking terrified and disoriented. Again she appealed to the nurse.

"You can come during visiting hours," the nurse repeated. "I'll write them down for you if you like."

Just then a neuropsychologist came into the room. "Ma'am," she said to Tonia, "this is your husband's rehabilitation, not yours. Leave the work to us and just think of him as away on deployment."

Tonia knew the comment was meant to help, but anger rose in her. What could she do to make them understand that Kenny had made progress because she had been so closely involved in his care? She glanced at her husband. His eyes still betrayed his confusion and apprehension, but suddenly something ignited when their gazes locked. Now she saw a glimmer of the true Kenny, the proud Marine, who knew what it was to stand and fight. She was a Marine in a way too. Over this past month or so, she'd fought through the red tape and the stresses that were overwhelming the military medical system. She'd been in the trenches, battling to make sure Kenny got the best care. She'd done things she'd no idea she had the strength and determination to do. Something had taken root inside her. She had changed. In the glance that passed between them, Kenny seemed to be saying that they were going to keep fighting, the two of them, because their strength was in their love, and nothing could beat that; nothing can defeat love, and now was not the time to back down.

"He is not on any deployment, and I'm going to be at my husband's side for the duration," she told the therapist. "If you won't help me do that, I'll find people who will."

That's when she remembered the business cards.

She started calling the numbers, many of them congressional representatives and staffers, and explained her plight, a situation that could not possibly be unique. She contacted the local Marine Corps reserve unit and convinced them to exert influence on hospital administrators, not just for her but also for other families. She signed up as a hospital volunteer, thus eluding the hated barrier of visiting hours. And she helped the hospital create a program to raise money to provide more housing for patients' loved ones. Tonia Sargent, the high school-educated aerobics teacher and loyal Marine wife, became a crusading advocate.

"I guess I went to war," she admits, giving a rueful but satisfied smile.

Because of Tonia's foresight in handling her husband's affairs—she declined to sign documents that would have discharged Kenny from active duty at the time of his wounding and transferred him to the Veterans Administration—he was able to retire with a full military pension after twenty-one years. He does not work, and may never again, yet his recovery has been nothing short of miraculous, considering the severity of his injuries. He spends his days cooking, cleaning and keeping an eye on the girls, who are his joy, says Tonia. "Kenny feels incredibly blessed to be with them."

And Tonia? She's back teaching aerobics, the only thing that is the same about her life today. Kenny is not now, and never will be, the man he was before he went to Iraq and caught a bullet—one of thousands of bullets that have found US soldiers in this past decade of war.

That's why Tonia is still fighting her own war. She speaks to church groups and Rotary Clubs about the challenges of life after active duty, for the wounded and unwounded alike.

"No matter when these conflicts end," Tonia tells her audiences, "the warriors who come home will need more than slogans and campaign promises, more than bumper stickers and ribbon magnets on cars. They'll need resources to get the care they require. Support for family members taking part in that care. Prayer. A lot of prayer."

It is strange how war is so much about love: love of country and a way of life, love of the men and women in your
unit, love of the families left behind. Love of God, who sees
them through the loneliness, horrors and boredom. And most
of all, perhaps, the fierce and invincible love each of them
has for the very life they are willing to lay down for their
country.

My long war against my demons did not compare to what a
soldier faces in even one hour on the battlefield. Still, what
I found so moving about Tonia and Kenny's story was the
healing love that bonded them at his bedside. It helped me to
recall some pivotal events of my life, and how they have become
a part of me and my story.

The first was when I was about five and went to the hospital to have my tonsils and adenoids removed, a common
procedure then for children with asthma, which I had. I remember seeing, through a waning haze of pain meds, my
father tiptoeing into my darkened room, carrying a green
flatbed Lionel model-railroad car with sticks lashed to it by
twine to simulate timber. He put it down on the bedside table. We shared a love of railroads and model-train sets, and
young though I was, I sensed something compelling in the
way he offered it, a tenderness I'd never seen. He sat with
me for a long time without really saying anything, but he so
clearly was reacting to my helplessness. He didn't need to
speak, and besides I couldn't talk. But the car was a symbol of
something we shared and he knew I would understand, perhaps, something he could never say: that I was his son and he
loved me.

The summer I was twelve, I was hit by a car while riding my bike. The impact shattered my pelvis and fractured my skull, and to this day I can still totally scare myself by summoning the memory of being rushed to the hospital gasping desperately for breath—the accident caused a nearly fatal asthma attack—my mother in the back of the ambulance begging me to stay alive, and the sirens screaming in my ears as I lost consciousness.

I awoke days later with our parish priest, Father Walling, leaning over me murmuring prayers. We were alone, my family having taken a break from their vigil, and he looked as shocked as I was when my eyes popped open. But it was a visit later by another man, old Mel, that I have never forgotten.

Mel was as important to my education at the time as any teacher. Mel drove our school bus, and I was the safety boy. With my white AAA belt and the privilege of riding standing up in the aisle, I was Mel's enforcer. It was my first taste of power, and I could get carried away. In fact, Mel told me I was causing more disruption than I was preventing. The first rule of authority, he said, was to be fair. "Don't be an instigator, Eddie, be a peacemaker. Be humble." When things got out of my control, old Mel would pull the Blue Bird school bus over, ram the three-foot-high gearshift into park, turn around, and simply stare. I was always amazed at how that worked. Mel was tough, and he was toughest on me.

A self-described Georgia cracker, Mel moved up north to work in an auto factory. After he retired from the line, he took a job driving the bus. He was a great driver, despite having grown up in the South, where they never had to cope with the blizzards and snowdrifts of the annual Michigan ice age. Once school was out, Mel spent all his time at his fishing shack way up north. Mel loved fishing. He didn't come south for any reason until it was time to drive the bus again.

This year, though, he did. I remember turning my head and being shocked to see him standing in the doorway, his old ball cap in his hands, a stunned and sad expression on his hangdog face. Of course I was not a pretty sight myself, with all my bandages, flat on my back, attached to a gruesome traction device that I thought might have been dusted off from its last use during the Spanish Inquisition. Mel hovered there for a moment, cleared his throat several times, came in, and pulled a chair over to the bed. He smelled of sweat and fish, and that didn't bother me a bit. I was just glad to see him.

In that gravelly Southern drawl we kids all loved to imitate when he was out of earshot, he told me that a) I was going to be all right no matter what, because I was as tough as he was, and b) I would not lose my job as his safety boy. The latter bit of information, I think, was why he had driven hundreds of miles to see me; he was afraid how worried I might be about that.

And then he put his head in his hands and wept.

No matter what deep reservoir of feeling my condition breached in old Mel—and whatever it was, I was surely too young to understand such adult things—his outburst moved me in a way I couldn't stop thinking about for a long time afterward. There was something there, some shared experience of humanity, the mystery of love and loss, that connected me to him. My lying in that hospital bed stirred something in him and I could feel it, not as some kid frightened by adult emotions, but as one human connected ineffably to another.

The outburst subsided as quickly as it had erupted. Mel stood up, tugged his ball cap back on his balding pate, and took his leave. "See you in the school year, Eddie," he said, with a squint that denoted earnestness. He must have noticed just then all the prayer cards on my table, because he added, "I ain't much of a prayin' man, but I was raised Baptist and I still know how to send one up when I need to."

With that he was gone, headed north for a couple more weeks of fishing.

I wonder what Mel would have thought of me and the condition I was in when I was admitted to St. Luke's that Memorial Day weekend in 1986 after collapsing on Broadway in what used to be called, in the old British navy, the "rum fits." Certainly it was grounds for dismissal from the safety-boy corps. I'm sure it would have made him very sad to see me like that, and I'm certain in the course of his own long life he'd seen a friend or a family member fall into the same straits. He probably never thought it could have been me though. You just never know what little boys are going to turn into.

We all know people who are in trouble with alcohol or drugs or some other destructive obsession from which they cannot seem to free themselves. These people can change, they can be saved, and they need your help. They need to know you believe in them. I want to believe my old school-bus driver would have still had faith in me. As it turns out, plenty of folks did.

I was stunned by all the people who visited me at St. Luke's. They weren't sad or shocked. They were happy to see me, relieved that I was alive—and, they let me know over and over again, totally confident that I would get better, that this slip wasn't the end of my sobriety or my sanity. It was the beginning of something, something strong and good and lasting.

"I've known you for years," one friend said, "and except for a little wear and tear I've never seen you look better." She laughed. "All right, so you look like crap. But there is something different this time." Again and again I heard that I was going to be all right. I heard it so much I came to believe it.

The first thing I needed to do was shed my shame the way a snake sheds its skin, because it was shame that had kept me drinking once I'd started again in Copenhagen. I had called my mother as soon as I got back to the States, before I did anything. I couldn't imagine what I had put her through— again. Because what I had done to her caused me the greatest shame. I couldn't help thinking back to that night I called her from the World Trade Center, when I thought I'd reached the end of my rope. That had been hard. This was harder.

"Mom, it's me. I'm back. I'm okay. I'm sorry."

There was a long pause. I wondered if she was crying. My mother wasn't a crier and if she started now I wasn't sure I could handle it. But her voice came back clear and strong. "I knew you were going to be all right," she said. "I don't know why. I just knew it."

"I bet you said a few prayers to St. Jude though," I tried to joke. To old-school Catholics like my mother, St. Jude was the patron saint of lost or hopeless causes. When I was a teenager, Mom would sneak her statue of St. Jude into my room. I would evict him the minute she wasn't looking. What kid wants to be thought of as a lost cause? Inevitably St. Jude would reappear and just as inevitably, I would remove him. It got to be a kind of game between us, a spiritual chess match, her hiding the statue and me tearing my room apart looking for it. And beneath that game was a very serious struggle.

"I asked God to be with you," she said. "That's all. Just that you were not alone. I didn't want you to go through whatever you were going through alone."

The call ended quickly after that because I couldn't think of anything else to say but that I was sorry and the word began to sound meaningless to me the more I said it. Many years would pass before I felt I had made proper amends to my mother for all that I had cruelly put her through, the disappearances and the hospitalizations, the wildness.

I was alone with her shortly before she died a decade later in an Alzheimer's unit where she spent her final few years, battling the disease that plagues my family. Her mind was so destroyed that I wasn't sure there was anything left to call a mother. She hadn't really spoken in a long while. Time and again, though, a little glimmer of Estelle Rossiter Grinnan would briefly emerge from all the tangled ganglia, a flash of self.

Now, as I sat by her bed, she was very near death. There was nothing at all to be done but feed her an occasional ice chip and push the wisps of pure white hair off her wrinkled forehead. When we moved her into the unit, I'd unearthed St. Jude from a jumble of things in a closet and brought him along, a little worse for wear. His right hand, which had held up two fingers, had been amputated at some point, and a chip in his shock of hair made him look balding. His iconic green cloak was still reasonably well-preserved. He now occupied a spot on Mom's nightstand, just a statue bought many, many years before at a religious gift shop, not a god or a thing imbued with spiritual powers, only ceramic material formed into the image of a man, one statue out of thousands, comfort for the hopeless.

"Remember that game we played, how you used to put St. Jude in my room?" I asked, not expecting an answer. "He's in your room now, Mom. Checkmate."

Mom's eyes came open, as green as grass, and it made me feel overwhelmingly grateful that I could sit here with her, having been sober now a number of years. She'd seen me marry Julee, and she loved her daughter-in-law. These sober years with Mom had been a great blessing in my life. I felt I had unfinished business though.

"I didn't want you to be alone," I explained, even as I thought how selfish it was to unburden yourself to the dying. "I don't know how to say I'm sorry for all the terrible things I put you through. I wasn't an easy kid, was I?"

The corners of her mouth seemed to curl ever so slightly into a smile. Or at least I wanted to think so.

"I love you," I said. "I've always loved you no matter how I acted and I always knew you loved me even when I didn't love myself."

She raised her head slightly, slowly. Her lips moved and she said the last word I would ever hear her say, softly but clearly.

"Love."

I was sitting with my beleaguered sponsor in a day room at St. Luke's, ready to be released from captivity. It had been a three-day stay, I had managed to dodge the dreaded spinal tap and was feeling close to being my old self. Pretty soon the discharge papers would be completed and I would be on my way. My sponsor was taking me for lunch and a meeting.

"Why did I pick up a drink again?" I asked him.

"You didn't really pick up a drink so much as you took back your will."

This was the kind of Delphic declaration he often made that drove me crazy. He chuckled at my exasperated expression.

"Look," he said, "addiction is a disease of relapse. We relapse when we think we're more qualified to be in charge of our lives than God. The drink is the end of a slip, remember, not the beginning. Edward, I don't think you ever really surrendered your will, not completely. You stayed dry for a couple of years; you made progress. You didn't drink when you ignored my advice and took that dangerous trip to Baltimore to confront Daria. But is that being sober?" He paused for emphasis and to tap me on the arm, hard. "Your biggest problem is that you haven't been humble."

The tune wasn't new. He'd sung this aria many times before. But what could be more humbling than the state I found myself in now?

"You don't think sitting here with my butt hanging out of a hospital gown is humbling?" I demanded.

He laughed. "There's a difference between humiliation and humility. Begging for spare change and picking cigarette butts up off the street, which you were doing just a few years ago, is humiliating. But it didn't humble you, did it? You're still proud and stubborn and even arrogant at times and it gets you high and it gets you drunk. And the fact is, you don't have many drunks left in you. You're not going to survive much longer unless you get humble. For you it's a matter of life or death and don't kid yourself. Look around. This is as good as it gets if you keep binging."

I stared at the floor. I knew he was right; I just wasn't confident I could really do what he asked. How was I to become humble, to find the fearlessness to admit my life was unmanageable and had to be surrendered to a power greater than myself? I'd always felt that that was a kind of living suicide, to give up control. Yet my own will was destroying me. Was that what the experience with the light was all about? A metaphysical or even hallucinatory phenomenon, a light from above or within that was as much survival mechanism as it was a spiritual awakening?

"Humility comes with self-acceptance, Edward. You must look at yourself and your life honestly but without the self-centered shame, and I know how hard that is for you."

Well, there it was. I had a fatal case of terminal shame. I flashed back to the hotel room in Denmark. It hadn't been my life I'd wanted to end so much as the overpowering sense of shame, the kind of naked shame that turns you inside out and lays bare every hateful thing about you for the world to see. Shame that is not survivable.

"Love your sobriety," he said. "Love your Higher Power, however you define it. Love your fellow drunks whether they are sober or not because you share more in common with them than with anyone else. Love the clothes on your back and the food on your table and every blessing deserved and undeserved. Love everything and everyone who helps you stay sane and sober. Love will keep you humble, and humble people can change."

My sponsor's plan for me was so simple it was almost confusing. Find a job, almost any job, and just settle in for a year. "Learn how to be of service," he said. Not in some trendy Soho restaurant or chasing the adrenaline buzz of the next freelance gig. Something simple and steady.

First there was the matter of my present employment with the Danes, which had not been officially concluded since they didn't want to fire me in the hospital. Jenny, my boss, had been one of my most supportive visitors, and she was urging me to fight.

I wasn't so sure, and I didn't want Jenny jeopardizing her own position by being so outspoken. So a day after leaving St. Luke's I presented myself to one of the Hanses, who was president of North American operations. I'd been to his office before and had admired the massive Scandinavian desk that he'd had shipped over from Copenhagen. The wood was a beautiful blond hue with darker swirls, and as we sat across the no-man's land of that impressive piece of office furniture, I felt myself getting lost in the swirls.

"As you must know," he said in his painfully careful English, "your behavior is entirely unacceptable, and while we are quite relieved that you are okay, we cannot see a way to justify your continued employment under the circumstances."

I think he expected me to fight, to show anger or tearful remorse, but I kept staring at the swirls and thinking how absurd it was that I would even be sitting here. This part of my life already seemed ancient, like the site of some archeological dig.

"I hope you can understand that this is a difficult decision for us because you have done such good work and we appreciate. . . . "

"Listen," I interrupted, "I'd fire me too, in a heartbeat. I don't think I'd even be having a conversation with me. I embarrassed you and I am sorry and I certainly can't blame you for cutting me loose, so please don't worry about it."

What I didn't tell Hans, and what had amazed me throughout the whole discussion, was that I felt no shame whatsoever. Where normally I would have been groveling and beating my breast, now I just wanted to move on with as much dignity as possible.

Hans looked both shaken and relieved, and as I rose to leave he nearly jumped up out of his high-backed leather chair and thrust out his hand.

"By the way," I said, "I suppose I owe you a debt of gratitude for sending those Interpol officers to my room. I can't really explain it to you now, but it made all the difference."

He cocked his head. "No," he said, walking me to the door, "there was nothing to do with Interpol. We called no one."

"You didn't send them?"

"No, absolutely not. Maybe your family was looking for you."

But they didn't call Interpol either, because I asked. Neither did the hotel staff or anyone else I subsequently thought might have had reason to summon the international police. To this day I cannot tell you how those two agents—whoever they were—came to knock on my door at the exact moment they did.

A week or so after saying good-bye to Hans and his fellow Hanses, I had my clumsy but serendipitous encounter with that portly cocker spaniel and his owner, the flashy blonde with the amazing eyes, on West 72nd Street. I swore I'd never get involved with someone in the entertainment business (remember, she was on her way home from an audition); I'd spent too much time around theater types not to realize that most of them were crazier than I was. Then again, I swore I would never do a lot of things. Besides, Julee and her mom had already decided that she had just met the man she was going to marry. It just took me a while to catch on.

I started looking for jobs in earnest, per my sponsor's suggestion. I got an interview at Conde Nast's *Vanity Fair*, which had recently been resurrected after several decades in publishing cryogenesis. My interrogator stared at my résumé as if there had been some awful mistake in calling me in, or maybe one of her colleagues was playing a tasteless joke. After a perfunctory parsing of my qualifications, she slid my résumé aside with her arched fingertips and said rather clinically, "O-kay." I braced myself, certain that there was a trap door under my chair and her shoe was frantically searching beneath her desk for the lever that would activate it. The whole interview took less time than the elevator ride to get there.

"That was exactly the wrong place to go," my sponsor said. "You're lucky they weren't interested, and I'm shocked that you were. There is nothing humble about Conde. Try saying yes to something a little less grandiose. Just say yes before you can say no. Try it."

And then came a strange call from a job recruiter I'd sent a letter to: Would I be interested in something called *Guideposts*?

Guide what?

I wasn't completely unfamiliar with it, I realized, vaguely aware that Jenny read it; I thought I'd seen an issue in her briefcase. And once I'd dated a woman whose mother sent it to her as a gift; I thought I remembered Martin Sheen on the cover and his story about having a heart attack while making *Apocalypse Now*. The recruiter proceeded to describe the magazine.

"You mean it's a religious magazine?" I interrupted. I'm sure she could hear the hesitancy rising in my voice.

No, absolutely not, she insisted, not religious. Spiritual. True, first-person stories of hope and inspiration. "They are storytellers," she said, sounding as if she might be reading from a crib sheet. "It's about real people who are changed and uplifted by the events and challenges of their lives, everyday people and celebrities alike, a magazine where people's spiritual values meet their daily lives."

I'd spent most of my life telling stories, mostly some version of my own, so perhaps the opportunity to help other people tell theirs would be liberating. It would only be for a year . . . if that. Just until I could catch my breath and work on my résumé.

Which is how I found myself sitting in the office of *Guideposts* Editor-in-Chief Van Varner high above Third Avenue in midtown Manhattan. He was hunched over his desk, writing quickly, and then erasing furiously and writing again. Yes, a brilliant editor at work. I sat quietly and respectfully, not wanting to intrude on his genius. Eventually, however, I could not restrain myself from taking a peek at what he was so hard at work on.

It was a betting form. He was picking horses for that afternoon's races at Aqueduct.

That was interesting. And that's how my *Guideposts* interview began.

Van, of course, as I was to soon learn, was not a degenerate gambler but a transplanted Kentucky gentleman who stayed in touch with his Churchill Downs roots—he attended his first Derby when he was still in a stroller—by playing the horses. It was a harmless hobby financed by loose change that he found or the deposit money he got back on returnable cans and bottles. Any winnings he garnered he usually gave to a good cause.

Van didn't ask me so much about my writing experience as he asked me about myself. Which, I learned later, was how he was interviewed for his job at the magazine back in the year that I was born. "I sat with Dr. Peale in his office at their Manhattan apartment. I'd just lost my job as a book editor at a big publishing house. He asked me a few basic questions then leaned forward and said, 'Tell me, are you a happy man?'"

"I gave the question some thought," Van related, "because I knew it was in fact a very serious question, a question that meant a lot to Dr. Peale because it defined how you perceive life. Finally I said, truthfully, 'Yes, I believe I am.' Dr. Peale leapt from his chair, threw open the office door, and cried out to his wife and partner in everything, 'Ruth! Come here right now and meet a happy editor!'"

Van didn't ask me that first day if I was happy. I think he knew, being one of the most perceptive people I would ever meet, that it was a question I couldn't really answer. On a certain level Van knew what was up with me. The one thing he did want to know was if I cared about people, about their lives and how they thought about things.

"No one here will ever ask you what you believe personally," he said. "But I don't think you'll stick around if you don't believe in something, and you must respect the readers' beliefs at all times."

As it turned out Van lived in a venerable old Upper West Side apartment building called the Beresford, which was right around the corner from where I lived at the time. I stopped by that night on my way to meet Julee for Chinese and picked up a manuscript that needed work. "You'll be a big star in Creston," Julee laughed, referring to her hometown back in Iowa, where everyone read *Guideposts* and thought *Vanity Fair* was a ladies' underwear catalogue.

I suppose my audition went well enough—though we never published the piece I worked on—and Van offered me a job a few days later as an assistant editor, almost as low as you could go on the masthead. And even though I had come to expect the offer and planned to accept, my mind suddenly began to whir with doubts. Could I really fit in at a place called *Guideposts*? Was this work I could believe in? I knew I would grow miserable if it wasn't. Would it matter to me that some people in the New York publishing world would snicker at the idea of a magazine like this one? Or more likely simply never have heard of it? I was about to turn thirty-three; was this the step I wanted to take? I was desperate to do something honest and right for once. I didn't just want to grab at anything.

It was as if my brain was starting to hyperventilate. One thought rose up and crowded out the others, a notion my sponsor had planted. I said yes before I could say no.

I stayed at *Guideposts* for a year. Then another. And of course I'm still here.

What kept me? The stories. *Your* stories.

The power of our stories is transformative. Our stories give voice to our lives. In my early years at the magazine I traveled the country talking to people about their stories, helping to form them into publishable pieces, and I came to know some of the most extraordinary people I will ever meet. Their stories—and their faith—changed me. I have laughed with people and cried with people and prayed with people. Some of them I have told you about in this book. I believe that everyone has a *Guideposts* story, a story of change. *You* have a *Guideposts* story.

Stories are our roadmap through life, our record of growth, and how we come to recognize and understand ourselves and the great loving power at work in our lives, for it is this power that touches our every moment. When we finally tell our stories, it changes us; it puts us into spiritual focus. On some level everyone needs to tell their story, and that's why we have so many thousands of submissions each year.

Never could I have imagined how these stories would not just alter the course of my life but also influence the very essence of who I am. But stories can do that, when told with love and honesty and faith. They have deepened me spiritually and as a human being. I have been blessed by these stories more than I could ever have dreamed, and they inspired me to finally share my own. Julee told me when I agreed to write this book that if I didn't honestly tell my own story, with all the bits of flesh still sticking to the bones, then the effort wouldn't be worth it. She was right.

I've spent many years studying stories, and I've learned that all stories, from Aeschylus's *Oresteia* to a comic-book adventure, in order to be stories, require change. Change drives action, internally and externally, and life never stops changing. That's why stories—our own and others'—can hold such valuable life lessons and wisdom for us. I have used the stories in this book to demonstrate the power of human beings to change the most difficult things about their lives and themselves, to face adversity and emerge better, stronger, more faith-filled people for it. Through their stories and my own, I've tried to identify the nine most dynamic aspects of personal change: Honesty, Willingness, Imagination, Commitment, Faith, Forgiveness, Acceptance, Resilience, and Love. And I've proposed that the outcome of powerful personal change is happiness.

Some might say that happiness is a shallow concept or fleeting state. Some of my Buddhist friends claim that it is mostly a Western construct. I disagree. When are we humans more at peace than when we are happy; more fully alive in the moment than when we are free of worry or regret or sorrow?

If I were asked the same question that Dr. Peale posed Van in his interview, what would I say?

What would you say?

As I write this, I think of a certain moment in my life that embodied my own personal change. It occurred not so long ago. Millie, my golden retriever puppy, was asleep in front of the wood stove on a chilly spring night at our house in the Berkshire Hills of western Massachusetts. Asleep is not the word for it. More like zonked. Crashed. As only a puppy who has had a very busy and exciting day can be. Earlier she had had her first visit to the *Guideposts* offices—my dogs have often come to work with me. How exhilarating it was to meet all those new people and new smells . . . *So this is where he goes every day!*

Then it was into the Jeep for the three-hour ride up to the mountain cabin, Millie's first visit there too. She was a little carsick on the way up, and the look on her face when I finally pulled into the driveway was like someone who had just gotten off a bad amusement-park ride. As soon as she hit the ground, though, she was off like a shot, tearing down the hill out back, straight for the woods.

"Millie!" I yelled.

Coyotes, bears, mountain lions. Skunks!

"*Millie!*"

All the books say not to run after a puppy; they like to be chased. Stay still and call them in a firm, commanding voice. I immediately ran after her, yelling hysterically.

"Millie!"

She made a sharp right turn into a neighbor's yard and raced around to the back porch where she encountered a black lab named Simon through the kitchen window. Simon came out and played and chased for the next forty-five minutes until they both dropped from exhaustion.

I cooked on the grill that night and made a miniburger for Millie to add to her dinner. First time for that too. And now here she was, breathing deeply and snoring gently by the stove, as content and oblivious as can be. Through the window I watched the sun set, the horizon streaked with orange and stars spackling the sapphire sky.

All at once I want to freeze everything in time—this moment, this day, Millie's breathing, this incredible feeling of peace and contentment that has swept over me. I want to grab this feeling and hold it so tight I will always remember what this moment feels like. I don't care if time ever moves again because I would be perfectly happy living in this moment forever.

Was that the happiest moment in my life? By no means. Do I always feel like that? Certainly not. Yet there was a time in my life when I could not have lived in that moment, could not have discovered the joy and serenity it held. I was not a person who could be at peace. So happiness may not be so much a constant state but rather the capacity to fully experience life's most profound and joyous moments, and to be able to discover these moments of joy and wonder that are there for us to embrace, moments when we touch God. The personal change I have undergone was utterly necessary for me to have discovered those moments when I am truly alive, truly happy, a happiness that is not transitory but transcendent. Now close your eyes and think about such a moment, inhabit it again, and experience its joy and serenity. That is happiness.

I have called this book a not-by-yourself-help book because I believe that through our stories we help each other change and grow, shaping our future and thus transforming the world. For a long time I doubted I could ever change, that I was a captive of an immutable fate. If there was anyone for whom change seemed impossible, it was me. And yet I changed. Against all odds, I grew. And so can you.

Acknowledgments

||||||||||||||||||||||||||||||||||||||||||||||||||||||||||||||||||||||||||||||||||||||||||||||||||||||||||||||||||||||||||||||||||||||

N o writer works in a vacuum, certainly not this writer, and it is hard to know where to start when it comes to thanking the people without whom you'd be completely adrift. First and foremost, I'd like to acknowledge the best magazine staff in the world and thank them for their forbearance in the face of any disruption that may have been occasioned by the writing of this book; and especially my executive editors Rick Hamlin and Amy Wong for their wisdom, insight and friendship.

Of the many people who also read the manuscript-in-progress and helped it—and me—along the way I would particularly like to thank Colleen Hughes, Linda Raglan Cunningham, Debbie Macomber, Evan Balzer, Dick Hopple, David Matt, Philip Charles-Pierre, Elizabeth Sherrill and Kelly Mangold.

For encouragement, advice, support, inspiration and humor: Evelyn Freed, Fulton Oursler Jr., John Temple, Doug Pratt, Carl Raymond, David Morris, Elizabeth Kramer

Gold, Andrew Attaway, Pablo Diaz, Bill McGlynn, Anne Adriance, Dave Teitler, Audrey Razgaitis, Julie Mehta, Georgia Morrissey, Cynara Charles-Pierre, Marion Bond West, Celeste McCauley, Nancy Galya, Amy Molinero, Lettie Teague, John Guare, Kathleen Callahan, Christine Wallace, Michael O'Neill, Patty Weissman, Howard O'Brien, Len Horovitz, Bob Y., John Noonan, Janine Scolpino, Jenny Wade, Leigh Kearney, Andrea Craig, Keren Baltzer, Sally Fischer, Marlene Kahan, Karen Nourse, Zach Bennett, Jeff Chu and my extremely patient editor Toni Sciarra.

I am deeply indebted to the Peale family: John, Maggie and Liz, and to the memory of their parents Norman Vincent Peale and Ruth Stafford Peale, and Paul Everett.

I owe particular thanks to Guideposts Senior Vice President Rocco Martino, who encouraged me to write this book without knowing what would be in it.

The problem with a page like this is not where to begin but when to end. There are so many people in my life to whom I am obliged for their love and understanding, I can barely count them all, and so many whose names I've forgotten or never knew but were there just when I needed them. So to all those angels, thank you; you know who you are.

And one last prop for my wife Julee Cruise. I'm thinking of those late weekend nights at the office when I would pick up the phone and hear her say, "So, ah, how's *War and Peace* coming along?"

Thanks, Jules.

Online Resources

Visit EdwardGrinnan.com to watch video interviews with the author, read his blog "Edposts," send your comments to him, and find links to follow him on Facebook and Twitter.

You'll also be able to share your own story of transformation and discover free inspiring e-books, including a collection of stories featured in *The Promise of Hope* and Edward Grinnan's favorite readings from the devotional book *Daily Guideposts*.

Guideposts, a nonprofit organization, touches millions of lives every day through products and services that inspire, encourage and uplift. Our magazines, books, prayer network and outreach programs help people connect their faith-filled values to their daily lives. To learn more, visit Guideposts.org or GuidepostsFoundation.org.